Studies in Arts-Based Educational Research

Volume 2

Series editor

Barbara Bickel, Southern Illinois University, USA

International Editorial Board

Kakali Bhattacharya, Kansas State University, USA
Pam Burnard, University of Cambridge, UK
Mindy Carter, McGill University, Canada
Tabitha Dell'Angelo, The College of New Jersey, USA
Walter Gershon, Kent State University, USA
Peter Gouzouasis, The University of British Columbia, Canada
Alexandra Lasczik, Southern Cross University, Australia
Morna McDermott McNulty, Towson University, USA
Richard Siegesmund, Northern Illinois University, USA
Sean Wiebe, University of Prince Edward Island, Canada

Series Description:

The volumes in this series inform the readers of the expansive research being conducted using a variety of forms of Arts Based Educational Research, drawing from all disciplines and all forms and practices—the literary, visual, and performing arts.

The series includes Arts Based Educational Research that takes place in academic and non-academic settings, as well as be based in practices that are individual and collaborative, private and public. The epistemological, ontological and axiological explorations of the methodologies as well as issues of the representation and dissemination of Arts Based Educational Research will be engaged with and explored. The hinge connecting the arts and research in this Arts Based Educational Research book series is education, being understood in its broadest sense, as learning/transformation/change that takes place in diverse formal and informal settings, as having an impact on and with humans in such a way as to limit and/or assist their conscious awareness and produce new understandings for them to act with and upon the world.

More information about this series at http://www.springer.com/series/13575

Kathleen Pithouse-Morgan
Daisy Pillay · Claudia Mitchell
Editors

Memory Mosaics: Researching Teacher Professional Learning Through Artful Memory-work

Springer

Editors
Kathleen Pithouse-Morgan
School of Education
University of KwaZulu-Natal
Durban, South Africa

Daisy Pillay
School of Education
University of KwaZulu-Natal
Durban, South Africa

Claudia Mitchell
Department of Integrated Studies
 in Education (DISE)
McGill University
Montreal, QC, Canada

and

School of Education
University of KwaZulu-Natal
Durban, South Africa

ISSN 2364-8376 ISSN 2364-8384 (electronic)
Studies in Arts-Based Educational Research
ISBN 978-3-319-97105-6 ISBN 978-3-319-97106-3 (eBook)
https://doi.org/10.1007/978-3-319-97106-3

Library of Congress Control Number: 2018955913

© Springer Nature Switzerland AG 2019
This work is subject to copyright. All rights are reserved by the Publisher, whether the whole or part
of the material is concerned, specifically the rights of translation, reprinting, reuse of illustrations,
recitation, broadcasting, reproduction on microfilms or in any other physical way, and transmission
or information storage and retrieval, electronic adaptation, computer software, or by similar or dissimilar
methodology now known or hereafter developed.
The use of general descriptive names, registered names, trademarks, service marks, etc. in this
publication does not imply, even in the absence of a specific statement, that such names are exempt from
the relevant protective laws and regulations and therefore free for general use.
The publisher, the authors and the editors are safe to assume that the advice and information in this
book are believed to be true and accurate at the date of publication. Neither the publisher nor the
authors or the editors give a warranty, express or implied, with respect to the material contained herein or
for any errors or omissions that may have been made. The publisher remains neutral with regard to
jurisdictional claims in published maps and institutional affiliations.

Cover artist: Sun Kyoung Kim

This Springer imprint is published by the registered company Springer Nature Switzerland AG
The registered company address is: Gewerbestrasse 11, 6330 Cham, Switzerland

We dedicate this book to all the teacher-researchers we have worked with over the years in South Africa, Canada, and other parts of the world. Their courageous and creative explorations of memory, the arts, and professional learning have been an inspiration for this book. We especially remember Phezi (Hypesia Zamile) Chiliza, a teacher-researcher who was so passionate and tireless in her efforts to support South African early childhood teachers in creative arts teaching and learning. Through her own memory-work, she learned that "creativity... is an innate ability that every human being possesses and that should be nurtured at school and outside of school" (Chiliza 2015, p. 97).[1]

---

[1] Chiliza, H. Z. (2015). *Facilitating creative arts teaching and learning with Foundation Phase teachers: A subject advisor's self-study* (Unpublished master's thesis). University of KwaZulu-Natal, South Africa. Retrieved from http://researchspace.ukzn.ac.za/handle/10413/13666.

Series Editor's Foreword

Using Artful Memory-work to Research Teacher Professional Learning

When Series Editor-in-Chief Barbara Bickel initiated this book series with Springer editor Jolanda Voogd on behalf of the Arts-Based Educational Research Special Interest Group (ABER SIG) at the American Educational Research Association (AERA), I was invited to serve on the Editorial Board, with a team of wonderfully generous, and kind colleagues. It was a timely development for the expanding field of ABER, which seemed to be magnifying internationally, and certainly in my home country of Australia. The series has now endured through the terms of three Chairs of the ABER SIG (including myself) and is powering onwards. I am most encouraged that the series is maturing and enlarging and that worthy collections like this suite of memory mosaics are afforded this forum to share and elevate such important work.

I am also thrilled that this book is positioned globally in both the southern and northern hemispheres so as to be authentically international and diverse. I am also delighted to note that the work of 21 new and emerging scholars/teacher researchers in South Africa and Canada have been foregrounded in this collection through ABER practices such as collage, film, drawing, narrative, poetry, photography, storytelling, and television.

In reviewing and reading this work, what became immediately clear is the authenticity of the structures of book—the editors and authors have positioned the metaphor of the mosaic so beautifully, in that the content and form are entwined and coherent, and create and ensure multiple emergent and generative readings. This is the best of ABER in my view—where form and content hold hands and together generate complex outcomes including a somewhat unique praxis that foregrounds practice *as* theory, art *as* critical, and makes complex conceptual frameworks visible.

Kathleen Pithouse-Morgan, Daisy Pillay, and Claudia Mitchell have assembled a suite of chapters and authors from South Africa and Canada engaging the elegant metaphor of mosaic as a way into framing teacher professional learning in an artful way, drawing from memory-work as a central premise. The editors by way of mentoring and mutual learning have chosen to write into and around each chapter as a way to connect resonances, scholarship, and theory so that although each chapter transcends the collection (as all rigorous scholarship ought), they are also linked, mosaic-like to each of the other writings and positions. The result is an elegant, interesting, and deeply useful assemblage of ABER scholarship. I do hope you enjoy reading and engaging with the work as much as I have.

Southern Cross University, Australia   Alexandra Lasczik

Acknowledgements

As editors of *Memory Mosaics: Researching Teacher Professional Learning Through Artful Memory-work*, we are appreciative of the contributions of many people. We are grateful to the chapter authors for their innovative research and their readiness to work together to open up understandings of connections made with, between, and through memory, the arts, and teacher professional learning. We would also like to thank the specialist peer reviewers who gave readily of their time and expertise. We acknowledge Moira Richards for her comprehensive and skilful editorial support. And we are grateful to Barbara Bickel and the International Editorial Board and International Advisory Board for this opportunity to contribute to the *Studies in Arts-Based Educational Research* book series. We also thank Jolanda Voogd, Helen van der Stelt, and their colleagues from Springer for their support. In addition, we thankfully acknowledge support and grant funding from the National Research Foundation of South Africa (Incentive Funding for Rated Researchers, Grant Number 90832) and the University of KwaZulu-Natal's University Teaching and Learning Office (Grant number: CRG6).[2]

---

[2] We acknowledge that any opinion, findings, conclusions, or recommendations expressed in this material are those of the authors and therefore, the funders do not accept any liability in regard thereto.

Contents

Memory Mosaics: New Voices, Insights, Possibilities for Working with the Arts and Memory in Researching Teacher Professional Learning 1
Kathleen Pithouse-Morgan, Daisy Pillay and Claudia Mitchell

"To Seek Out *Something More*": Knowing the Teacher-Researcher Self Differently Through Self-narrative Writing and Found Photographs 15
Daisy Pillay, Sagie Naicker and Wendy Rawlinson

Working with Photographs: Seeing, Looking, and Visual Representation as Professional Learning 35
Claudia Mitchell, Katie MacEntee, Mary Cullinan and Patti Allison

Picturing a More Hopeful Future: Teacher-Researchers Drawing Early Memories of School 55
Kathleen Pithouse-Morgan, Hlengiwe (Mawi) Makhanya,
Graham Downing and Nontuthuko Phewa

Collaging Memories: Reimagining Teacher-Researcher Identities and Perspectives 77
Daisy Pillay, Reena Ramkelewan and Anita Hiralaal

Seeing Through Television and Film: The Teacher's Gaze in Professional Learning 95
Claudia Mitchell, Bridget Campbell, Stephanie Pizzuto
and Brian Andrew Benoit

Creative Nonfiction Narratives and Memory-Work: Pathways for Women Teacher-Researchers' Scholarship of Ambiguity and Openings 113
Daisy Pillay, Mary Cullinan and Leighandri Moodley

The Promise of Poetry Belongs to Us All: Poetic Professional Learning in Teacher-Researchers' Memory-Work 133
Kathleen Pithouse-Morgan, S'phiwe Madondo and Edwina Grossi

Stories Blending, Flowing Out: Connecting Teacher Professional Learning, Re-membering, and Storytelling 155
Kathleen Pithouse-Morgan, Sandra Owén:nakon Deer-Standup
and Thokozani Ndaleni

Ethically Significant Moments in Stirring up Memories 175
Claudia Mitchell, Sifiso Magubane, Casey Burkholder
and Sheeren Saloojee

Index 193

Contributors

Patti Allison Department of Language and Literacy Education, University of British Columbia, Vancouver, Canada

Brian Andrew Benoit Department of Integrated Studies in Education, Faculty of Education, McGill University, Montreal, Canada

Casey Burkholder Faculty of Education, University of New Brunswick, Fredericton, Canada

Bridget Campbell School of Education, University of KwaZulu-Natal, Durban, South Africa

Mary Cullinan Department of Integrated Studies in Education, Faculty of Education, McGill University, Montreal, Canada

Sandra Owén:nakon Deer-Standup Department of Integrated Studies in Education, Faculty of Education, McGill University, Montreal, Canada

Graham Downing School of Education, University of KwaZulu-Natal, Durban, South Africa

Edwina Grossi School of Education, University of KwaZulu-Natal, Durban, South Africa

Anita Hiralaal School of Education, University of KwaZulu-Natal, Durban, South Africa; School of Education, Durban University of Technology, Pietermaritzburg, South Africa

Katie MacEntee Faculty of Environmental Studies, York University, Toronto, Canada

S'phiwe Madondo School of Education, University of KwaZulu-Natal, Durban, South Africa

Sifiso Magubane School of Education, University of KwaZulu-Natal, Durban, South Africa

Hlengiwe (Mawi) Makhanya School of Education, University of KwaZulu-Natal, Durban, South Africa

Claudia Mitchell Department of Integrated Studies in Education, Faculty of Education, McGill University, Montreal, Canada; School of Education, University of KwaZulu-Natal, Durban, South Africa

Leighandri Moodley School of Education, University of KwaZulu-Natal, Durban, South Africa

Sagie Naicker School of Education, University of KwaZulu-Natal, Durban, South Africa; New Age Strategies, Durban, South Africa

Thokozani Ndaleni School of Education, University of KwaZulu-Natal, Durban, South Africa

Nontuthuko Phewa School of Education, University of KwaZulu-Natal, Durban, South Africa

Daisy Pillay School of Education, University of KwaZulu-Natal, Durban, South Africa

Kathleen Pithouse-Morgan School of Education, University of KwaZulu-Natal, Durban, South Africa

Stephanie Pizzuto Department of Integrated Studies in Education, Faculty of Education, McGill University, Montreal, Canada

Reena Ramkelewan School of Education, University of KwaZulu-Natal, Durban, South Africa

Wendy Rawlinson School of Education, University of KwaZulu-Natal, Durban, South Africa; Department of Media Language and Communication, Durban University of Technology, Durban, South Africa

Sheeren Saloojee School of Education, University of KwaZulu-Natal, Durban, South Africa

List of Figures

"To Seek Out Something More": Knowing the Teacher-Researcher Self Differently Through Self-narrative Writing and Found Photographs

Fig. 1 Sagie as an able-bodied person (Photographer, Andrew Naidoo, with permission) 19

Fig. 2 Sagie as a person with a disability (Photographer, Nithia Naidoo; Copyright, African News Agency Pictures (*The Herald*), with permission) 22

Fig. 3 Seated on the trencadis bench (Photographer, Marí Peté, with permission) 26

Fig. 4 Imagining aesthetic communication pedagogy (Photographer, Marí Peté, with permission) 27

Working with Photographs: Seeing, Looking, and Visual Representation as Professional Learning

Fig. 1 Sarah's collage (Photographer, Jean Stuart, with permission) 41

Fig. 2 Into the light (Photographer, Mary Cullinan, with permission) 44

Fig. 3 Helping each other to stay afloat, despite the rapids and rocks (Photographer, Mary Cullinan's participant, with permission) 45

Fig. 4 Awkward yet majestic (Photographer, Mary Cullinan's participant, with permission). 46

Fig. 5 Independent and strong (Photographer, Mary Cullinan's participant, with permission). 47

Fig. 6 Melvin Charney—Canadian Centre for Architecture Sculpture Garden, Montreal, Canada (Photographer, Mary Cullinan's participant, with permission). 48

Picturing a More Hopeful Future: Teacher-Researchers Drawing Early Memories of School

Fig. 1 Memories of early schooling (Drawing, Hlengiwe Makhanya, with permission) 60
Fig. 2 Welcome to school (Drawing, Graham Downing, with permission) 64
Fig. 3 The new school (Drawing, Graham Downing, with permission) 65
Fig. 4 Toothbrush (Drawing, Graham Downing, with permission) 66
Fig. 5 A learner hiding under the desk (Drawing, Nontuthuko Phewa, with permission) 70
Fig. 6 Teachers carrying sticks (Drawing, Nontuthuko Phewa, with permission) 71

Collaging Memories: Reimagining Teacher-Researcher Identities and Perspectives

Fig. 1 Reena's collage: The cabbage-head (Collage, Reena Ramkelawan, with permission) 82
Fig. 2 Anita's collage portrait: Exciting connections (Collage, Anita Hiralaal, with permission) 86
Fig. 3 Anita's only photograph of herself as a young child (Photographer, Roy Ramjewan, with permission) 87

Creative Nonfiction Narratives and Memory-Work: Pathways for Women Teacher-Researchers' Scholarship of Ambiguity and Openings

Fig. 1 Teatime meant support to my mother's friends (Photographer, Mary Cullinan, with permission) 117
Fig. 2 Lac La Ronge, Saskatchewan (Photographer, Mary Cullinan's participant, with permission) 119
Fig. 3 Reinventing myself... rewriting script (Photographer, Mary Cullinan's participant, with permission) 121
Fig. 4 Leighandri's memory drawing (Drawing, Leighandri Moodley, with permission) 123
Fig. 5 Kerusha's artefact (Photographer, Leighandri Moodley, with permission) 126
Fig. 6 Elizabeth's artefact (Photographer, Leighandri Moodley, with permission) 127

List of Figures xvii

Stories Blending, Flowing Out: Connecting Teacher Professional Learning, Re-membering, and Storytelling

Fig. 1   Big book, creation story: Corn, beans, squash, and strawberries (Photographer, Sandra Owén:nakon Deer-Standup, with permission).. 161

Fig. 2   The *mbawula's* flickering flames (Photographer, Thokozani Ndaleni, with permission)............................... 165

Fig. 3   The family bond, the *isithebe* (Photographer, Thokozani Ndaleni, with permission).. 166

Ethically Significant Moments in Stirring up Memories

Fig. 1   Sifiso: The student by day, warrior by night. This is a photograph of myself (on the left) with my two friends who were pretending to be fighting 179

Memory Mosaics: New Voices, Insights, Possibilities for Working with the Arts and Memory in Researching Teacher Professional Learning

Kathleen Pithouse-Morgan, Daisy Pillay and Claudia Mitchell

Abstract "New Voices, Insights, Possibilities for Working with the Arts and Memory in Researching Teacher Professional Learning" begins with a prologue that tells a story of how the book editors—Kathleen Pithouse-Morgan, Daisy Pillay, and Claudia Mitchell—have engaged with their own learning, as well as with what the book can offer to others. The chapter goes on to retrace research connections between memory-work, the arts, and professional learning. Next, the book editors look back at their personal, professional, and scholarly connections as a way to signal their ongoing collaborations across Canada and South Africa. They also draw attention to political and social links between Canada and South Africa. Thereafter, the editors explain how each of the subsequent nine chapters was composed from juxtaposing several "mosaic" pieces written by 21 new and emerging scholars in South Africa and Canada. This is followed by a synopsis of each chapter. To conclude, the editors highlight the scholarly contributions of *Memory Mosaics*.

Keywords Arts-based research · Canada · Memory-work
Teacher professional learning · South Africa

K. Pithouse-Morgan (✉) · D. Pillay · C. Mitchell
School of Education, University of KwaZulu-Natal, Durban, South Africa
e-mail: pithousemorgan@ukzn.ac.za

D. Pillay
e-mail: pillaygv@ukzn.ac.za

C. Mitchell
Department of Integrated Studies in Education, McGill University, Montreal, Canada
e-mail: Claudia.mitchell@mcgill.ca

© Springer Nature Switzerland AG 2019
K. Pithouse-Morgan et al. (eds.), *Memory Mosaics: Researching Teacher Professional Learning Through Artful Memory-work*, Studies in Arts-Based Educational Research 2, https://doi.org/10.1007/978-3-319-97106-3_1

1 A Dialogic Prologue: "When We Create a Mosaic, What Do We See, What Do We Learn?"

This prologue offers a "narrative dialogue" (Anderson-Patton and Bass 2002, p. 103) as a means of telling a story of how we—Kathleen Pithouse-Morgan, Daisy Pillay, and Claudia Mitchell—have engaged with our own learning as the editors of this book, as well as with what the book can offer to others. We chose a narrative dialogue format, drawing on the literary and performing arts, to exemplify how growth can happen through conversation among educational researchers. In the literary arts, dialogue can help readers to understand more about the characters in a story and to see how development takes place through exchanges between different characters (Coulter and Smith 2009). In a performance, a monologue "comes forward as a 'what is,'" while a dialogue "stages 'what might be'" (Pelias 2008, pp. 191–192). Our dialogue illustrates how collaborative inquiry with the 21 teacher-researcher contributors to this book has furthered our understanding of what might be made possible and visible though infusing the arts into researching the ways in which the past influences teaching and how memory can become a tool for future-oriented teacher professional learning.

Kathleen: Each chapter of this book brings together new and emerging voices from different contexts in South Africa and Canada to explore the intersection of the arts, memory, and teacher professional learning.

Daisy: When we create a mosaic of these disparate pieces ….

Kathleen: … What do we see?

Daisy: Each piece is about teacher professional learning, but when we put them together …

Kathleen: … What do *we* learn?

Claudia: Well, in the Canadian pieces that I've been working with, everybody is taking up social justice questions. For instance, in Casey Burkholder's use of cellphilms with preservice teachers, she was asking, "Whose stories are left out of history?" In Brian Benoit's critical viewing and re-viewing of a popular television series, he was enquiring, "Whose stories, in terms of class, are left out?" And Patti Alison curated a photograph album to interrogate her own white settler history. So, I see it as the arts and memory working together as a way to look into critical issues of social justice such as exclusion and colonisation. Somehow, the arts give permission to really take this up.

Daisy: In the chapter with Sagie Naicker and Wendy Rawlinson, I came to recognise how the combination of self-narratives and found photographs was opening and expanding pathways for unlearning prejudices and different forms of disability and self-closure. For Sagie who is physically disabled, and Wendy who felt disabled by her white, middle-class experiences, these visual encounters became opportunities for reflection, and self-awareness, and the possibility to grow in fulfilling ways.

Kathleen: The arts allow us to experience and make visible experiences of exclusion and colonisation in ways that are powerful and also personally and professionally meaningful. One of the most striking realisations for me in working with the teacher-researchers from South Africa has been the grave injustice of a lack of access to the arts. In South Africa, historically, black people were denied access to the arts in schools. Many of our teacher-researchers have no formal background in the arts because that was impossible for them. But, the arts are a resource that belongs to everybody.

Claudia: Another thing that I noticed was how the chapter on ethical dilemmas highlights lived experiences of ethics, as opposed to the procedural. For instance, Sifiso Magubane's story of going to the family of his dead friend to ask for permission to use his photograph revealed an embodied aspect of ethics.

Kathleen: It's also an emotional experience of ethics.

Claudia: I feel like I had not really thought about emotion and memory in quite that way before. The emotion of the pieces in the ethics chapter seemed really critical in terms of implications for doing this kind of research. It's about how we understand ethics differently and what we often leave out of our writing about research ethics—the omissions.

Daisy: For me, many of the pieces were about artful memory-work as an act of self. For example, in the chapter on collaging memory, for both of the teacher-researchers collage making became a performance, an act. Anita Hiralaal recalled her first trip to an art shop to buy a canvas. She commented on how, for the first time, she felt like an artist. What also came out of that chapter was that collaging is such an accessible approach.

Claudia: It is absolutely. You don't need any digital technology, or …

Daisy: Through cutting and sticking found materials to make a collage, anybody can visually story who they want to be.

Kathleen: What comes though so strongly in many pieces is how freeing it can be for adults to start engaging with the arts in ways that were often denied them as children and young people. This then opens up new ways for teacher-researchers to see and engage differently with memories. Because the arts allow us to notice and to do things that can't be done otherwise.

Daisy: For Anita, she was at quite an advanced stage in her study, but she couldn't really see what was happening until she made a collage portrait. She started to make connections between the personal and professional that allowed her to reimagine herself as a teacher educator. She saw how she had been constrained by a fixed idea of what she should do to be in control of the classroom.

Claudia: That's really interesting. So, as she was doing the collage …?

Daisy: For the first time, she realised how her personal history was shaping the need to be controlling in the classroom.

Claudia: So, did she go back into her childhood?

Daisy: Exactly, back into her childhood. Then she realised how much agency resided in her to move those pictures around as she realised that she didn't *choose* to teach like that. And that she could now make different choices.

Claudia: This is *why* I am and this is what I *could* be.

Daisy: So, artful memory-work frees us to imagine new possibilities. It's in the doing, in that actual making, that we can practise what is possible. With Anita, this collaging space allowed her to practise being a creative teacher educator.

Kathleen: Artful memory-work can change how we teach and how we think about teaching.

Daisy: And that transformation can be seen in the artwork, in how the images evolve. As we shift and play around with the pictures, the transition is so visible.

Kathleen: In working with Sandra Owén:nakon Deer-Standup and Thokozani Ndaleni on the storytelling chapter, it was remarkable to see how their experiences on continents apart were so similar, but of course also diverse. Thokozani reflected on how working with artefacts and storytelling helped him to think in a different way about what it means to be an English language teacher educator in South Africa. When he read Sandra's piece, he saw how people in Canada had had similar experiences of oral storytelling to his own, and that really opened his eyes to the educative value of storytelling, but also to issues of language. Sandra is working to breathe new life into her indigenous language and it made Thokozani think about how his home language of isiZulu could become a resource for teaching English with isiZulu-speaking students—and how he can draw on his students' indigenous knowledges and contexts. So, that's why this professional learning is so important. Because these teacher-researchers are our resource for the future.

Claudia: And in all the chapters, the teacher-researchers are very passionate about the work.

Kathleen: For example, in the chapter on drawing memories of school, there is a piece by Graham Downing, who is a graphic designer, and also pieces by Hlengiwe (Mawi) Makhanya and Nontuthuko Phewa who had never really drawn seriously before doing their research. But for all of them, the passion and enthusiasm about the drawings and the process of drawing is similar. So, maybe for these teacher-researchers, the power of artful memory-work is not so much to do with perceived artistic ability, or the beauty of the product. It's to do with the feeling of being engrossed and seeing differently or more keenly.

Daisy: When I discussed the collage making with Reena Ramkelewan, she said it was "magical." It was a magical act of self.

Claudia: That act of self would fit in nicely with the chapter on working with photographs. For instance, Katie MacEntee was using photographs to go back to her participants who recognised themselves though looking at photographs they had taken some years before.

Kathleen: There is that connection between the past, present, and future. The arts can help us to understand the past in new ways in order to practise, in new ways, in the present and future.

Claudia: And it's important that these pieces are not written by just any researchers, they are all *teacher*-researchers.

Kathleen: So, they are living out educational and social change, and driving that change. Ultimately, it's the teachers who make that difference.

Daisy: Once we have seen the possibilities, there's always hope.

2 Retracing Research Connections Between Memory-Work, the Arts, and Professional Learning

Memory-work was first conceptualised as a social science research methodology through a process of collective inquiry on female sexualisation undertaken by a group of feminist women in Germany, led by Frigga Haug (1987). Haug's memory-work practice involved collective inquiry by a group of women who wished to explore a common research question that was "a burning issue" for all involved (Haug n.d., p. 2). The process required individual writing of memories combined with collective reading aloud, oral brainstorming, and discussion (Haug n.d.). The inquiry was aimed at reencountering particular memories of lived experiences with a sense of curiosity and alternative possibilities in order to gain a new sense of orientation and direction for the future (Haug 2008). Memories were understood as embedded in, and conditioned by, the social world and so memory-work was intended to free researchers to take purposeful action within and in response to social conditions and forces (Haug 2008).

Significantly, even though Haug offered a comprehensive description of each aspect of her group's collective memory-work practice (Haug n.d.), she advocated "freedom for individuals attempting to do memory work to change the method for themselves, remaining within—or critically expanding—the theoretical framework of the process" (n.d., p. 2). Haug's invitation to change and expand the method and theoretical framing of memory-work was taken up in relation to professional learning by Mitchell and Weber (1999) who conducted groundbreaking research on memory-work as a mode of teacher professional learning in the 1990s. Mitchell and Weber worked with Canadian schoolteachers to examine how memories of childhood and schooling might have influenced their teaching, and how they might engage critically and creatively with these memories as "a powerful and highly effective means of self-transformation and a catalyst for professional growth" (Mitchell and Weber 1999, p. 232).

Mitchell and Weber (1999) conceptualised professional learning through memory-work as "a pedagogy of reinvention"—"a process of going back over something in different ways and with new perspectives, of studying one's own experience with insight and awareness of the present for purposes of acting on the future" (p. 8). This also speaks to the notion of productive remembering (Mitchell et al. 2011a; Strong-Wilson et al. 2013): "the idea of how memory and the past can be a productive learning space for the present and the future" (Mitchell et al. 2011b, p. 1). The energy and optimism inherent in these concepts of a pedagogy of reinvention and productive remembering resonate with an approach to professional learning that focuses on teachers (or other professionals) initiating and directing their own learning to enhance their continuing growth and to contribute to the wellbeing of others (Easton 2008; Pithouse-Morgan and Samaras 2015; Webster-Wright 2010). This approach has developed through dialogue between scholarship of professional learning and pedagogic practice in a "reciprocal process wherein one enables the other" (Hooks 1994, p. 59). It aims to acknowledge and facilitate the agency of teachers in processes of professional learning that can contribute to transformative education.

Furthermore, while Haug's memory-work method centred on the composition and editing of written memory accounts, Mitchell and Weber's (1999) research on memory-work and teacher professional learning brought in the use of visual and arts-based methods and resources such as drawing, photography, video making, and script writing. Their work demonstrated how visual and arts-based methods and resources could allow teacher-researchers to make visible and tangible their own and other teachers' memories in relation to vital educational and social questions (Mitchell and Weber 1999).

3 Building on Our Own Longstanding, Transcontinental Connections

As editors from the two countries represented in this book, our connections with each other, and with researching teacher professional learning through artful memory-work, run deep. Our scholarly collaborations began with our work together at the University of KwaZulu-Natal in South Africa that dates back to 2003, when Claudia was Chair and Professor in the School of Education, and continued through meetings, conferences, projects, student exchanges, and publications in both Canada and South Africa in the ensuing years. Kathleen, for example, was a postdoctoral fellow at McGill University in 2007–2008 with Claudia as her mentor. As part of her postdoctoral project, Kathleen edited with Claudia and our colleague, Relebohile Moletsane, the book, *Making Connections: Self-Study and Social Action* (Pithouse et al. 2009), which includes sections on "The Self in Memory" and "Creative Re(Presentations) of the Self." Kathleen also convened with Claudia Mitchell and two other researchers at McGill, Teresa Strong-Wilson and Susann Allnutt, an international symposium on productive remembering, which led to two books.[1] That symposium was followed up by the publishing of a themed issue of the *Journal of Education* with South African teacher-researchers writing on "Memory and Pedagogy," guest edited by Kathleen, Daisy, and Claudia (Pithouse-Morgan et al. 2012). Subsequent themed issues of *Educational Research for Social Change*[2] and *Perspectives in Education*[3] brought together the work of an international group of educational researchers, many of whom were exploring visual and arts-based research methods and memory-work. More recently, the book, *Object Medleys: Interpretive Possibilities for Educational*

---

[1]*Memory and Pedagogy* (Mitchell et al. 2011b) and *Productive Remembering and Social Agency* (Strong-Wilson et al. 2013).

[2]Themed, "Enacting Reflexivity in Educational Research" (Pithouse-Morgan et al. 2014a).

[3]Themed, "Self-study of Educational Practice: Re-Imagining Our Pedagogies" (Pithouse-Morgan et al. 2014b).

Research, edited by Daisy, Kathleen, and Inbanathan Naicker (Pillay et al. 2017)[4] combined "object pieces" written by education scholars working across South Africa, Canada, and the United Kingdom. This book offers diverse approaches to object inquiry in educational research, including memory-work and arts-based methods.

We reference these personal, professional, and scholarly connections as a way to signal our ongoing collaborations across Canada and South Africa. But these connections are not just about our personal connections as editors and indeed are not just about a serendipitous connection between a country in the Global North and a country in the Global South. Over the last 70 years, there have been many political and social links between Canada and South Africa, some that have been generative and productive and some less so. On the side of what we would regard as productive, Canada was one of the countries that South Africa looked to for support in establishing its democratic school system through the financial assistance and technical support of the Canadian International Development Agency (CIDA). This was in relation to the South African Schools Act (Department of Education 1996), establishing national and provincial educational structures, and the setting up of the Gender Equity Task Team (see Wolpe et al. 1997), which helped to frame the gender machinery at the National Department of Education and related structures in the provinces.[5] However, we would be remiss if we did not also highlight the less positive connections, in that our two countries share some shameful bonds in relation to our colonial histories. Here we refer to the colonial and then apartheid structures of South Africa that were only dismantled in 1994, and we also acknowledge that Canada has the legacy of the reservation system, which meant that many Indigenous people were denied basic rights to language and culture. The residential schools that Indigenous children were forced to attend left deep scars that are still being felt. In many ways, both Canada and South Africa remain haunted by the past, with apartheid continuing to have an impact in South Africa more than 20 years after the first democratic elections and, in Canada, the legacies of a colonial history still being lived out. Both countries have attempted to deal with the past through their Truth and Reconciliation Commissions (South Africa from 1995–1998 and Canada 2008–2015) with Canada having established a Call to Action, which calls for universities and education systems more broadly to develop specific strategies for indigenising educational structures (https://www.aadnc-aan dc.gc.ca/eng/1450124405592/1450124456123). In essence, decolonisation is very much on the contemporary agenda of both countries. And so it is not surprising that when we began to conceive of an artful collection of mosaic pieces based on memory-work and teacher professional learning, we saw that a number of the contributors across the two country contexts were dealing with social justice issues in education that pertained to inclusion/exclusion and (de)colonisation.

---

[4]Inspired by Claudia's pioneering body of work on objects in social research (Mitchell 2011; Mitchell and Reid-Walsh 2002; Mitchell and Weber 1999).

[5]Here we refer to CIDA's South Africa programme beginning in the mid 1990s, which included Canada's support to the South African Qualification Authority (SAQA), support to teacher education, and the McGill University and the South African Department of Education partnership, the Canada-South Africa Education Management Programme (CSAEMP). CSAEMP was involved in supporting SAQA and the Gender Equity Task Team.

4 Composing Memory Mosaics

Memory Mosaics: Researching Teacher Professional Learning Through Artful Memory-Work builds on connections between memory-work, the arts, and professional learning research to offer imaginative and expressive explorations of teacher-researchers' memories and histories in relation to wider social and cultural concerns, and across diverse contexts. Each of the subsequent nine chapters was composed from juxtaposing several "mosaic" pieces written by 21 new and emerging scholars in South Africa and Canada. These teacher-researchers have diverse educational backgrounds and are teaching various subjects in schools and higher education institutions. They have engaged in memory-work using arts-based methods and resources from a variety of standpoints and using diverse approaches. Some have done self-focused research, drawing on their own memories and personal histories, while others have facilitated memory-work with other teachers. Their work demonstrates a range of arts-based research practices and sources including collage, film, drawing, narrative, poetry, photography, storytelling, and television.

In art, mosaic usually takes the form of "decoration of a surface with designs made up of closely set, usually variously coloured, small pieces of material" (Waage and Nordhagen 2000, para. 1). The individual parts are combined to a new, unique whole. The mosaic pieces in this book present exemplars of artful professional learning research and illustrate innovative research methods and practices. In the spirit of academic mentoring and reciprocal learning, the book editors have written around these distinctive pieces in each chapter to position them, mosaic-like in terms of varied contexts and vantage points, to highlight resonances across the pieces, and to connect them to scholarly conversations at the intersection of memory-work, the arts, and professional learning research. Like multifaceted mosaics composed of broken pottery, glass, and tile fragments, teacher-researchers' visual and narrative juxtapositions, layered accounts, and multiple tellings have been assembled as patterned pieces to form an original arrangement in each chapter. Each chapter, as an assemblage of mosaic pieces, is related to the other mosaic chapters around it, but is not subsumed by them, which allows for both continuity and fluidity within the book as a whole. Collectively, the chapters illustrate the multidimensionality and complexity of processes of teacher professional learning through artful memory-work.

Observing quality standards for scholarly publication was crucial to our work on this edited volume. The mosaic chapters offer original research and were individually reviewed by independent peer reviewers who contributed prepublication guidance and expertise. Together, the editors and authors revised the chapters in response to the peer review recommendations.

5 An Overview of the Chapters

"'To Seek Out *Something More*': Knowing the Teacher-Researcher Self Differently Through Self-Narrative Writing and Found Photographs" by Daisy Pillay, Sagie Naicker, and Wendy Rawlinson showcases the power of found photographs for evoking, constructing, and reconstructing memory in written self-narratives. The exemplars are drawn from Sagie Naicker's and Wendy Rawlinson's doctoral research in South Africa. Sagie drew on selected photographs to examine how his disability identity influenced his leadership practice, and his journey as an activist seeking social justice for people with disabilities. Wendy's found photograph evoked a bodily experience of being transported to a more imaginative space that triggered her curiosity for aesthetic pedagogical adventuring in her racially diverse classroom. Taken as a whole, the chapter demonstrates how, drawing multi-methodologically on self-narratives and the visual meaning making perspective of found photographs, the scholarship of self-awareness of teachers' ways of being, knowing, and doing can make significant contributions to teacher professional learning.

The next chapter, "Working with Photographs: Seeing, Looking, and Visual Representation as Professional Learning" by Claudia Mitchell, Katie MacEntee, Mary Cullinan, and Patti Allison, focuses on the use of photography in memory-work in teachers' professional learning, drawing on exemplars produced by three teacher-researchers. Katie MacEntee worked with preservice teachers at a South African university using photo elicitation. The teachers look back on what they learned in a project on sexuality education using the arts. Mary Cullinan, studying at a Canadian university, also used a type of photo elicitation but in so doing "co-constructed" with her participants, all late entry women reflecting on coming into doctoral study, the meanings of these experiences. Patti Allison, also at a Canadian university, engaged in the process of curating a photo album based on family photographs and in so doing engaged in a decolonising process. In looking across the three mosaic pieces, we get a sense of the ways in these methods offer what could be termed as deeply "emotive" work.

"Picturing a More Hopeful Future: Teacher-Researchers Drawing Early Memories of School" by Kathleen Pithouse-Morgan, Hlengiwe (Mawi) Makhanya, Graham Downing, and Nontuthuko Phewa brings together three exemplars from teacher-researchers who have used memory drawing as an arts-based method for self-study research. The three mosaic pieces offer diverse yet also complementary stories brought forth by South African teachers' drawings of early memories of school in the 1970s, 1980s, and 1990s. The drawings and accompanying written reflections offer access to poignant stories of the past, with a shared ethical purpose of engendering new and more optimistic stories for the future. Overall, the chapter illustrates the usefulness and impact of memory drawing as an emotional entry point for teachers' future-oriented remembering.

In "Collaging Memories: Reimagining Teacher-Researcher Identities and Perspectives," Daisy Pillay, Reena Ramkelewan, and Anita Hiralaal explore teacher-researcher identities and perspectives through the piecing together of lived experience and practice using collage. The exemplars are drawn from ongoing doctoral research by two emerging South African scholars, Reena and Anita. Reena's mosaic piece reveals how collage making assisted her in recognising the multiple and layered selves that constitute her life and work as a teacher-researcher in a public primary school. Anita's piece shows how creating a collage portrait helped her bring together memories of critical experiences and significant people who influenced her in becoming a certain type of teacher educator. Together, Reena's and Anita's accounts of collaging memories show how collage making can reinvigorate critical moments of the past for new perspectives to inform teacher-researchers' selves and practices.

"Seeing Through Television and Film: The Teacher's Gaze in Professional Learning" by Claudia Mitchell, Bridget Campbell, Stephanie Pizzuto, and Brian Andrew Benoit draws together three exemplars for using film and television in teachers' professional learning. Bridget Campbell, working at a South African university, embarked on the use of two teacher films, *Freedom Writers* and *Dead Poets Society*, to enrich her understanding of her work with the preservice teachers in her class. Then Stephanie Pizzuto, as a master's student at a Canadian university, used a popular television series from her childhood, *Boy Meets World,* to deepen an understanding of the teacher she now wants to become. Brian Benoit, also at a Canadian university, explored the way he used repeated viewings of a local television series he remembered from an earlier time, *Les Bougon*, to engage in memory-work and critical autoethnography in relation to class structures.

The following chapter, "Creative Nonfiction Narratives and Memory-Work: Pathways for Women Teacher-Researchers' Scholarship of Ambiguity and Openings" by Daisy Pillay, Mary Cullinan, and Leighandri Moodley, draws on exemplars of memory-work and creative nonfiction narratives presented by two teacher-researchers from their graduate studies. Mary, a Canadian teacher and late-entry doctoral student, used personal photos and metaphorical images to evoke memories of how women saw their journey as late-entry doctoral students in order to come to a closer understanding of her life and place in academia. Leighandri shares two creative narratives she composed with South African women novice teachers in her master's study to bring her to a deeper understanding of her own story as a novice teacher. The mosaic pieces illustrate ways in which memory-work and creative nonfiction narratives can facilitate new understandings of both past and present, generating new narratives that can change the future.

"The Promise of Poetry Belongs to Us All: Poetic Professional Learning in Teacher-Researchers' Memory-Work" by Kathleen Pithouse-Morgan, S'phiwe Madondo, and Edwina Grossi builds on the developing scholarship of poetic professional learning in the social sciences by exploring two exemplars of South African teacher-researchers' poetic engagement with memory and pedagogy. The mosaic pieces by S'phiwe Madondo and Edwina Grossi, which exemplify professional learning by way of poetry, offer windows into poetic explorations of these teacher-researchers' own memories and histories in relation to varied educational and socio-cultural contexts and concerns. The pieces illustrate poetic inquiry as a mode of working deliberately and imaginatively with memories to produce evocative insights into teaching and learning. They also offer encouragement to teacher-researchers who might not have a formal background in the literary arts to start to play with composing poems as research data, representations, and interpretations.

The penultimate chapter, "Stories Blending, Flowing Out: Connecting Teacher Professional Learning, Re-Membering, and Storytelling" by Kathleen Pithouse-Morgan, Sandra Owén:nakon Deer-Standup, and Thokozani Ndaleni, offers written research accounts of engaging with oral storytelling as an arts-based community and family practice. The chapter brings together mosaic pieces by two teacher-researchers, who, on different continents, have delved into teacher professional learning in relation to re-membering through mythical and personal stories. The mosaic pieces are complemented by a dialogue piece, which portrays how communicating with each other across continents and cultural contexts deepened and extended Sandra and Thokozani's mindfulness of the educative potential of connecting re-membering, storytelling, and teacher professional learning. The chapter reveals how, as teacher-researchers retell their own stories and listen to others' stories, they can make new sense of their past and present learning, and reimagine stories of the future.

The closing chapter, "Ethically Significant Moments in Stirring Up Memories" by Claudia Mitchell, Sifiso Magubane, Casey Burkholder, and Sheeren Saloojee, points to the issue of ethics in artful engagement as an area that is under-explored in memory-work and self-study. Sifiso Magubane, a South African teacher-researcher, considers the emotional challenges in getting permission to use the photograph of a close friend of his who has died. Casey Burkholder, studying at a Canadian university, considers some of the tensions in preservice teachers producing cellphilms about their own personal histories and, especially, the politics of exclusion. Finally, Sheeren Saloojee, who is completing a doctoral study at a South African university, addresses an issue seldom discussed in relation to vulnerability in social research—that of the emotional well-being of the researcher, especially in relation to what it means to carry around and represent the stories of the participants. The three mosaic pieces highlight situational ethics and ethics of the personal, both aspects of "doing most good" and "doing least harm" that rarely appear in any guide or any ethics policy.

6 Closing: What Have We Seen? What Have We Learned?

Memory Mosaics communicates new voices, new insights, and new possibilities for working with the arts and memory in researching teacher professional learning. Each chapter offers a multidimensional, polyvocal exploration of interrelationships between the arts, lived educational experiences, and pressing social and cultural concerns. The peer-reviewed book chapters call attention to both the educational significance and challenges of working with memory and the arts in relation to professional learning. They also illustrate a variety of innovative and artful approaches to educational memory-work. As a collective, the chapters serve as an accessible and imaginative methodological toolkit and resource for artful inquiry into teachers' remembered selves, experiences, and practices.

When memories, lives, and art forms interconnect, they breathe life, agency, and colour into teacher professional learning. Placed side by side, the mosaic chapters serve as momentary glimpses of past–present lives moving through space and time, creating pathways for new ideas and perspectives, and offering multiple meanings and many voices. Overall, the book offers a sense of future-oriented remembering in relation to how artful memory-work can be used generatively for professional learning research in diverse educational contexts. The chapters demonstrate how artful memory-work can engender unique insights into teacher professional learning, with implications for personal, professional, and social transformation. Critically, the book as a whole highlights ways in which arts-based approaches to memory-work can play a critical role in pedagogies of reinvention and decolonisation, particularly in communities that have been marginalised from mainstream educational research. As Maxine Greene (1998) explained, "engagements with the… arts [can] release the imaginative capacity into play [and foster] a commitment to the risky search for alternative possibilities" (pp. 47–49).

But there is also a converse and unexpected outcome of this work in that the various chapters help us to dig deeper into the ways in which memory-work through art forms such as photography, drawing, collage, television, and film contributes to deepening an understanding of the arts and artful representation. To take an example from photography, the various exemplars help to frame the idea of "truth" (Is this right? or What truths have I been erroneously living with?) and, also, an acknowledgement of the significance of co-constructions of knowledge through the visual. In many of the chapters, emotion is prominent. The art forms themselves evoke emotion and the various authors explicitly acknowledge emotion in different ways, ranging from "stirring up memories" to recognising how deeply felt and long-held emotions might play a role in the decisions we make as teachers. In placing the chapter on ethical moments as the last chapter, we see that there is a case for saying, art = ethics. This may be a position held in artistic circles, but it a message that is driven home in the examples offered in the mosaic pieces. Finally, there is the role of recognition or recognising ourselves in various art forms. On one hand, recognition or recognising ourselves in art may not be a totally new idea. On the other, it is perhaps the personal descriptions of these "up close" instances of recognition that are rare and yet so important in professional learning. Thus, we are left with the idea of not just how art can be used in teacher memory-work studies, but what memory-work studies can say about art and artful inquiry.

References

Anderson-Patton, V., & Bass, E. (2002). Using narrative teaching portfolios for self-study. In N. Lyons & V. K. LaBoskey (Eds.), *Narrative inquiry in practice: Advancing the knowledge of teaching* (pp. 101–114). New York: Teachers College Press.

Coulter, C. A., & Smith, M. L. (2009). The construction zone: Literary elements in narrative research. *Educational Researcher, 38*(8), 577–590.

Department of Education. (1996). *South African Schools Act (Act 108 of 1996)*. Pretoria: Government Press.

Easton, L. B. (2008). From professional development to professional learning. *Phi Delta Kappan, 89*(10), 755–761.

Greene, M. (1998). Art and imagination: Overcoming a desperate stasis. In A. C. Ornstein & L. S. Behar-Horenstein (Eds.), *Contemporary issues in curriculum* (2nd ed., pp. 45–53). Needham Heights: Allyn & Bacon.

Haug, F. (1987). *Female sexualization: A collective work of memory* (E. Carter, Trans.). London: Verso.

Haug, F. (2008). Memory work. *Australian Feminist Studies, 23*(58), 537–541.

Haug, F. (n.d.). *Memory-work as a method of social science research: A detailed rendering of memory-work method*. Retrieved from http://www.friggahaug.inkrit.de/documents/memorywork-researchguidei7.pdf.

Hooks, B. (1994). *Teaching to transgress: Education as the practice of freedom*. New York: Routledge.

Mitchell, C. (2011). *Doing visual research*. London: SAGE.

Mitchell, C., & Reid-Walsh, J. (2002). *Researching children's popular culture: The cultural spaces of childhood*. London: Routledge.

Mitchell, C., Strong-Wilson, T., Pithouse, K., & Allnutt, S. (2011a). Introducing Memory and Pedagogy. In C. Mitchell, T. Strong-Wilson, K. Pithouse, & S. Allnutt (Eds.), *Memory and pedagogy* (pp. 1–13). New York: Routledge.

Mitchell, C., Strong-Wilson, T., Pithouse, K., & Allnutt, S. (Eds.). (2011b). *Memory and pedagogy*. New York: Routledge.

Mitchell, C., & Weber, S. (1999). *Reinventing ourselves as teachers: Beyond nostalgia*. London: Falmer Press.

Pelias, R. J. (2008). Performative inquiry: Embodiment and its challenges. In J. G. Knowles & A. L. Cole (Eds.), *Handbook of the arts in qualitative research* (pp. 185–193). Thousand Oaks: SAGE.

Pillay, D., Pithouse-Morgan, K., & Naicker, I. (Eds.). (2017). *Object medleys: Interpretive possibilities for educational research*. Rotterdam: Sense Publishers.

Pithouse, K., Mitchell, C., & Moletsane, R. (Eds.). (2009). *Making connections: Self-study and social action*. New York: Peter Lang.

Pithouse-Morgan, K., Mitchell, C., Pillay, D. (2012). Editorial: Memory and pedagogy special issue. *Journal of Education, 54*, 1–6. Retrieved from http://joe.ukzn.ac.za/Libraries/No_54_2012/Complete_issue.sflb.ashx.

Pithouse-Morgan, K., Mitchell, C., Pillay, D. (2014a). Editorial. *Educational Research for Social Change (ERSC), 3*(2), 1–4. Retrieved from http://ersc.nmmu.ac.za/articles/Vol_3_No_2_Editorial_pp_1_to_4_November_2014.pdf.

Pithouse-Morgan, K., Mitchell, C., & Pillay, D. (2014b). Self-study of educational practice: Re-imagining our pedagogies [Editorial]. *Perspectives in Education, 32*(2), 1–7.

Pithouse-Morgan, K., & Samaras, A. P. (2015). The power of "we" for professional learning. In K. Pithouse-Morgan & A. P. Samaras (Eds.), *Polyvocal professional learning through self-study research* (pp. 1–20). Rotterdam: Sense Publishers.

Strong-Wilson, T., Mitchell, C., Allnutt, S., & Pithouse-Morgan, K. (Eds.). (2013). *Productive remembering and social agency*. Rotterdam: Sense Publishers.

Waage, F. O., & Nordhagen, P. J. (2000). Mosaic. In *Encyclopaedia Britannica*. Retrieved from https://www.britannica.com/art/mosaic-art.

Webster-Wright, A. (2010). *Authentic professional learning: Making a difference through learning at work*. Dordrecht: Springer.

Wolpe, A., Quinlan, O., & Martinez, L. (1997). *Gender equity in education: Report of the Gender Equity Task Team*. Pretoria: Department of Education.

"To Seek Out *Something More*": Knowing the Teacher-Researcher Self Differently Through Self-narrative Writing and Found Photographs

Daisy Pillay, Sagie Naicker and Wendy Rawlinson

Abstract "'To Seek Out *Something More*': Knowing the Teacher-Researcher Self Differently Through Self-narrative Writing and Found Photographs" by Daisy Pillay, Sagie Naicker, and Wendy Rawlinson showcases the power of found photographs for evoking, constructing, and reconstructing memory in written self-narratives. The exemplars are drawn from Sagie Naicker's and Wendy Rawlinson's doctoral research in South Africa. Sagie drew on selected photographs to examine how his disability identity influenced his leadership practice, and his journey as an activist seeking social justice for people with disabilities. Wendy's found photograph evoked a bodily experience of being transported to a more imaginative space that triggered her curiosity for aesthetic pedagogical adventuring in her racially diverse classroom. Taken as a whole, the chapter demonstrates how, drawing multi-methodologically on self-narratives and the visual meaning making perspective of found photographs, the scholarship of self-awareness of teachers' ways of being, knowing, and doing can make significant contributions to teacher professional learning.

Keywords Identity · Memory-work · Photographs · Self-narrative writing
South Africa · Teacher professional learning

D. Pillay (✉) · S. Naicker · W. Rawlinson
School of Education, University of KwaZulu-Natal, Durban, South Africa
e-mail: pillaygv@ukzn.ac.za

S. Naicker
e-mail: sagie@newagestrategies.co.za

W. Rawlinson
e-mail: wendyr@dut.ac.za

S. Naicker
New Age Strategies, Durban, South Africa

W. Rawlinson
Department of Media Language & Communication, Durban University of Technology, Durban, South Africa

© Springer Nature Switzerland AG 2019
K. Pithouse-Morgan et al. (eds.), *Memory Mosaics: Researching Teacher Professional Learning Through Artful Memory-work*, Studies in Arts-Based Educational Research 2, https://doi.org/10.1007/978-3-319-97106-3_2

15

1 Introduction

Writing stories of self can serve as an "act of deliberate remembering" (Mitchell 2011, p. 45) of critical events and past moments to make memories available in self-narratives, which then can become research artefacts in and of themselves. As such, self-narrative writing offers teacher-researchers an alternate vantage point to unravel the complexity of teachers' lives and teaching practices, and an opportunity to engage more critically with personal, social, and educational lived experiences (Bullough 1994).

Hatch and Wisniewski (1994, p. 130) cautioned, however, that self-narratives shape and limit how teachers construct their own versions of their lived experiences because they are "bound by discourse structures to a limited range of expression and understanding." Visual methods can compensate for these limitations, and can offer teacher-researchers a way of seeing and studying self from yet another vantage point (Mitchell 2011; Mitchell et al. 2009). Visual ways of knowing in self-narrative accounts can reveal the embodied connectedness between the past and present, and the personal and professional in an integrated, dynamic, and nonlinear view of self and who one is in the world (Krall 1988).

The potential for visual meaning making in writing teachers' self-narrative accounts "lies in harnessing the power of images to bring things to light in both personal and public ways" (Mitchell et al. 2009, p. 119). In addition, Till (2008) identified teachers' visual meaning making in self-narrative accounts as sites for seeing truth, which, Boulton-Founke (2014) pointed out, can incite moments of disruption of the normative through affective engagement. Drawing on visual knowing "connects us to the self, yet distances us from ourselves" and in these in-between moments of slippage, teachers may imagine new and different ways of being and doing as teacher" (Mitchell et al. 2009, p. 119).

As Weber (2008) explained, visual meaning making in research can centre on "found material," which can include "personal photographs from [researchers'] own lives [that become] springboards for ... insightful work" (p. 48). This chapter draws multi-methodologically on self-narratives and the visual meaning making perspective of found photographs. The chapter uses self-narrative accounts and found photographs to access, examine, and reflect on memories and past experiences, and to inquire reflexively into imagining teacher-researchers' lives differently. The exemplars are drawn from Sagie Naicker's and Wendy Rawlinson's doctoral research. These exemplars illustrate how the meaning making potential of found photographs of self, and narrative accounts of self, can combine to embody excitement and emotion for knowing teacher-researcher self differently.

2 The Construction of the Chapter

The chapter writing was facilitated by Daisy Pillay, a teacher educator, educational researcher, and graduate supervisor working to support teacher learning and teacher change. In her own professional learning and scholarship, Daisy has engaged in

"To Seek Out *Something More*": Knowing the Teacher-Researcher ... 17

collaborative co-construction to engage reflexively with visual and written narratives of self as expressive spaces for autobiographical remembering that involves cognitive, motivational, and affective aspects (Pillay and Govinden 2007; Pillay and Pithouse-Morgan 2016; Pillay and Saloojee 2012). For this mosaic chapter, she facilitated the integration of two autobiographical teacher explorations, which draw on critical reflections of self-narratives and found photographs.

To begin the process, Daisy invited Sagie Naicker and Wendy Rawlinson to develop short mosaic pieces on looking at, or working with, their own photographs from their respective doctoral theses. Sagie's thesis (Naicker 2014a) was completed several years ago, and Wendy's is currently work in progress. Inspired by their own personal histories, Sagie and Wendy worked over an 8-month period to write about, and reflect critically, on their found photographs and the narrative accounts of the lived experiences related to them. They explored how they could use the "embodied aesthetic engagement" of their found photographs as "objects and social documents" (Mitchell and Allnutt 2008, p. 252) to engage critically with social injustices, and to implement socially just practices and discourses in their respective contexts.

During this period, Sagie, Wendy, and Daisy conversed regularly via e-mail and face-to-face about how the combination of self-narratives and found photographs were opening expanding pathways for unlearning prejudices and different forms of self-closure. In time, these conversations included possibilities for teacher change.

The chapter is organised into three sections. In the first two sections, are Sagie's and Wendy's self-introductions and their narrative exemplars, which were composed from their critical reflections on their self-narrative writing and found photographs of themselves. The third section includes all three authors' voices selected from the audio taped face-to-face conversations and e-mail conversations. These selections are analysed for the connections between the mosaics about knowing teacher-self differently, and for suggesting potential and possible development for researching teacher professional learning.

3 The Mosaic Pieces

Sagie Naicker's Self-Narrative
I am (Dhanasagaran) (Sagie) Naicker, an Indian man raised in a South African traditional Indian family steeped in culture, tradition, and values. My father strongly supported and promoted education because it was linked to progress and a way to cope with limited opportunities in an apartheid, race differentiated society. After completing my initial teaching degree, I went on to complete my honours and master's degrees in education. After teaching for a few years, I became a school counsellor and, thereafter, moved into school leadership and management. I have served as a superintendent of education management (SEM), leadership and management coach, director of The South African Institute of Sathya Sai Education (SAISSE), and as

founder chairperson of the Forget-Me-Not Sports Club for the Disabled. In 2011, I enrolled for a doctoral degree.

Drawing from the literature that suggests the value of reflection for educational leaders, I decided to undertake a self-study for my doctorate after I experienced a critical incident as a director of SAISSE. The self-study forced me to withdraw from the hurly-burly, frenetic leadership activities I was immersed in, and to look within for answers to questions that puzzled me. I created a digital memory box consisting of photographs, newspaper articles, and documents to act as memory prompts to remember events, evoke memory and emotion (Naicker 2014b). On gathering the artefacts, I found myself reminiscing as I started to rebuild connections with the past and started to reflect on the way I have changed and grown.

The dialectics of the actual self (images of the present self), ought self (others' images of self), and ideal self (images of the future possible self) were studied (Higgins 1987) to gain insights into my identities as a leader, and how these identities have shaped and influenced my leadership practice. In this mosaic piece, I examine what it is to be regarded as a person with a disability, how this identity influenced my leadership practice, and my journey as an activist seeking social justice for people with disabilities. I rely on two photographs, one of me as an able-bodied person and the second, as a person with a disability, to engage with my exploration and meaning making.

On Becoming a Paraplegic

I was 25 years old, and I was making progress in life. By then I had bought a brand-new car, taken over the bond payments for the family home, enrolled for post graduate study, was in a steady relationship, and was attracted to humanitarian work inspired by my deepening interest in spirituality. I was physically active and played volleyball in a league, football for the school staff team, and regularly jogged to keep fit. I was interested in the social and emotional well-being of my learners, and was appointed as a school guidance counsellor in a high school. I was blissfully unaware that this was all to change: that my life as a "normal" or "able-bodied" person was about to be radically disrupted, and was soon to be replaced with a new identity as a person with a disability.

Little Did I Know …

Little did I know that the last photograph that I would have of me standing up without assistive devices was taken at the official opening of the Sathya Sai Welbedacht Upliftment Project. On December 2, 1985, I was involved in a car accident and my life as I knew it changed forever. The nurses told me that I had injured my spinal cord, and the doctors told me that I would never walk again. I had become a paraplegic and the struggle to reclaim my life had just begun.

> This photograph was taken on 23 November 1985, nine days before the life-changing and life-defining accident. When I look at this photograph, I feel depressed; the hardships, physical pain, and challenges that I experience as a paraplegic overwhelm me. (Naicker 2014a)

The reference to the photograph (see Fig. 1) is poignant because it reveals my present self—longing for the completeness that was independent and free of mobility

Fig. 1 Sagie as an able-bodied person (Photographer, Andrew Naidoo, with permission)

assistive devices. Higgins' (1987) self-discrepancy theory suggested that the actual self strives towards becoming an ideal self. In this particular instance, there is a contradiction because I express the desire of going backwards instead of forwards because my ideal self in an able body is located in the past. The pain and hardship of being trapped in a body that is disabled with mobility impairment, and the barriers I experience daily, drives me to moments of extreme frustration. O'Connor et al. (2004) concluded that for paraplegics, even simple routine tasks demand a lot of energy and effort. I find the activities that able-bodied people take for granted, such as standing, walking, running, stepping over curbs, and climbing stairs, very difficult because both public and private places are not adapted for people with mobility impairments.

Blanes et al. (2009, p. 19) were of the view that "these barriers have a negative impact on the QoL [Quality of Life] and self-esteem of persons with SCI [Spinal Cord Injury]." In addition to the partial loss of sensation, I find the loss of normal urinary and bowel function, and increased spasticity quite stressful. I concur with Blanes et al. (2009, p. 19) who argue, "problems associated with an impaired body, such as pain, fatigue, urinary tract infections, spasticity and susceptibility to pressure ulcers, have a significant impact upon the lives of many people with SCI." The accident that led to my paraplegia has changed my life forever.

An Intelligent Mind Trapped in a Disobedient Body

I struggled to negotiate between the desire to function as an able-bodied person with an "intelligent mind" trapped in a "disobedient body" (Chib 2011, p. 9). The labels, a *person with a disability*, a *paraplegic*, and being *differently abled*, determined by my medical status redefined who I was. O'Connor et al. (2004, p. 11) were of similar view that medical status plays a significant role in defining feelings of difference, which "emerged as an important and disturbing aspect of living with paraplegia … related to being simultaneously invisible and overly visible in the eyes of the community."

> I recalled the initial reaction of my colleagues and learners when I returned to work as a paraplegic. It was a huge adjustment facing my colleagues, some of whom were very supportive and others just felt awkward around me … I worried my principal to give me challenging assignments as I felt he was not fair to me because I thought that he saw me as someone who was less capable.
>
> At the physical level, I appeared to be very conspicuous—people stared at my unusual swing-through gait with my crutches, and as I wheeled myself in a shopping mall. Paradoxically, I was invisible in the workplace and I initially struggled to gain the respect of my colleagues and seniors. I learnt that I would have to prove to my colleagues that I was competent, and was a valuable member of the team. I therefore worked very hard to debunk the stereotype that people with disabilities are not capable and do not add value at the workplace. (Naicker 2014a)

Only the Outer Me Had Changed

I threw myself into my work because I was determined to dispel the notion that I was not capable because I was now a paraplegic. In time, my colleagues learned that only the outer me had changed, but the old me was still very much the same.

I struggled to negotiate the balance of desiring independence and at the same time admitting that I needed help in some matters because of physical limitations. Like O'Connor et al. (2004, p. 414), I agree that people living with disabilities, makes them acutely aware of the limits to their independence, and that I need to establish a "balance between relying on others and maintaining personal control."

In time, I came across many well-intentioned people who did not feel pity for me but just saw me as a strong, independent person with mobility impairment. I made conscious efforts to overcome these barriers and appear to be "normal." I usually accepted environments that did not accommodate my special needs and tried to fit in without attracting too much attention to myself, even if it meant compromising my self-worth by accessing meeting and conference rooms through rear entrances that sometimes took me through unpleasant, restricted spaces. Watson (2002) aptly described the way I tried to fit in society when he wrote:

> People who have an impairment or chronic condition, it is argued, suffer a loss of self and go through a process during which they negotiate their lives in such a way to be ordinary as possible and so retain some contact with desired life-worlds. (p. 513)

Daring to Dream

Driven by a desire to be able-bodied and normal, I was hopeful that I would walk again without my elbow crutches. I believed that I would be able to integrate back into mainstream society and that I would be accepted without being made to feel that I was different. When a journalist interviewed me in 1988, I expressed this desire.

> I was delighted when I retrieved this newspaper article from the photographer (Fig. 2). Hope, courage, and determination are signified in this photograph. I did not realise then that the journey would be long and difficult and would eventually lead to the point where I am now more wheelchair bound. Notwithstanding this, I have no regrets for daring to dream that I could become normal again. (Naicker 2014a)

Disability Activist: My Personal–Professional Growth and Leadership Practice

My first-hand experience as a paraplegic, coupled with the heightened sense of justice and fair play that I described earlier, played a significant role when I helped co-found the Forget-Me-Not Sports Club for the Disabled. I made the following observation:

> When I chatted with a few other people who were disabled, I learnt that they did not work, did not have friends outside the disability sector, did not play sport, and spent most of their time at home. Their families did not have the means to take them out and they lived a very insular life divorced from mainstream society. As people with disabilities, we felt different from able-bodied persons as society saw us as people who were less fortunate and lesser beings who didn't count for much. (Naicker 2014a)

The Forget-Me-Not Sports Club has, for the last 28 years, acted as an advocacy group campaigning for the rights of people with disabilities and empowered people with disabilities to resist oppression and inequality. Initially, the club started out as a self-help organisation but over the years, it evolved into a self-organised entity that started to question the inequalities in society, and reflect its desire for its members to be included in mainstream society. We felt "discriminated against and marginalised because of [our] disability and had very limited access to fundamental socioeconomic rights such as employment, education, and appropriate health and welfare services" (Howell et al. 2006, p. 48).

As a club, we sought a transformed society where we would be treated with "dignity and equal access for personal development" (Siyabulela and Duncan 2006, p. 307). In this leadership experience, the vision was driven with the intention of making a difference, addressing a need, and serving others. Drawing on the success of Sri Sathya Sai Baba, my spiritual guide whose vision of free health care, drinking water, and education became a reality, I crafted a vision to emulate my spiritual guide.

In spite of the trials and tribulations that I have faced as a person with a disability, I regard it to be a positive and fulfilling experience because it afforded me the possibility to grow. Gardner et al. (2005) maintained that such life changing experiences accelerate authentic leadership development, and they described these moments as trigger events, which are opportunities for reflection, self-awareness, and self-regulation. In my personal history narrative, I recounted my life experiences

Fig. 2 Sagie as a person with a disability (Photographer, Nithia Naidoo; Copyright, African News Agency Pictures (*The Herald*), with permission)

and discussed the different leadership roles I have played, notwithstanding the fact that I am classified as a person with a disability.

Conclusion

The motor accident that led to my becoming a paraplegic at the peak of my youth altered my being significantly. Even though 29 years have gone by, I still experience a sense of otherness because paraplegia differentiates me from able-bodied people. Through the embodied processes of personal narrative self-study, leadership issues that challenged and puzzled me were reconstructed, deconstructed, and critically

"To Seek Out *Something More*": Knowing the Teacher-Researcher ...   23

reexamined to generate a more complete picture. My reflections are consistent with Gardner et al.'s (2005) exposition of authentic leadership theory, and I maintain that the trigger event for seeing truth (Till 2008) as a paraplegic enhanced my personal growth and ultimately my leadership practice—becoming an activist championing the personal, social, and educational rights of people with disabilities.

Wendy Rawlinson's Self-Narrative

I am Wendy Rawlinson and I have worked in education for the last 25 years. Trained in secondary education, I taught in a high school for a short period before moving on to lecture in higher education, teaching at two quite different technikons.[1] In 2001, I moved to the United States to teach for five years before returning to South Africa in 2007. I am currently a communication lecturer teaching classes of predominantly black African undergraduate students at a university of technology in South Africa. For my doctoral study, I am drawing on memory-work and personal history narrative to remember critical past–present experiences of my life that have fashioned me to be the teacher I am, so that I may open up thinking and understanding of what it means to be a communications lecturer in a diverse undergraduate class—and to debunk the stereotypes I held about the black African students who were failing the communications course that I teach. A photograph of myself, sitting on the trencadis bench in Park Guell, Barcelona, after attending a conference in 1995, served as a visual prompt for reflecting critically on my life as a communications teacher and the meanings and understandings I had come to adopt over time about my life as a teacher and my communication practices. Writing my narrative and inserting the "I" was my real struggle.

Growing Up White, Middle Class, and Privileged

Growing up in the 1960s during apartheid, my experiences of mixing with people of other races was confined to interaction with labourers, like our gardener. Black people didn't live in our area but some domestic helpers caught buses home. I wondered why the few black people who got onto the buses walked to the back of the bus and sat on the last seat. Our gardener, Charlie, came on Saturdays to work for us and although he was a jovial fellow, we had limited conversations with him because we couldn't speak isiZulu. Mom always gave him a delicious lunch but one nagging question that always plagued me was, "Why did he eat out of a tin plate?" Our interaction was limited because of language barriers, and the separateness of race and class (Soudien 2004).

White Middle-Class Education: A Seamless Transition ...

I started school in 1958 as a learner in a white school in a white neighbourhood. A whites-only school didn't seem strange to me because it represented my world. I considered this pleasant, orderly school environment normal. I never questioned the white middle-class educational landscape because that was what I grew up with—in

---

[1] "Technikons were South African institutions oriented to occupationally directed higher education. The intention was to teach high-level skills and knowledge to add on to the more practical training offered in technical colleges" (Harrison 2009, p. 259).

apartheid South Africa race would determine where one could live (Jacklin 2001) and white schools were allotted spacious and resource-filled classrooms.

My privileges continued into my teaching and lecturing life in historically white institutions. I started teaching in 1975, at an all-white boys' high school until my son was born in 1977. I then took up a position as a lecturer at a historically white technikon in 1982, with an all-white staff and student complement. The transition to higher education was relatively easy and I enjoyed being a lecturer in a collegial environment, lecturing to older students. The staff and students all seemed to share the same values.

It was a seamless move from an all-white school to an historically white institution (HWI). Because the institution comprised an all-white student and staff complement, and everyone spoke English, there was very little diversity and teaching was seamless (Jacklin 2001). I taught a prescribed curriculum, and the students were willing to learn the content I delivered and pass the exam. I felt safe and secure in my teacher role. After an unsuccessful application for a different position within the institution I made a decision to teach elsewhere.

An Outsider: "I Can't Help Being Born White!"

After leaving my position at the white technikon in 1990, I moved into an historically black institution. My position as white lecturer was inscribed with power, derived from my historically privileged race group and language (Christie and Collins 1982). The phrase *historically black* establishes a distinction between the type of educational institution with which I have been familiar in the past, and one which I now had to take up to continue my teaching career—as a single parent. Technikons and universities were organised along race and ethnicity, and black students were forced to attend those institutions in black areas that had been designated as black institutions. Funding was racially skewed and unequal, which meant a disparity existed between the resources and facilities at black and white technikons and universities. A lower status was accorded to black higher education institutions (Reddy 2004). Deciding to take up a position that was available here meant that I had to adjust to a different sociocultural context from that of the privilege and status I enjoyed at the white technikon where students and staff were of the same race and language, and possessed a similar cultural capital.

My struggle is best illuminated in the anecdote below, which I vividly recall in 1991 because it was a dilemmatic moment in which my white middle-class values were in tension with my professional responsibility as a communication lecturer. In allowing students to speak on a topic they had selected to develop their oral communication skills rather than prescribe what students should know about the subject, I was unprepared for a speech on Bantu Education, which was a controversial subject because it had, in essence, defined an unequal system of education during the apartheid era. Sipho was discussing the legacy of this act that had left negative imprints on his life .

"To Seek Out *Something More*": Knowing the Teacher-Researcher …

Lesson on Oral Presentation

Sipho (pseudonym): "Blacks were only fit for labour. We were considered not worthy of receiving a higher education. Maths wasn't necessary because we would be working in the fields. This … was the policy of Bantu Education." I shifted uncomfortably in my seat; it was true, but did he have to labour the point? I understand—it was a despicable policy.

Sipho: "We blacks didn't deserve an education it seems." The sarcasm in his voice was unmistakable. I could see Sipho's rapid breathing as the pitch of his voice rose a few notches.

Sipho: "Less than human! The whites did this—took away our power!" he continued. His anger was palpable.

Me: I wanted to scream out, "It isn't my fault!" I finally blurted out "I can't help being born white!" His voice was trembling, but I felt as if all eyes in the room were fixed on me.

Me: I cried out "I'm sorry … I'm sorry for the enforcement of such an evil system!" I felt as if the temperature in the room rose: as if a giant boiler had been switched on, and I alone was simmering in the suffocating liquid. (Personal journal)

I have never before been in a situation like that, where I felt anger so palpably. I felt as if I became a physical representation of the suffering inflicted on all black people and hence "the enemy." I trembled at the barrage of words that seemed to spew out at me. I felt like I became a target receiving intense hate arrows from the student. I understood in that moment how hostility and injustice, generated during apartheid, simmers under the surface, waiting to erupt in every situation of social and educational life in the South African context.

As an outsider and the only white in the room (McVee 2004), I felt targeted. The fear that I was outnumbered and not understood overwhelmed me. In negotiating this tension that I was experiencing as these multiple issues played themselves out in the classroom, all I could say was "I'm sorry." I felt out of my depth in the classroom where I felt I lost all control as a lecturer because I became defensive of my whiteness (Jansen 2009). Unexpectedly being confronted with my race and emotions shook my idea of my effectiveness as a teacher in the classroom. Up to this point, I had believed I was a good teacher—then I was suddenly confronted with my race and emotions that shook my idea of who I was as teacher in the classroom (Jacklin 2001). I was not only confronted with the deep-rooted effects of apartheid legislation, but also with my white privilege (Warren and Hytten 2004), and how particular values crippled me from understanding my students and the power of their voices enabled through oral speaking.

"Admitting I Am Sorry": Exploring New Meanings and Understandings

In considering a comment from a critical friend, "Why are you so defensive?" I recognised that defending my white privilege (McIntosh 1990) acknowledged how I have operated and became complicit in reproducing certain rules of apartheid in South Africa, as privileged white female.

The photograph of me seated on the trencadis bench, taken in Barcelona in 1995 (Fig. 3), is the artefact I chose from my personal narrative to inspire the juxtaposing and exploration of meanings and understandings of my life as communication lecturer, teaching predominantly black African undergraduate students.

Fig. 3 Seated on the trencadis bench (Photographer, Marí Peté, with permission)

> As I gaze at the trencadis bench with its multicoloured tile fragments, its vibrant patterns, and its sinuous shape, I recall how it contrasts my life, which reflects unidimensional, linear, and fixed teaching practices. Through reflexivity, invited by my bodily presence on the bench, I begin to question my traditional fixed notions of being a teacher that I carry with me, and my white privilege, expectations, and assumptions. (Personal journal, March 2014).

To Dream of the Kind of Teacher I Can Become

The memory of my body comfortably couched on the bench (Fig. 3) transported me to the imaginative, dreamlike space of Park Guell. The blurring of time enabled the recall of this magical experience, which happened 22 years ago—and jolted me to challenge myself and my fixed views of communication practices, which I enacted daily in my classroom.

> The space–time moment re-spatialises, in a flash, my desire for unknowing my traditional teacher-self that I struggle with as a white and privileged individual, and to revise what I want to be and know, and how I want to be known as a communication lecturer. I am inspired to imagine the potential magic of a new classroom that defies the rigid technicist's systems and actions I have called upon in my disembodied professional practices for so long. I imagine transforming my classroom into a colourful space: not monochromatic, but multifaceted and connected like the trencadis shards that make up the intricate patterns of the bench.

Fig. 4 Imagining aesthetic communication pedagogy (Photographer, Marí Peté, with permission)

Through confronting the limitations of my privileges and beliefs, I recognise that I can be a different teacher, nontraditional teacher, capable of changing my classroom where there are no hierarchies between white and black, where there are no more deficient learners and disadvantaged students who are judged as English second-language speakers and, by default, inferior. Instead, I imagine a classroom where many voices are valued—beyond race, class, culture, and cultural capital.

The photograph (Fig. 4) is of myself on the trencadis bench. Nestled on the bench, my embodied experience probes the depths of my encounter in Park Guell, transcending linear boundaries while confronting my comfortable limitations (Falzon 1998). I become free to think more broadly about new ways of being and becoming. In freeing my thought from what it silently thinks (Foucault 1985), I renew the choices at my disposal and choose to act in a different way, unhindered by my fixed values, beliefs, and perspectives. (Personal journal)

Conclusion

Writing my narrative and inserting the I was a struggle because I felt vulnerable including personal portrayals of my life into my professional experiences. However, it was only when I acknowledged that teacher identity is a tangled web of influences steeped in personal and professional experiences (Bukor 2013), that I was able to fully understand my communication practices.

The photo of me seated on the trencadis bench in a fairy-tale park setting jolted my researcher-self and evoked a bodily experience of being transported to a more imaginative space that triggered my curiosity for aesthetic pedagogical adventuring in my racially diverse classrooms.

I recognise that personal–professional learning can benefit from artful inquiries into the self, and that attention to material culture can be a beneficial and freeing means to learning (White and Lemieux 2015). I was able to examine my prejudices, attitudes, and assumptions that, prior to then, had not been under the gaze. The self-reflexivity prompted by the arts- based methods triggered emotions, feelings, and a probing of beliefs as a traditional teacher with fixed stereotypes of who my students are. Through the process of reflexivity, I am now able to negotiate a poetics, a creative space where alternate communication classes can take place, and a space where I can transcend my limitations—to live and teach more fully as a communication educator.

4 A New Assemblage for Knowing Teacher-Researcher Self Differently

In our face-to-face and e-mail conversations, we—Sagie, Wendy, and Daisy—shared and discussed developing points of synergy that we saw through juxtaposing Sagie's and Wendy's self-narrative pieces. We shared and discussed how our encounters with found photographs and written self-narratives opened up ways, first, to provoke and disrupt "what is" (Mitchell and Allnutt 2008, p. 260)—normative understandings of to be, know, and act as teacher-researchers—and second, how we could think about and enact teaching and researching differently. In the section below, we map out selected points of continuity that evolved from our conversations and deepened and expanded our learning about pathways to perform and embody (Boulton-Founke 2014) knowing the teacher-researcher self as an emancipatory and creative experience. To close this section, Daisy offers a poetic reflection on our co-learning.

4.1 Seeking Selves Outside of Recognition

We discovered that the found photographs developed a gravitas because of the intensity of the representation, and the value they accrued. Sagie expressed this as follows: "I was delighted when I retrieved this newspaper article from the photographer." Sagie was able to create moments to remember and to create a powerful memory of his tragic accident. Such memories are the kinds that trigger emotion that troubles and provokes reflexive inquiry into "what was" or "what is," and to suggest, "what could be" (Mitchell and Allnutt 2008, p. 260). Sagie wrote in his e-mail conversation with Wendy and Daisy, "This understanding that identity is 'composed of multiple, context-dependent selves represented in an interrelated memory network' McConnel et al. (2012, p. 380), demanded from me a stepping back, a stepping away, and through a closer and deeper studying and exploration of the photograph, it brought to the surface the existential desire to seek answers to the questions: 'Who am I?' 'What am I?' and, 'What can be improved?' In response Wendy replied, "I am also inspired to imagine the potential magic of a new classroom that defies the rigid technicist's systems and actions I have called upon in my professional practices for so long. I imagine transforming my classroom into what I desire it to be, and can create—a colourful classroom: not monochromatic, but multifaceted like the trencadis shards that make up the bench."

4.2 A Transgressive Jolt from the Familiar Teacher-Self

We learned that found photographs of a personal event possess the past (Krall 1988) and remain in the person's life story. In this reflexive visual encounter, we encountered our teacher-selves connecting with passionate feeling to the memory experience. This passionate feeling jolted us into opening up possibilities for a new and different perspective to reconnect and realign the personal–professional, mind–body, past–present, and the emotional–cognitive. Then, when we used self-narrative writing around the found photographs, we discovered that, together, they served as a conduit and voice for the imagination and the invisible in a momentary, embodied act by intellectuals (Emihovich 1994).

Provoking affective bodily memories had an empowering effect for both Wendy and Sagie. Wendy found herself wanting to improve her pedagogical skills in a way that would challenge her disembodied stance in the context she was teaching. Wendy now confesses that "awareness of my whiteness prompted an intentional effort to take an ethical stance to transform both myself and my practices, and to move beyond them (Foucault 1985)." Sagie describes the photo of himself on crutches, thus: "My first-hand experience as a paraplegic heightened my sense of justice and fair play as a leader. I take disability as a challenge that offers me opportunities to transcend limitations and become a fuller being." Like Gadamer (1976), we recognise how our past lived experiences can shape and inform our beliefs and perspectives in the choices we make, hope for, or avoid as teacher-researchers. Simultaneously, we recognise that we can take possession of any such moment lingering in memory as it "flashes up" (Benjamin 1968, p. 257), to reveal hidden features of the present and past (Denzin 2007). We realise that we can create a new and different version of the past, and a new version of self as teacher from these significant revelations.

4.3 Photographs and Narratives of Self as Pedagogical Spaces

We agree with Ayers and Ayers (2014) that teachers need to be aware of their teaching selves, their choices, and the preferences that inform their pedagogical practice. Writing self-narratives with found photographs provides teacher-researchers opportunities to face up to themselves, and to dwell in their own struggles from a more embodying perspective, which could inform their teacher identities differently (Vinz 1997).

Wendy's growing self-awareness is expressed in her remark, "The introduction of arts-based methods paved the way for me to use creative methods such as collage and artefacts in my classroom in order to shift power hierarchies in the classroom, and to foster greater connection and participation of students." Sagie has developed a new perspective and perception of himself as a different kind of teacher leader: "Leading the Forget-Me-Not Sports Club for the Disabled not only enhanced my leadership development but also provided the opportunity to challenge the stereotypes I had associated with disability." We believe that our experiences of the impact of our reflexive self-narratives have bridged the distance between the private and the societal, and allowed us an affable and cohesive view of the present and "a more complete understanding of the human condition" (Krall 1988, p. 478).

4.4 Weaving Different Stories for Embodied, Generative Learning

From the conversations that took place between the three authors, Daisy selected phrases and words to create two free verse poems, "Disability Enables" and "Total Design," which provided impetus for further reflection on the learning generated by weaving together Sagie's and Wendy's stories.

Disability Enables

Disability, empowering,
disability enables
Disability, something more
transformation of self
Lying under the surface
invisible, powerful

Visual memory of photographic images of dis/abled self, and the meaning of self in self-narrative writing, serve as sites, not just for "seeing truth" (Bennett 2003, p. 29), but also for feeling and thinking truth. We found that when we were feeling and thinking truth, we experienced moments of slipping in and out of the normative and linear dis/abled self recalled through this affective engagement (Boulton-Founke 2014), to seek out *something more*. Researching teacher learning artfully for disruption, and through the affective dimension, can make available the "invisible of the visible thought" (Sheerin 2009, p. 73), and the less clearly articulated desires and interests that create and invite (Boulton-Founke 2014) knowing the teacher-researcher self differently.

> **Total Design**
>
> different stories
> seemingly disparate
> woven to fit.
> to enhance the total design.
> the beauty of mosaic patterns,
> side by side

Researching teacher professional learning in visual, storied ways, is an ongoing, nonlinear, complex, and seemingly disparate process. As mosaic patterns, the beauty of different stories woven side by side can connect to create a total design of embodied, generative teacher-researcher learning.

4.5 Finishing Touches

We have experienced how the power of found photographs can evoke and construct memory in self-narratives, which enable a number of possibilities. These possibilities can include a deepening of the essence of being unique, a provocation of *what is* known, (Mitchell and Allnutt 2008), and of possibilities for unknowing (Vinz 1997), as well as "what could be" for knowing the self and being in the world.

Visual and narrative ways of making meaning of teachers' everyday lives and practices hold the power to provoke the imagination and to reflect in order to develop greater awareness and understanding of one's perspectives and desires and even dreams (Greene 1988). Reflection can emancipate (Krall 1988), when we can "think with a [life] story" (Bochner 1997, p. 436), or when we "open ourselves to ourselves" (Ellis and Bochner 2000, p. 761) and engage in "thoughtful recovery of [our] educational experiences" (Krall 1988, p. 467). Such emancipatory reflections inform ways of freeing up embedded meanings, struggles, desires, dreams, and lingering events.

As Bullough (1994) highlighted, we cannot ignore our life histories and our personal experiences as teacher-researchers. It follows that we need to explore our lived experiences to understand how our values and beliefs, perspectives, and perceptions influence the choices we make daily—personally, socially, and professionally. We understand that such knowledge is deeply embodied, and requires risk taking and vulnerability.

When we study self critically, "the formative contextualised experiences of our lives influence how we think about" and act as teacher-researchers (Samaras et al. 2004, p. 905). These influences open up pathways for professional growth in ways that not only end up changing oneself, but also serve "as impetus for tackling the wider social problems that contextualise our individual [teacher] lives" (Mitchell et al. 2009, p. 119).

We believe that when we draw multi-methodologically on self-narratives and the visual meaning making perspective of found photographs, an important scholarship of self-awareness is developing. The scholarship of self-awareness of teachers' ways of being, knowing, and doing can make significant contributions to teacher professional learning.

By assembling Sagie's and Wendy's self-narratives and their found photographs, we were able to explore how the "past surfaces in our 'everyday'" (Talya Chalef as cited in Till 2008, p. 107) and how, as teacher-researchers, they chose to deal with these entanglements. When we work artfully, with memories elicited through chosen photographs, we can see "truth … that registers the pain of memory as it is directly experienced to communicate a level of bodily effect" (Bennett 2003, p. 29). This powerful effect reveals our own complicity and can produce new understandings for self knowing, and personal and social change as teachers.

Acknowledgements We are thankful to our peer reviewer, Joan Lucy Conolly (Durban University of Technology, South Africa), for her encouraging and insightful feedback on this chapter.

References

Ayers, R., & Ayers, W. (2014). *Teaching the taboo: Courage and imagination in the classroom.* New York: Teachers College Press.

Benjamin, W. (1968). *Illuminations.* New York: Harcourt, Brace & World.

Bennett, J. (2003). The aesthetics of sense memory: Theorising trauma through the visual arts. In S. Radstone & K. Hodgkin (Eds.), *Regimes of memory* (pp. 27–40). London: Routlege.

Blanes, L., Carmagnani, M. I. S., & Ferreira, L. M. (2009). Quality of life and self-esteem of persons with paraplegia living in São Paulo, Brazil. *Quality of Life Research,18*(1), 15–21. https://doi.org/10.1007/s11136008-9411-9.

Bochner, A. P. (1997). It's about time: Narrative and the divided self. *Qualitative Inquiry,3*(4), 418–438.

Boulton-Founke, A. (2014). Narrative form and Yam Lau's Room: The encounter in arts-based Research. *International Journal of Education & the Arts, 15*(17). Retrieved from http://www.ijea.org/v15n17/.

Bukor, E. (2013). The impact of personal and professional experiences: Holistic exploration of teacher identity. *Working Papers in Language Pedagogy (WoPaLP),7,* 48–73.

Bullough, R. V., Jr. (1994). Personal history and teaching metaphors: A self study of teaching as conversation. *Teacher Education Quarterly,21*(1), 107–120.

Chib, M. (2011). *One little finger.* New Delhi: Sage.

Christie, P., & Collins, C. (1982). Bantu Education: Apartheid ideology or labour reproduction? *Comparative Education,18*(1), 59–75.

Denzin, N. K. (2007). *Searching for Yellowstone: Performing race, nation, and nature in the New West.* Walnut Creek: Left Coast Press.

Ellis, C., & Bochner, A. P. (2000). Autoethnography, personal narrative, reflexivity: Researcher as subject. In N. Denzin & Y. Lincoln (Eds.), *Handbook of qualitative research* (2nd ed., pp. 733–768). Thousand Oaks: Sage.

"To Seek Out *Something More*": Knowing the Teacher-Researcher … 33

Emihovich, C. (1994). Distancing passion. In J. A. Hatch & R. Wisniewski (Eds.), *Life history and narrative* (pp. 37–48). London: Falmer.

Falzon, C. (1998). *Foucault and social dialogue: Beyond fragmentation*. New York: Routledge.

Foucault, M. (1985). *The use of pleasure: The history of sexuality* (Vol. 2, R. Hurley, Trans.). New York: Pantheon.

Gadamer, H.-G. (1976). *Philosophical hermeneutics* (D. E. Linge, Ed. & Trans.). Berkeley: University of California Press.

Gardner, W. L., Avolio, B. J., Luthans, F., May, D. R., & Walumbwa, F. (2005). "Can you see the real me?" A self-based model of authentic leader and follower development. *The Leadership Quarterly,16*(3), 343–372. https://doi.org/10.1016/j.leaqua.2005.03.003.

Greene, M. (1988). What happened to imagination? In K. Egan & D. Nadener (Eds.), *Imagination and education* (pp. 45–55). New York: Teachers College Press.

Harrison, L. (2009). A tinker's quest: Embarking on an autoethnographic journey in learning "doctoralness". In K. Pithouse, C. Mitchell, & R. Moletsane (Eds.), *Making connections: Self-study & social action* (pp. 253–268). New York: Peter Lang.

Hatch, J. A., & Wisniewski, R. (Eds.). (1994). *Life history and narrative*. London: Falmer.

Higgins, E. T. (1987). Self-discrepancy: A theory relating self and affect. *Psychological Review, 94*(3), 319–340. http://psycnet.apa.org/doi/10.1037/0033-295X.94.3.319.

Howell, C., Chalklen, S., & Alberts, T. (2006). A history of the disability rights movement in South Africa. In B. Watermeyer, L. Swartz, T. Lorenzo, M. Schneider, & M. Priestley (Eds.), *Disability and social change: A South African agenda* (pp. 46–84). Cape Town: HSRC Press.

Jacklin, H. (2001). *Teachers, identities, and space*. Retrieved from http://www.oerafrica.org/system/files/Being%20a%20Teacher%20readings_Section%20One_Reading%203.pdf?file=1&type=node&id=9154&force=.

Jansen, J. D. (2009). *Knowledge in the blood: Confronting race and the apartheid past*. Cape Town: Juta.

Krall, F. R. (1988). From the inside out: Personal history as educational research. *Educational Theory,38*(4), 467–479.

McConnell, A. R., Shoda, T. M., & Skulborstad, H. M. (2012). The self as a collection of multiple self-aspects: Structure, development, operation, and implications. *Social Cognition,30*(4), 380–395. https://doi.org/10.1521/soco.2012.30.4.380.

McIntosh, P. (1990). Unpacking the knapsack of white privilege. *Independent School,49*(2), 31–36.

McVee, M. B. (2004). Narrative and the exploration of culture in teachers' discussions of literacy, identity, self, and other. *Teaching and Teacher education,20*(8), 881–899.

Mitchell, C. (2011). *Doing visual research*. London: Sage.

Mitchell, C., & Allnutt, S. (2008). Photographs and/as social documentary. In J. G. Knowles & A. L. Cole (Eds.), *Handbook of the arts in qualitative research* (pp. 251–263). Thousand Oaks: Sage.

Mitchell, C., Weber, S., & Pithouse, K. (2009). Facing the public: Using photography for self-study and social action. In D. Tidwell, M. Heston, & L. Fitzgerald (Eds.), *Research methods for the self-study of practice* (pp. 119–134). New York: Springer.

Naicker, D. (2014a). *Piecing together the leadership puzzle: A self-study of practice* (Unpublished doctoral dissertation). University of KwaZulu-Natal, South Africa. Retrieved from http://researchspace.ukzn.ac.za/handle/10413/12642.

Naicker, S. (2014b). Digital memory box as a tool for reflexivity in researching leadership practice. *Educational Research for Social Change (ERSC), 3*(2), 51–65. Retrieved from http://ersc.nmmu.ac.za/view_edition.php?v=3&n=2.

O'Connor, D. L., Young, J. M., & Saul, M. J. (2004). Living with paraplegia: Tensions and contradictions. *Health and Social Work,29*(3), 207–218. https://doi.org/10.1093/hsw/29.3.207.

Pillay, D., & Govinden, B. (2007). "In search of home": Practices of the self in selected teacher narratives. *Journal of Education,42*(1), 125–139.

Pillay, D., & Pithouse-Morgan, K. (2016). A self-study of connecting through aesthetic memory-work. In J. Kitchen, D. Tidwell, & L. Fitzgerald (Eds.), *Self-study and diversity II: Inclusive teacher education for a diverse world* (pp. 121–136). Rotterdam: Sense Publishers.

Pillay, D., & Saloojee, S. (2012). Revisiting rurality and schooling: A teacher's story. *Perspectives in Education,30*(1), 43–52.

Reddy, T. (2004). Higher education and social transformation: South Africa case study. *Council on Higher Education.* Retrieved from http://www.che.ac.za/media_and_publications/research/higher-education-and-social-transformation-south-africa-case-study.

Samaras, A. P., Hicks, M. A., & Berger, J. G. (2004). Self-study through personal history. In J. J. Loughran, M. L. Hamilton, V. K. LaBoskey, & T. Russell (Eds.), *International handbook of self-study of teaching and teacher education practices* (Vol. 2, pp. 905–942). Dordrecht: Kluwer.

Sheerin, D. (2009). *Deleuze and Ricoeur: Disavowed affinities and the narrative self.* London: Continuum.

Siyabulela, K., & Duncan, M. (2006). Psychiatric disability and social change: An insider perspective. In B. Watermeyer, L. Swartz, T. Lorenzo, M. Schneider, & M. Priestley (Eds.), *Disability and social change: A South African agenda* (pp. 291–310). Cape Town: HSRC Press.

Soudien, C. (2004). "Constituting the class": An analysis of the process of 'integration' in South African schools. In L. Chisholm (Ed.), *Changing class: Education and social change in post-apartheid South Africa* (pp. 89–114). Cape Town: HSRC Press.

Till, K. E. (2008). Artistic and activist memory-work: Approaching place-based practice. *Memory Studies,1*(1), 99–113.

Vinz, R. (1997). Capturing a moving form: "Becoming" as teachers. *English Education,29*(2), 137–146.

Warren, J. T., & Hytten, K. (2004). The faces of whiteness: Pitfalls and the critical democrat. *Communication Education,53*(4), 321–339.

Watson, N. (2002). Well, I know this is going to sound very strange to you, but I don't see myself as a disabled person: Identity and disability. *Disability & Society,17*(5), 509–527.

Weber, S. (2008). Visual images in research. In J. G. Knowles & A. L. Cole (Eds.), *Handbook of the arts in qualitative research* (pp. 40–53). Thousand Oaks: Sage.

White, B. E., & Lemieux, A. (2015). Reflecting selves: Pre-service teacher identity development explored through material culture. *Learning Landscapes,9*(1), 267–283.

Working with Photographs: Seeing, Looking, and Visual Representation as Professional Learning

Claudia Mitchell, Katie MacEntee, Mary Cullinan and Patti Allison

Abstract "Working with Photographs: Seeing, Looking, and Visual Representation as Professional Learning" by Claudia Mitchell, Katie MacEntee, Mary Cullinan, and Patti Allison, focuses on the use of photography in memory-work in teachers' professional learning, drawing on exemplars produced by three teacher-researchers. Katie MacEntee worked with preservice teachers at a South African university using photo elicitation. The teachers look back on what they learned in a project on sexuality education using the arts. Mary Cullinan, studying at a Canadian university, also used a type of photo elicitation but in so doing "co-constructed" with her participants, all late entry women reflecting on coming into doctoral study, the meanings of these experiences. Patti Allison, also at a Canadian university, engaged in the process of curating a photo album based on family photographs and in so doing engaged in a decolonising process. In looking across the three mosaic pieces, we get a sense of the ways in these methods offer what could be termed as deeply "emotive" work.

Keywords Canada · Memory-work · Photographs · Photo album
Photo elicitation · South Africa · Teacher professional learning

---

C. Mitchell (✉) · M. Cullinan
Department of Integrated Studies in Education, McGill University, Montreal, Canada
e-mail: claudia.mitchell@mcgill.ca

M. Cullinan
e-mail: Mary.cullinan@mail.mcgill.ca

C. Mitchell
School of Education, University of KwaZulu-Natal, Durban, South Africa

K. MacEntee
Faculty of Environmental Studies, York University, Toronto, Canada
e-mail: macentee@yorku.ca

P. Allison
Department of Language and Literacy Education, University of British Columbia, Vancouver, Canada
e-mail: pralison07@gmail.com

© Springer Nature Switzerland AG 2019
K. Pithouse-Morgan et al. (eds.), *Memory Mosaics: Researching Teacher Professional Learning Through Artful Memory-work*, Studies in Arts-Based Educational Research 2, https://doi.org/10.1007/978-3-319-97106-3_3

1 Setting the Scene

This chapter examines the ways in which working with photographs, such as family photos, and specific forms of photo-elicitation including working with found images can contribute to artful memory-work in professional learning. Building on the work of scholars in visual studies, the chapter highlights the significance of seeing, looking, and visual representation in autoethnographic engagement and memory studies. The use of photographs in memory-work and self-study approaches to professional development builds on the work of Mitchell and Weber (1999) where teachers "looked back" at their own school photographs as an entry point to deepening an understanding professional identity. More recent work has included Brian Benoit's critical autoethnographic memory-work studies based on going back to the schools of his childhood and photographing these schools. The process of taking the pictures is itself a memory-work prompt (Benoit 2016a, b).

The chapter is made up of three mosaic pieces. The first exemplar comes out of Katie MacEntee's doctoral fieldwork with preservice teachers at a university in South Africa. In that work, she used a type of photo-elicitation as a memory prompt. The preservice teachers had all participated in a series of "youth as knowledge producers" arts-based workshops on collage, image theatre, and photovoice as tools for engaging young people in addressing HIV and AIDS. Several years after the preservice teachers had had this training, and had worked as student teachers in rural schools, Katie drew on a series of process photos from the arts-based workshops to engage in remembering and assessing what they had learned.

Mary Cullinan, a resource teacher in a primary school, reports on her doctoral work at a Canadian university with late-entry women doing a Ph.D.—including many women whose postgraduate work was in education. In the study, she drew on the use of photographs in narrative inquiry. Conducting face-to-face and Skype interviews with the participants, she realized that visual images alongside the spoken narratives served to deepen an understanding of their memories of learning and their struggles and accomplishments. Many of the participants selected a visual image that they shared with Mary. Some of these images were family photographs, while others were more metaphoric, found images. Other participants were keen to have Mary select possible metaphoric images that would represent their experiences (of building bridges, falling into deep holes, weathering the stormy seas, and so on). What the approach highlights is a type of photo-elicitation combined with a recognition of the significance of images of objects and things in evoking experiencing of adult learning.

In the third exemplar, Patti Alison writes about engaging in a curating an album project as an approach to engaging in self-study and memory-work in relation to her own process of decolonization as a Canadian. The idea that photographs colonize is something that many visual anthropologists have written about (Hartmann et al. 1999; Lutz and Collins 1993). The curating an album project described elsewhere (Mitchell and Allnutt 2008; Mitchell and Pithouse-Morgan 2014; Mitchell et al. 2009; Reinikainen and Zetterström-Dahlqvist 2016; Smith 2012) was not originally conceived of as a group activity so much as a project of personal identity and cultural production. The visual artefact produced in the album project is a small photo album, typically framed in a Dollar Store (discount shop), 10 by 15 cm photo album containing plastic sleeves. The format is simple: a title page, a typed or handwritten curatorial statement fitting into one plastic sleeve, each photo fitted into a plastic sleeve on one side of album and the caption for that photo in the plastic sleeve directly facing it, typically a process explanation in a plastic sleeve near the end, sometimes an author's statement and something about the author or artist.

2 What Difference Does This Make? Photo-Elicitation Interviews as Memory-Work Snapshots

by Katie MacEntee

The Youth as Knowledge Producers project ran from 2008 to 2010 through the Centre for Visual Methodologies for Social Change (CVMSC) at the University of KwaZulu-Natal (UKZN), South Africa. It was headed up by Jean Stuart with overlap with a related project, "Every Voice Counts," led by Naydene de Lange. The concept of youth as knowledge producers (YAKP) draws on the work of Lankshear and Knobel (2006) who referred to young people's visual media productions as representations of cultural knowledge and resources for social change. YAKP had three main goals: (1) to engender a practice of self-study and reflexivity with regards to preservice teachers' approaches to HIV education, (2) to provide training for preservice teachers in participatory arts-based methodologies for HIV education, and (3) to provide opportunities for preservice teachers, as peer educators, to gain practical experience facilitating these methodologies in different educational contexts (Centre for Visual Methodologies for Social Change 2010).

Over the course of three years, 2008–2010, a total of 44 preservice teachers who were enrolled in UKZN's faculty of education participated in the study. The study can be described to have had two phases. In 2008, the first phase, 20 participants were trained in collage, drumming, hip hop, forum theatre, photovoice, and participatory video as means of addressing South Africa's AIDS epidemic through a participatory pedagogy for sexual health education. In 2009, these participants themselves facilitated two participatory visual workshops. The first workshop was with a counselling education class in the faculty of education at UKZN. The second workshop was at a rural high school approximately two hours' drive away from the university. For this component, the preservice teachers worked in pairs to carry out participatory visual workshops with learners.

In 2010, I was invited by the YAKP research team to be involved with the second phase of the project. I conducted a 2-day collage training session attended by two of the original preservice teachers along with 24 new participants. Collage is an artistic practice that involves cutting and pasting disparate images (usually found images from magazines, books, or newspapers) and arranging them in such a way as to create a new holistic image. Following this training, five participants volunteered to cofacilitate a collage workshop on youth activism and HIV and AIDS attended by 18 learners from two rural high schools. In the week following the workshop, members of the research team, two of the preservice teachers, and I returned to the rural area to attend a presentation of the learners' collages during school assemblies and at a community event organized for World AIDS Day (MacEntee 2011).

The Photo-Elicitation Process: Reacting to and Reflecting on Photographs
In 2012, I returned to UKZN. With the support of the YAKP research team, I was interested in assessing the outcomes, both immediate and ongoing, for preservice teachers who had learned about participatory visual methodologies in the context of addressing HIV and AIDS. I was able to track down seven of the original YAKP preservice teacher participants. Of these seven, three were able to participate in the assessment. Monique and Sarah[1] had both joined YAKP to participate in the collage training in 2010. At the time of the assessment, Monique was in the final months of the 4-year teaching program and was specializing in drama and sports sciences. Sarah was in her third year and was concentrating on languages—Afrikaans and English. David had joined YAKP in 2008 and had taken part in all the YAKP trainings, and had been a member of the facilitation team with counselling class. In 2010, he had attended the collage training and cofacilitated the collage workshop alongside Sarah, Monique, and me. At the time of the assessment, David was working on a master's in education at UKZN. With each of these three students, we considered the question: "what difference do the arts make to HIV and AIDS education?"

My assessment methodology drew on the participatory visual framework followed by YAKP. Wanting to engage the participants in a process of looking back, I used photo-elicitation interviews that asked participants to look at photographs taken during the YAKP activities in 2010. Looking at the photographs elicited a looking back and remembering of events from the workshops. It also elicited a looking forward at the consequences of participating in YAKP since the project had ended. In this mosaic piece, I focus on the photo-elicitation data that depicts this concomitant looking back and forward.

Photo-elicitation interviews have been made popular by scholars such as Harper (2002) and Banks (1999), although Collier (1957) described a similar procedure 40 years earlier (Richard and Lahman 2015). The method involves documenting participants' reactions and reflections to researcher-generated photographs. Prosser and Schwartz (2003) stressed that researcher-generated photographs are subjective visual records of an event. The images represent the photographer's individual viewpoint and what she or he considered of value to document during the YAKP training and workshop. Recognizing this limitation, I chose 20 photographs from a collection of over 220 that I thought would give a sense of the range of YAKP activities we carried out in 2010. The collection included images of the participant trainings, images of the preservice teachers' collages, the groups of rural learners that the facilitators worked with closely, and the learners' collages. The pictures were a mixture

---

[1] I used pseudonyms for all participants.

of candid and posed photographs. Some photographs showed people's faces and others focused on the workshop settings and the artistic process or the collages under construction.

I conducted the photo-elicitation interviews with each participant one-on-one at UKZN. The meetings were approximately 90 min each. The interviews were audio recorded and then transcribed verbatim. According to Harper (2002), photo-elicitation "mines deeper shafts into a different part of the human consciousness than do word-alone interviews. It is partly due to how remembering is enlarged by photographs and partly due to the particular quality of the photograph itself" (pp. 22–23). Drawing on these ideas, I began the interview by explaining to the participant that I was interested in their responses to the photographs, that I hoped the pictures would help jog their memories of events from several years earlier, and to let me know if they had questions or if they did not remember what was happening in a photograph. For the interviews with Monique and Sarah, we started the interview sitting side-by-side and scrolling through the photos on my laptop. The photographs were arranged chronologically in a digital album, with photos of the training in collage method followed with photos of the rural workshop when the participants were cofacilitators. After three or four photographs, if the participant was silent, I would ask a probing question: "Do you remember this part of the training?" "Does anything in this image jump out at you?" or "What are you thinking about as we look at these photographs?" With David, who had been involved with YAKP since 2008 and participating in activities that I did not have photographs for, I started the interview asking him to relate his experiences in the earlier years and then introduced the photographs when his recounts had reached 2010.

Looking Back and Looking Forward Through Photo-Elicitation

While participants all looked at the same 20 images, not surprisingly, they reacted to different images. However, the process of reaction was often similar, with the participant looking to establish the context of the photograph and then, with some prompting, tracing memories or thoughts that the image evoked. Establishing context was usually done by asking a question. For instance, when Sarah saw a photograph of herself sitting at a table with a group of learners, she asked, "Oh, weren't we helping the learners there sign those forms—ethics and stuff?" Because I was present at the events, although I was seldom in the picture and may have been behind the camera taking the photo, the participants looked to me to confirm their interpretation of the photograph. This tendency to want to "check in" may highlight the power dynamic of the interview process. My role as interviewer and in a sense the owner of the photographs put me in a position of power, being able to confirm or deny the participant's interpretation. It also suggests that using the researcher-generated visual documentation of the YAKP events could have fixed the participants' memories to a particular image or interpretation of an image. It is likely that having participant-produced images may have disrupted this dynamic. My strategy at the time was to focus less on the participants' exact remembering of events, and instead use these check in questions as an opportunity to prompt reflections on the issue that they had identified, regardless if this was what was depicted in the photograph or not.

Therefore, in follow up to Sarah's question about ethics, I asked, "Yes, how did that go, the ethics and consent process, for you?" To this prompt, Sarah explained that asking learners for consent, rather than just telling them what to do as might be done when using a more teacher-centred approach, helped strengthen her rapport with the learners. She felt the consent process made the visual process more transparent and it helped instill the participatory, learner-centred intentions at the workshop.

Seeing Their Photographs of Collages Again, and Reflections on Collaboration
Responding to images of the training sessions, participants were often struck by the pictures of the collages that they made. David excitedly exclaimed, "Yup, that is ours!" (Interview transcript, p. 25). His use of the plural pronoun, *ours*, denotes the collaborative process of collage making and the ongoing shared ownership of the final product. Monique also remembered and was excited about the collage her group produced, "We did something very creative in our group. I remember that! I remember!" (Interview transcript, p. 2). Sarah laughed when she saw her collage for the first time since the training. She explained:

> I'm laughing because these pictures, you kind of make them say whatever you want them to say. Like for that one, the one with the children, we kind of said that they are orphans who have been effected by the disease. And I think we also talked about the stigmas attached within the communities themselves. And then you find that sometimes these children, especially if it's in a rural area, they have to deal with all the burdens with raising their smaller brothers and sisters without any assistance because people in the community kind of point fingers. (Interview transcript p. 10)

Prompted by the photograph, Sarah's memory illustrates how the group came together around the collage process. She recounted the production process as having engaged them in a verbal discussion on the social impacts of the epidemic as well as a visual negotiation of how to represent these issues in their collage (Fig. 1).

Images of People, and Reflections on Learning
The participants' most vivid responses were made when they looked at photographs taken at the rural workshop. Monique said, "Some of the children's faces [I remember] so clearly. Even though she is looking down now I remember her face" (Interview transcript, p. 4). In particular, the images of the facilitation team and the young people who the participants met over the weekend elicited the most dynamic ideas on how the YAKP process had affected them. The learnings from the weekend stayed with the participants long after YAKP was over. When seeing a picture of another of the cofacilitators showing the students her birth control pills, Sarah reflected:

> [She] said something that caught me totally off guard. Um, maybe because personally, myself, I hadn't started using contraceptives then. But since, I've started to accept. Hey, why not use them? Because, really, especially amongst the African community, I mean, contraceptives, especially for young people, it's a myth. They just believe in abstinence and nothing else … I didn't know how the learners were going to respond, what they were going to say. You know, I was a bit nervous myself! … Maybe these things aren't so bad after all. I mean, I've started. It was easier after that, for me to start using them because I realize … young people are using these things! There's nothing wrong. (Interview transcript, p. 7)

Fig. 1 Sarah's collage (Photographer, Jean Stuart, with permission)

When Sarah watched her peers talk candidly about contraception, she was nervous how the youth would respond. She was nervous of her own response to this frank discussion. But when the conversation was met openly by the young people she realized that the topic might not be as dangerous as she originally thought it would be. Since YAKP, Sarah has become more open and accepting of young women using contraceptives.

For Monique, viewing a picture of the group of students who she worked with prompted her to articulate what the learners taught her:

> I actually remember these pictures... Because that was something that I wasn't aware of ... where they come from was very rural, so they told me. And they weren't used to luxurious things. ... And it also made me look at the lens that children—and I say children because they are still in school ... and you think that they are innocent but really they do understand what is happening around them. So that was something that was really shocking for me. (Interview transcript, p. 5)

Returning to the title of the project, Youth as Knowledge Producers, this example illustrates the knowledge exchange from learner to educator that can occur through the participatory visual process. Later in the interview, Monique returned to this example again, explaining how it has continued to influence her teaching practice, her intention as a teacher to be a support to learners, and to listen to their experiences in order to begin to address their challenges—where they are at.

Conclusion

As Harper (2002) observed, this research also found that not all photographs were automatically evocative and different participants were drawn to respond to different photos. Because the participants and I were both present when a photo was taken, the participants seemed to gain confidence in their contributions to the interview process when they were able to verify with me their interpretation of the photos visual content. My responses to these questions required some sensitivity in order to not have my own interpretation of the photograph take over or marginalize that of the participants. I also wanted to avoid fixing the participants' interpretations of the ideas in the moment that was photographed. My responses, therefore, emphasized the ideas, issues, and memories the photograph evoked rather than whether or not the participant's interpretation of the photographs was accurate or complete.

Photo-elicitation interviews are best understood as a snapshot, of a moment in time, of participants' understanding at the time of the interview. In this sense, the participants' reflections on their understandings of their YAKP experiences were fluid or shifting. Their responses to the photographs denoted the passage of time and their reflections encompassed their past experiences (such as their collaborative process in the training or at the workshop), the present (their description of how this experience has influenced their actions and beliefs at the time of the interview), and their future intentions (how they intend to approach learners in the future). If the photo-elicitation activity were to happen again, participants would likely echo these responses while also providing new responses and new ideas on the impact of YAKP, based on their new experiences and perspective of life at the time of the interview. The YAKP project, therefore, has left an ongoing impression on the preservice teachers. David articulated this well when he stated: "The impact has been made on me. But I think you can't really tell the impact because you have put tools in the hands of people who are being exposed to hundreds of learners every day of their lives" (Interview transcript, p. 28).

3 What Does Support Look like?

by Mary Cullinan

I began my doctoral research, *Echoes of Late-Entry Women in Academia: A Narrative Inquiry* (Cullinan 2015), by collecting the narratives of women who had returned to university later in life to pursue doctoral studies. In the research, I was particularly interested in the lived experiences of these "late-entry" women, as I termed them, of the journey through doctoral studies. Initially, I began by collecting the stories through oral interviews. Some of these were face-to-face and some were through Skype. Before long, however, I began to find that their stories conjured up images in my mind as a listener. I reasoned that, surely, the women too, were either remembering images from long ago (as when they recalled their childhoods) or, in some cases,

Working with Photographs: Seeing, Looking, and Visual ...

images from nature (as when one compared the difference between a doctorate and a master's to "taking a leap over a vast chasm"). I could visualize these images and realized that I too had come up with images to describe my own late-entry process. I think back to one of my own rather theatrical images when asked about my feelings in the doctoral program. Instantly, the question brought to mind an image of jumping through hoops of fire.

I laughed as I produced the blazing image. Was it too dramatic? Was I exaggerating the whole affair? I didn't think I was. When I showed that image to other doctoral students, they all agreed. It was, at times, exactly how they felt. I also had another image that I felt described my place in time. It was a wooded path with a stream of light coming through (Fig. 2). When I shared this, I found again that many other women recognized the darkness as well as the light. Many of the images that women produced seemed to be a variation on the theme of "into the light." As I was visualizing these images, I found myself wondering if encouraging the women to actually present their images could assist others in appreciating the challenges and complexities of the late-entry woman's journey into academia. In general, the women were keen to provide images to illustrate their journey. In some cases, this was in the form of an evocative passage about their journey. In others, the women asked me to provide an image. I did so and, of course, each time asked for their approval of the image.

Some women produced images that depicted obstacles in their way: a ship on stormy seas, or a car headed into the night with only a beam of light ahead. Yet, almost always, there was light. As a woman investigating the challenges of doctoral study, I found these recurring images reassuring.

Although I have successfully defended my research and am now the extremely proud holder of a doctoral degree, these images, fraught with obstacles and worry, or in some cases, impending doom, bring me right back to where I was and how I felt such images described my feelings more than any words possibly could. I considered that images, real or imagined, might provide yet another view on women's accounts. Sometimes words just don't seem to convey our deepest true feelings. We can see this when we see the joy or the sorrow on a person's face, or when we utter those words: "I don't know what to say." Might images that go along with the women's stories help to bring readers to a deeper understanding of their stories? Might the teller feel that, yes, at times words are inadequate? Indeed, it seemed as though this were true. As soon as I offered the opportunity to the women to illustrate their journey with an image, many seized the opportunity. And I saw, at times, words were indeed inadequate. Using visual images allowed the women to provide yet another way of seeing and documenting their doctoral journey.

Here we see Marnie's[2] illustration of the importance of companionship, both in her words and image:

> In this picture (Fig. 3), I am part of a group that is madly paddling a raft on the Elaho River, trying to keep going forward and not fall into the river! This experience reminded me of the group of grad students (all women) with whom I worked. We named the group, "Study Sisters." The purposes were to support each other in our educational adventures and our

---

[2] All participants have pseudonyms.

Fig. 2 Into the light (Photographer, Mary Cullinan, with permission)

personal lives—to help keep each other afloat and moving forward in spite of the rapids and rocks we ran into along the way. Both experiences were exhilarating although, admittedly, one was much shorter than the other! (Cullinan 2015, p. 149)

From my many conversations with late-entry doctoral women students, I saw quickly that it would have been so easy for many women, myself included, to feel

Fig. 3 Helping each other to stay afloat, despite the rapids and rocks (Photographer, Mary Cullinan's participant, with permission)

disillusioned with the whole process of doctoral study. We were constantly questioned about the possible value of a newly minted PhD at a later stage in life. We were regularly reminded of the unlikelihood of ever recouping our financial investment. Yet, women forged ahead with their dream—one claiming she was making an investment in her intellect while another said the graduate dean had once told her to honor the highest in herself. She continued, "The dean said, for you, it is obviously the intellect." While some had external forces prodding them on, many women relied on internal fortitude. Some had the important support of family. Partner support figured prominently, as did support form peers and advisors. Yet, often, they referred to their internal fortitude, as we can hear echoed in these words from Sarah. She described an image of bright red tulips draped with feathery white snow:

> The image of these tulips in snow represents what I am trying to create (and therefore live the rest of my life) through growth in the Ph.D. program. While I have a lot of support of those around me, the journey sometimes holds the isolation and frostiness of winter. This photo speaks to the perseverance that is needed despite huge obstacles. It also speaks to patience and grace. (Cullinan 2015, p. 184)

Being an avid gardener, Sarah's image spoke to me. It immediately brought to mind the long dreariness of a Canadian winter and the hope of brightened spirits that these spring flowers bring. This, in many ways, is a metaphor for the conception, growth, and development of the thesis as well as some of the loneliness along the way.

Fig. 4 Awkward yet majestic (Photographer, Mary Cullinan's participant, with permission)

Another woman, Betty, likened herself to the giraffe, saying she was "awkward, yet majestic." We can hear the hesitancy, but the resolve, in her words as she described this picture (Fig. 4) she took while completing fieldwork in Africa:

> They are so tall, and their legs are so long, too. It reminded me of my awkwardness in the program. It really did, it made me think of that. How I'm growing different muscles, yeah I can do it too! You know, introducing myself into all these new worlds of activity. (Cullinan 2015, p. 158)

Images of nature abounded in the collection of photos. Jane compared herself to a heron on Dow's Lake in Ottawa (Fig. 5). She felt that she and the heron were similar. Her First Nations boyfriend said, "Maybe it's your spirit animal." Jane investigated. She said that one of the things about the heron is that it is independent and works on its own. She felt that definitely represented the kind of work that she was doing, even though she had to be self-disciplined, which she found difficult.

Jane explained:

> The heron wades in the water and brings things up from the water into the air, spanning these different realms of consciousness or awareness. The earth, of course, is like the ground that holds us all, that grounds us. And then, the water represents the unconscious mind. The heron brings things from the unconscious to the conscious. The heron sees opportunities where other birds don't. (Cullinan 2015, p. 157)

Fig. 5 Independent and strong (Photographer, Mary Cullinan's participant, with permission)

In preparation for our interview, Stephanie brought along a quote from Ouspensky (as cited in Shulman 1995) that she'd found in a book while she was studying, which helped inform her and, in turn, gave me something to mull over long after our talk together: "Think long thoughts, each of our thoughts is too short. Until you have experience from your own observation of the difference between long and short thoughts, this idea will mean nothing to you" (p. 54). Intrigued with this quote, I later asked Stephanie if she might like to supply an image to go along with it. She sent me the image below (Fig. 6). She provided the following words because she wanted to clarify what it meant to think long thoughts. Her image speaks to both the loneliness and perhaps also the danger, I thought.

> Single mother, caretaking daughter, full time worker, part time student—identities I juggled throughout my master's. Finished, I breathed out. Never again. But Ouspensky's suggestion (as cited in Shulman 1995) that each thought is too short, our thoughts should be much longer, pulled me back to do a doctorate—almost against my conscious will. Women carry

Fig. 6 Melvin Charney—Canadian Centre for Architecture Sculpture Garden, Montreal, Canada (Photographer, Mary Cullinan's participant, with permission)

bags. Women are interrupted. Women multitask. We so rarely have that opportunity to think a long thought—the pleasure and the pain of stretching a long thread forward—having your ideas spread out, connect, go deep. It's hard to describe how seductive and how precarious it is. (Cullinan 2015, p. 177)

Then there were images of crumbling bridges, vast canyons, and hazardous roads submitted as representative of the doctoral journey. Cindy, an ex-banker who had returned to academia found little support among her banking friends. They could not fathom why someone would leave a secure job in a bank for an insecure future in academia. She did, however, find tremendous support from her family. Yet, even though she was well supported by family, she felt quite alone at times:

My image? It is the view from the driver's seat of a car looking out on the flat highway on the snowy prairie. The highway is partly figurative—the journey is the Ph.D. I spent a lot of time driving between jobs to make ends meet. I did most of that driving in the winter. So, that is why the snow is there. Also, the process felt inhospitable at times, like there was the danger of negative consequences, that is, my progress or my project—the car—break down. It's a highway rather than a country road because I felt I had to go fast to keep up—stop only when there was a rest stop and keep my eyes on the road. The flat prairie is symbolic because I felt like I couldn't see where I was going. If there were mountains or some other goal at the end, I could see the distance decreasing but it always felt like I had to just keep going and going because someone else would decide when I had arrived at the end. I certainly didn't feel like it was smooth sailing. Things could randomly appear in the middle of the highway that would require sudden steering to avoid—like the time in real life on the QEW[3] when a ladder came flying off a van in front of me. But I did feel like I was driving in some way.

---

[3]Queen Elizabeth Way, a freeway in Toronto, Ontario, Canada.

No one but me was responsible for my sitting down at my desk every day and working. (Cullinan 2015, p. 194)

Indeed, many of the women often referred to the fact that, although the journey was difficult, they were the ones who'd put themselves on that road.

For my part, was it a never-ending journey? At times, it surely felt that way. However, it was worth every step. I have yet to find the image that really sums that feeling up. It was definitely a journey filled with questions about my ability to complete the doctorate. Slowly, I began to understand the true meaning of words like tenacity, endurance, and strength. Perhaps most important of all, as I learned how to cultivate my own inner strength, I was able to give voice and, I believe, make place for other women as they made their way through doctoral study. I still carry the women's stories in me; they are now a part of who I am. I began to answer the important questions that Laurel Richardson (1997) posed: "How do we put ourselves in our own texts, and with what consequences? How do we nurture our own individuality and at the same time lay claim to 'knowing' something? These are both philosophically and practically difficult problems" (p. 88). Being able to share women's stories helped me lay claim to knowing something. As a woman who set out with such concerns about my ability to fit in at the doctoral level, this is a significant claim to make. I am proud of my success. If I could only illustrate that warm feeling …

4 Curating an Album: Working with Family Photographs[4]

by Patti Alison

The protocol for this memory-work self-study project was as follows:

Part 1: Curating the Album

- Find (not take) 5–7 photographs dealing with social change.
- Bring copies of your photos to a "Curating an Album" group workshop. Share and discuss your photos in small groups. Help each other put the photos in an order that will show the issue of social change you have chosen. Discuss possible titles for the album in the small group.
- Following the workshop, arrange your photos in the order you feel best works for you.
- Write a curatorial statement of 100–150 words. Your curatorial statement is an opportunity to help guide the way audiences perceive your exhibition. It is a chance to communicate directly with viewers, help them understand your point of view, and get them excited and curious about the work they are about to experience.
- Create a title for your album.

---

[4]Components of this narrative are also found in Mitchell et al. (2017).

- Write a caption for each image. Each caption should be 2–3 sentences long about the theme. Captions are brief summaries of what the images mean and why they were chosen.

Part 2: Audiencing and Reflecting

- Present your own album to the rest of the group.
- Listen to and view the presentations of the others in the group on their albums.
- For the final, post production step, write a short reflection on various aspects of the whole process (from beginning to end—and including being part of an audience for the curated albums of the others). What was it like working with these images? What were the challenges? What part did you like doing best? Can one "picture" social change? Is there social change somewhere in you?

The photo album workshop that we did in our class at the University of British Columbia (Canada) and the subsequent creation of the album were illuminating experiences. I think the work presented in the "Curating Albums" PowerPoint offered by Claudia Mitchell, and in the video, *Our Photos, Our Stories, Ourselves* (Mak et al. 2006), demonstrated that the photo album project seemed to be able to bring out difficult aspects of the work being done by educators and health care workers in parts of South Africa.

I felt drawn to this project as soon as I realized we would have the opportunity to explore our own photographs and family ideas. I did feel a bit overwhelmed about finding the "right" photos because I have many, many print and digital photos. Additionally, I had some doubts about my ability to find a social change theme—what did that have to do with my family photos? I began looking at the idea of decolonizing or colonialism, which then helped me to whittle down the photos to 20–30 choices. I think the album activity began to have more value when looking through the lens of my master's courses. I was tempted to ask my sister for help with the project because she can be a great resource, however, I decided to let myself be guided by the photos.

My family is fortunate to have a wealth of photographs starting with my great-great grandparents. Both of my parents' families immigrated to Canada in the early 1900s from Scotland, and their paths can be traced through photos so I always enjoy going through them. However, this time, I began looking with a more critical eye as to what social change can be found in the images. According to family stories, our families left Scotland in order to find a better, more prosperous life. Although, the photographs show struggle and success, which can be seen as positive from a family point of view, I have begun to look more critically at what these images do not tell—the underlying story of Canada. My goal has been to decolonize myself and this activity, curating the album, was another step in that direction.

Another part of the process that I valued was the sharing and discussion with our classmates. I was nervous at first but once the discussion started, it seemed as if we could trust each other and share our tentative ideas. I am not sure I would have come to my theme if we had not had such a good discussion in the album workshop in which we engaged before we completed our albums; both group members were encouraging and provided effective feedback. Based on this aspect of the sharing in a small group setting, I actually looked forward to the audiencing portion of the assignment where we would be presenting our work to the whole class.

After experiencing the audiencing component of the project, I could see another layer to this activity. The two parts that had the most impact on me were the personal topics participants shared and the vulnerability that a project like this seems to bring to the surface. Before some students spoke, they prefaced their presentation with saying they felt "exposed" in the sharing. I think this response points to the authentic nature of this activity and perhaps the ability of this type of project to get at data that an interview situation may not be able to reveal.

A new learning from this activity is that social change can be found in pictures. This is a project that I realized that I could use with high school students—specifically with my Grade 10 and 11 English students. I planned to incorporate the album project into the First People's English course materials in the fall after the course at University of British Columbia, because I would be asking the students to do a social justice project. In the past, I have used a photo gallery walk in a section on stereotyping in one unit and now I plan to expand the walk into a more substantial album-type project. I think the different approaches noted in Mitchell and Allnutt's (2008) chapter, "Photographs and/as Social Documentary," can be applied in the classroom. For example, the "found" photos or the "transition" photos can be utilized in developing students' critical thinking about social change in areas such as colonialism, discrimination, or poverty (p. 259). Overall, completing the curating an album project was a valuable learning experience for me.

5   What Can We Learn from This Work with Photographs in Relation to Memory-Work and Self-study?

Clearly photographs can be very powerful tools for evoking the past and yet also for being future-oriented. In Patti's case, for example, the actual album production process has influenced her ideas for teaching in the future. In the different exemplars, the use of photographs varied from recent memory in their use in photo-elicitation, to even two or three years later as can be seen in Katie's mosaic piece, through to a distant past as found in Patti's work with family photographs. Perhaps one of the greatest surprises in the use of images in photo-elicitation is the role of the researcher in selecting the photos. It was Mary, as researcher, who found or selected some of the photos but as evoked by the narratives of the participants and as such creating something of a loop. Katie preselected the 20 photos from a digital collection of 220. The role of self-recognition is key in both, as so powerfully highlighted by one of the South African teachers: "Yup, that's ours." In the three exemplars, the role of production itself varied. At one end, Patti was engaged in the creative production of creating the album using photographs from the family album. Critically in her work is the idea of audiencing, a term used by Rose (2012) to draw attention to an additional layer of textuality in cultural production.

There is something about the collaborative nature of looking, whether this is one-on-one in the case of Katie and Mary's exemplars, or in a small group (Patti), that prompts a critical dialogue about the issues under investigation. We might also draw attention to how, in these collaborative interactions, there seems still to be a need for some type of facilitated direction (e.g., Katie's use of prompting questions in the interview process or the step-by-step protocol offered by Claudia in Patti's group). In Mary's work, there is a type of coproduction based on a very close and personal relationship between Mary and each of her participants as they negotiate a visual artefact. But this idea of coproduction is not absent from Katie's exemplar even though on the surface it might seem less apparent. Even if she has not written about it explicitly, the fact that she is also part of "doing memory"—both by virtue of the fact that she was so involved in the Youth as Knowledge Producers project as a whole and by virtue of the fact that she had to go through 220 photos to find 20 to use in the photo-elicitation activity—suggests a close relationship both to the viewers and to the viewing/looking process.

The three exemplars also help us to think about materiality as a dynamic in self-study and memory-work. On one hand, Patti worked with the original copies of the photos from her family album, making copies to use in the curated album. Her work is akin to what Annette Kuhn (1995) and others have written about in relation to the actual locating and handling of the photos. Katie and Mary, on the other hand, worked with digital and online images. While the participants did not manipulate or rework the images, perhaps their engagement is closer to what Strong-Wilson et al. (2016) wrote about in the various digital memory pieces they described in their work with teachers.

There is also some aspect of the process that may be problematic in terms of the sense of documentation, which also may tell us something about the compelling features of this work to self-study. For example, there was a concern expressed on the part of participants for capturing (and fixing) a "true" representation. Katie talks about struggling to keep participants from focusing too much on whether their interpretation of the photographs was accurate and, rather, to think more about the overarching ideas and memories a photograph evokes as part of self-study. Differently, Mary talks about images getting to a true emotion in a way that words cannot. And then, nearer the end, she admits that there are certain aspects of the journey that she has yet to find the right image to describe—the right one is out there and she just has to find it. In Patti's case, it is her references to decolonizing methods that prompted her to question the historical documentation of the photos (the fixing of her family's immigration story in narratives of struggle and resilience) and to dig more deeply into the history that was not pictured or privileged—which pictures were taken and which were not (as in the case of land displacement or forced migration of Indigenous peoples in Canada)?

Finally, the three exemplars highlight the intimacy potential of working with photographs and a sense of what might be termed *emotive* self-study. Looking at Katie's use of the photographs in YAKP, we get that sense of ownership, collaboration, and togetherness. In the symbolic images used in Mary's work, these images relate to a

Working with Photographs: Seeing, Looking, and Visual ...

particular (hopeful) struggle. In Patti's work this comes up again in relation to how the various teacher participants expressed the feeling of hesitancy at being exposed during their album presentations but yet, as she observes, appreciative of the authenticity of the activity. Taken together, these mosaic pieces point to the potential for richness in professional learnings.

Acknowledgement We thank Relebohile Moletsane (University of KwaZulu-Natal) for her insightful peer review of this chapter.

References

Banks, M. (1999). *Rethinking visual anthropology*. New Haven: Yale University Press.
Benoit, B. A. (2016a). *Understanding the teacher self: Learning through critical autoethnography* (Unpublished doctoral dissertation). McGill University, Canada.
Benoit, B. A. (2016b). Schools as artifacts: Critical autoethnography and teacher renewal. *McGill Journal of Education/Revue des sciences de l'éducation de McGill, 51*(3), 991–1225.
Centre for Visual Methodologies for Social Change (CVMSC). (2010). *Center for Visual Methodologies for Social Change: Annual report, September 2009–December 2010.* Retrieved from http://cvm.ukzn.ac.za/Libraries/Annual_Reports/Annual_Report_2009_-_2010.sflb.ashx.
Collier, J. (1957). Photography in anthropology: A report on two experiments. *American Anthropologist, 59*(5), 843–859.
Cullinan, M. (2015). *Echoes of late-entry women in academia: A narrative inquiry* (Unpublished doctoral dissertation). McGill University, Canada.
Harper, D. (2002). Talking about pictures: A case for photo elicitation. *Visual Studies, 17*(1), 13–26.
Hartmann, W., Silvester, J., & Hayes, P. (1999). *The colonizing camera: Photographs in the making of Namibian history*. Cape Town: University of Cape Town Press.
Kuhn, A. (1995). *Family photographs: Acts of memory and imagination*. London: Verso.
Lankshear, C., & Knobel, M. (2006). *New literacies everyday practices and classroom learning*. Maidenhead: Open University Press.
Lutz, C., & Collins, J. L. (1993). *Reading national geographic*. Chicago: University of Chicago Press.
MacEntee, K. (2011, May). *Participation in leadership: A critical analysis of participation in a youth-based collage workshop on HIV and AIDS in rural South Africa*. Paper presented at the Comparative & International Education Society, Canada.
Mak, M. (Director), Mitchell, C., & Stuart, J. (Producers). (2006). *Our photos, our videos, our stories* [Video production]. Montreal: Taffeta Productions.
Mitchell, C., & Allnutt, S. (2008). Photographs and/as social documentary. In G. Knowles & A. Cole (Eds.), *Handbook of the arts in qualitative research* (pp. 251–264). London: SAGE.
Mitchell, C., de Lange, N., & Moletsane, R. (2017). *Participatory visual methodologies: Social change, community and policy*. London: SAGE.
Mitchell, C., & Pithouse-Morgan, K. (2014). Expanding the memory catalogue: Southern African women's contributions to memory-work writing as a feminist methodology. *Agenda, 28*(1), 92–103. https://doi.org/10.1080/10130950.2014.883704.
Mitchell, C., & Weber, S. (1999). *Reinventing ourselves as teachers: Beyond nostalgia*. London: Falmer Press.
Mitchell, C., Weber, S., & Pithouse, K. (2009). Facing the public: Using photography for self-study and social action. In D. Tidwell, M. Heston, & L. Fitzgerald (Eds.), *Research methods for the self-study of practice* (pp. 119–134). New York: Springer.

Prosser, J., & Schwartz, D. (2003). Photographs within the sociological research process. In J. Prosser (Ed.), *Image-based research: A sourcebook for qualitative researchers* (pp. 115–130). London: RoutledgeFalmer.

Reinikainen, L., & Zetterström-Dahlqvist, H. (2016). Curating an exhibition in a university setting: An autoethnographic study of an autoethographic work. In D. Pillay, I. Naicker, & K. Pithouse-Morgan (Eds.), *Academic autoethnographies: Inside teaching in higher education* (pp. 69–83). Rotterdam: Sense Publishers.

Richard, V. M., & Lahman, M. K. (2015). Photo-elicitation: Reflexivity on method, analysis, and graphic portraits. *International Journal of Research & Method in Education, 38*(1), 3–22.

Richardson, L. (1997). *Fields of play: Constructing an academic life.* New Brunswick: Rutgers University Press.

Rose, G. (2012). *Visual methodologies.* London: SAGE.

Shulman, A. K. (1995). *Drinking the rain.* New York: Farrar, Straus & Giroux.

Smith, A. (2012). Take a picture: Photographs, dress, gender and self-study. In R. Moletsane, C. Mitchell, & A. Smith (Eds.), *Was it something I wore? Dress, identity, materiality.* Cape Town: HSRC Press.

Strong-Wilson, T., Mitchell, C., & Ingersoll, M. (2016). Exploring multidirectional memory-work and the digital as a phase space for teacher professional development. In M. Knoebel & J. Kalman (Eds.), *New literacies and teachers' professional development* (pp. 151–172). New York: Peter Lang.

Picturing a More Hopeful Future: Teacher-Researchers Drawing Early Memories of School

Kathleen Pithouse-Morgan, Hlengiwe (Mawi) Makhanya, Graham Downing and Nontuthuko Phewa

Abstract "Picturing a More Hopeful Future: Teacher-Researchers Drawing Early Memories of School" by Kathleen Pithouse-Morgan, Hlengiwe (Mawi) Makhanya, Graham Downing, and Nontuthuko Phewa brings together three exemplars from teacher-researchers who have used memory drawing as an arts-based method for self-study research. The three mosaic pieces offer diverse yet also complementary stories brought forth by South African teachers' drawings of early memories of school in the 1970s, 1980s, and 1990s. The drawings and accompanying written reflections offer access to poignant stories of the past, with a shared ethical purpose of engendering new and more optimistic stories for the future. Overall, the chapter illustrates the usefulness and impact of memory drawing as an emotional entry point for teachers' future-oriented remembering.

Keywords Arts-based methods · Memory drawing · Memories of school
Memory-work · South Africa · Teacher professional learning

> How can early memories of school, of teachers, of particular episodes … become part of our work as teachers? (Mitchell and Weber 1998, p. 46)

K. Pithouse-Morgan (✉) · H. Makhanya · G. Downing · N. Phewa
School of Education, University of KwaZulu-Natal, Durban, South Africa
e-mail: pithousemorgan@ukzn.ac.za

H. Makhanya
e-mail: hdbmhlongo@yahoo.com

G. Downing
e-mail: GDowning@vegaschool.com

N. Phewa
e-mail: nontuthu123@gmail.com

© Springer Nature Switzerland AG 2019
K. Pithouse-Morgan et al. (eds.), *Memory Mosaics: Researching Teacher Professional Learning Through Artful Memory-work*, Studies in Arts-Based Educational Research 2, https://doi.org/10.1007/978-3-319-97106-3_4

1 Teachers' Memory Drawing as a Pedagogy of Reinvention

In a retrospective essay (in Mitchell et al. 2011a), social researcher Claudia Mitchell described how a serendipitous foray (with long-term collaborator Sandra Weber) into working with a collection of children's drawings in the early 1990s grew into a pioneering transnational exploration of drawing as a research method. This multifaceted body of work by Mitchell and her colleagues now spans more than two decades (see, for example, Mitchell 2011; Mitchell 2017; Weber and Mitchell 1995, 1996). In reflecting on her enduring interest in this area, Mitchell identified four vital characteristics of drawing as an accessible and interactive social research method:

(a) "Simplicity. All you need is paper and a pencil or pen."
(b) The "tangibility" and "concreteness" of drawings. "We can lay out ... drawings and look at them and touch them. We can scan them and look at them on the computer screen."
(c) The "immediacy of drawings and their potential to move audiences."
(d) The "interpretive possibilities in drawings. ... Everyone can have an interpretation" (Mitchell et al. 2011a, p. 2).

This chapter builds on one particular aspect of Mitchell and her collaborators' work: drawing as a means for teacher-researchers to make visible and learn from their own and other teachers' early memories of school (Mitchell and Weber 1999). The intention of such memory-work is to explore how teachers' early memories of school, represented as drawings, can serve as resources for individual and collective teacher professional learning in relation to wider educational and social concerns. This is informed by a conception of teacher professional learning that focuses on teachers as professionals initiating and directing their own learning through dialogue and interaction to enhance their continuing growth and to contribute to the wellbeing of others (Pithouse-Morgan and Samaras 2015).

As Mitchell et al. (2011b) pointed out, "drawing as a research method is more than just ... making drawings. ... It entails participants drawing and talking (or writing) ... about the meaning embedded in their drawing" (p. 25). Combining memory drawing with personal reflection and collective discussion can generate professionally and socially valuable learning (Mitchell and Weber 1999). In particular, engaging individually and collectively with thought-provoking questions about what memory drawings suggest about the past, present, and future can generate "future-oriented remembering" (Mitchell and Weber 1999, pp. 221–223). Mitchell and Weber have conceptualised this as "a pedagogy of reinvention"—"a process of going back over something in different ways and with new perspectives, of studying one's own experience with insight and awareness of the present for the purposes of acting on the future" (1999, p. 8).

Drawing as a research method can be inspired by and overlap with scholarship on the use of visual arts and images in qualitative research (Mitchell et al 2011b; Weber 2008). However, when the main purpose of teacher memory drawing is for its processes and products to contribute to future-oriented professional learning, issues of aesthetics or artistry can be downplayed to alleviate anxieties that might inhibit drawing. For instance, Mitchell and Weber (1999) advised: "Do not worry about artistic ability. ... Even stick figures will do" (p. 130). Another way of looking at this advice is that, when teachers are reinhabiting and making visible their early memories of school through drawing, more childlike drawings such as stick figures can help to evoke a child's perspective and perceptions in an artful way.

2 Teachers' Memory Drawing as an Entry Point for Self-study Research

As a contribution to the scholarship of teachers' memory drawing as a pedagogy of reinvention, this chapter brings together three original exemplars from South African teacher-researchers who have used memory drawing as a self-study research method: Hlengiwe (Mawi) Makhanya, Graham Downing, and Nontuthuko Phewa. The exemplars and ensuing reflection and discussion were collated by Kathleen Pithouse-Morgan, a teacher educator with an interest in drawing as a method in self-study research (Pithouse 2011).

Self-study research concentrates on the researcher's own professional learning in a particular context, with the intention of enhancing the growth of professional practice and wisdom (Samaras 2011). It is based on a conception of teachers and other professionals as self-directed agents of their own learning who learn through interaction with others (Pithouse-Morgan and Samaras 2015). Self-study research methodology "entails multiple and diverse self-study methods" (Samaras 2011, p. 87). Samaras (2011) explained that "the method you choose depends on what you are trying to understand and how a particular method helps you achieve that understanding" (p. 88). As demonstrated by the three exemplars in this chapter, working with early memories of school through drawing is one method that can serve as a useful entry point for teachers' self-study research (Mitchell and Weber 1999).

Because of intriguing resonances and divergences in the use of memory drawing in self-study research by Mawi (Makhanya 2010), Graham (Downing 2014), and Nontuthuko (Phewa 2016), Kathleen requested that they each compose a brief mosaic piece for this chapter—in whatever configuration they preferred. The chapter was developed over a 6-month period from the three mosaic pieces and e-mail conversations between Kathleen, Mawi, Graham, and Nontuthuko. This allowed time to share, reflect on, and revise the mosaic pieces and associated understandings of working with memory drawing, self-study, and teacher professional learning. Using the mosaic pieces, together with viewpoints expressed in the e-mail correspondence, Kathleen drafted an initial version of the chapter. She shared this draft with her coauthors for their suggestions for improvement and revision. The final form of the chapter was developed through collaboration between the four authors, the book editors, and a peer reviewer.

3 Putting the Mosaic Pieces into Context

The three mosaic pieces, narrated in the first person, offer distinctive yet also complementary stories elicited by South African teachers' drawings of early memories of school in the 1970s, 1980s, and 1990s. Here, it is useful to highlight the point made by Mitchell et al. (2011b) about the importance of an awareness that every "drawing is produced by a specific individual in a particular space and time. ... [And that] the drawer's context (both present and past) must colour what is drawn, how it is drawn, and what the drawing represents" (p. 25). In a South African context, the recent history of apartheid (1948–1994) is omnipresent and is critical to a sociohistorical understanding of teachers' individual and collective early school experiences. Apartheid is an Afrikaans word that can be translated as *separateness.* In the apartheid era, the Nationalist government used racial classifications to disconnect and subjugate South African people (Clark and Worger 2016). A hierarchy of racialised privilege ensured that people designated as *white* profited from disproportionately greater government spending and access to superior facilities and resources in all spheres of life (including education), while people designated as *black African, coloured*, and *Indian* were disenfranchised and ruthlessly disadvantaged (Clark and Worger 2016). Notably, the repressive Nationalist government aimed to use education as an "anaesthetic instrument—designed to numb and deaden" (Pillay and Pithouse-Morgan 2016, p. 123) any potential dissent that might threaten its dominance (Nkomo 1990). Almost 20 years after the formal end of the apartheid regime, education in South African is still burdened by the effects of decades of deliberate impoverishment of educational provision for the majority, and by a legacy of anaesthetising apartheid education.

The next section of this chapter presents a brief orientation to Mawi Makhanya's use of memory drawing as a self-study research method and then presents her first-person mosaic piece. This is followed by an introduction to Graham Downing's research and then his mosaic piece. Thereafter, is an introduction to Nontuthuko Phewa's work, followed by her mosaic piece. Next, is Kathleen's poetic response to the three mosaic pieces. The chapter closes with a consideration of the educative implications of memory drawing.

4 Mawi Makhanya's Use of Memory Drawing

Hlengiwe (Mawi) Makhanya is a former schoolteacher and teacher educator. Since 2001, she has been employed by the South African Department of Education as a subject advisor to guide and advise foundation phase (Grades R–3) teachers. Mawi conducted a self-study for her master's research (Makhanya 2010) with the aim of improving her professional practice of supporting the teaching of literacy and numeracy in the foundation phase. As a starting point, she undertook memory-work to recollect and reflect on her lived experiences of schooling to better understand

Picturing a More Hopeful Future: Teacher-Researchers Drawing ...

what contributions her own learning experiences as a black African girl during the apartheid era made to her practice as a subject advisor. In addition, Mawi worked with a small group of foundation phase teachers so that she could better understand the influence of their past experiences. She introduced the teachers to memory drawing to prompt recall and discussions of their early childhood experiences of learning numeracy and literacy.

Learning from Teachers' Memory Drawings
by Hlengiwe (Mawi) Makhanya

Introduction

As a subject advisor, I am responsible to monitor teaching and learning and provide curriculum support to teachers in primary schools in my district. In this mosaic piece, I show how I used memory drawing as a way to begin to engage with a key question in my self-study research: "How can I better understand the experiences, practices, and needs of teachers in relation to the learning and teaching of literacy and numeracy in the foundation phase?" To respond to this question, I worked with a small group of three female foundation phase teachers from three different schools. Two of the teachers were teaching in under-resourced schools in rural areas. The third teacher was teaching in a semiurban area surrounded by informal settlement houses. These teachers, Mhlobo,[1] Mali, and Toto, did not know each other beforehand. At the time of the study, each teacher had more than 10 years of teaching experience. Their ages ranged from 38 to 47 years, and so their early schooling took place in the 1970s and 1980s during the apartheid era. Like me, these teachers are all black African and speak isiZulu as their mother tongue.

According to Weber (2008), visual images such as drawings can "help us to access those elusive, hard-to-put-into-words aspects of knowledge that might otherwise remain hidden or ignored" (p. 44). Furthermore, Derry (2005) explained that memory drawings can help to us to access memories and can offer a "multi-layered intellectual/emotional connection to [the drawn] experience" (p. 35). My intention in using memory drawing was for the teachers to access past experiences related to learning and teaching of numeracy and literacy and to share these with each other and me. I hoped to gain understanding of what had shaped their lives and practices. Additionally, I was interested in understanding possible connections between their experiences and my own. I also wanted to encourage the group to discuss these experiences in an open-ended way that would allow each member to learn and grow as a teacher.

Each teacher was asked to think back and draw early schooling experiences that might have helped or hindered her learning and teaching of literacy and numeracy. Adapting Onyx and Small's recommendations for memory writing (2001, p. 776), I asked the teachers to draw particular episodes from their past in as much detail as possible.

---

[1] For confidentiality, the names of the participants have been changed.

Fig. 1 Memories of early schooling (Drawing, Hlengiwe Makhanya, with permission)

Drawing Early Experiences of Learning Numeracy and Literacy

At the beginning, it was so tense when I explained to the teachers that I would like them to draw their early experiences. I first gave the instructions in English, but there was quietness after I asked my participants to draw. I thought that maybe the instructions were not clear or that the teachers did not understand me because of a language barrier. Thus, I went on to explain in more detail in our mother tongue. However, when we were discussing in isiZulu, I discovered that their hesitation was because they were afraid to draw. They looked at each other and confessed that they were not comfortable with drawing because it had not been part of their schooling. They said that they were not good at art. Like me, these teachers were schooled during the apartheid era where whites were given better education than black Africans, and art was not considered an important subject for black African schools (Christie 1991).

I assured the teachers that I was not expecting a "perfect" drawing but something from which they could tell their story. I then decided to draw first, and share my experiences as a starting point. After a long silence, I showed them what my drawing looked like (see Fig. 1). I explained that although I was also not confident in drawing, I felt that my drawing represented my early experiences well. After that, the teachers seemed to feel more confident and started to draw.

As the teachers were drawing, they were discussing things such as, "How do you draw learners[2] squashed on one bench?" Once the initial discomfort was overcome, the drawing process was creative and fun and I believe that this encouraged teachers to be actively involved in the research. I saw how drawing activates the mind and thus helped the teachers in the process of remembering. This was exciting for them because it helped them to remember what their former classrooms looked like, and how their former teachers taught them. The teachers' drawings also helped me to understand their perceptions of their experiences (Derry 2005).

The Teachers' Memory Drawings

The memory drawings produced by the teachers were shared and discussed in the group. Toto's drawing portrayed how, because they did not have a classroom, they were taught under a tree. When they had to write using their slates, they kneeled down to press on a bench. Toto mentioned that the days that she enjoyed most were in summer when it was raining and there was no school.

Mhlobo's drawing depicted her first school in a deep rural area. In her school, they used a local church as a classroom. Both Grade 1 and Grade 2 shared the church with one teacher who was responsible for teaching this multigrade class. Mhlobo remembered that they did not have reading materials and had no desks but, instead, used benches to sit and write on. She explained, "When I was doing Grade 1, we used to sit on the bench. When it was time for writing, we had to kneel down and write using a pencil. If you didn't have a pencil, you got punished, or were chased out of the classroom."

Mali's drawing showed her memories of how children learnt, and were tested on, spelling. They would be scattered outside in the schoolyard. The teacher would loudly shout out the words and all of them would spell out the words aloud together, without writing. Thereafter, they were allowed to write the spelling word. Mali recounted how, if someone got three words wrong, she or he was punished with three strokes.

The Discussion Prompted by the Memory Drawings

I wanted the participants, including me, to feel free to discuss how our drawings had helped to elicit our memories (Derry 2005). After the teachers had shared their drawings with the group, we discussed issues raised by the four drawings. We discovered that our early schooling experiences were similar.

The first issue our discussion highlighted was the types of classroom and the conditions of those classrooms. All members of the group attended primary schools during the apartheid era in under-resourced schools. Mhlobo and Toto's schools were in a rural area and, although Mali's school was in an urban township, it was also under-resourced.

Another key issue that came out of our discussion was the way in which we were taught phonics (letter recognition). In my experience as a foundation phase teacher, phonics is a cornerstone of language acquisition. It is important for learners to know and understand what they are learning about phonics and why they are learning this.

---

[2]In South Africa, students at schools are referred to as *learners*.

However, our former teachers all used a traditional, teacher-centred method. Our teachers would write "a, e, i, o, u" on the chalkboard and let the learners recite this repeatedly. The teachers would then wipe this off and ask learners to rewrite it onto their slates. This rote learning must have been believed to be the best method of teaching phonics because all of us had experienced it.

The teaching of reading was not evident in the early experiences of two members of the group. One participant said that her former teacher had had only one textbook called *Umasihambisane* [*Let us go together*], and that this teacher used to ask them to read without giving them the skills of reading. Learners were also punished for failing to read, and that created a culture within them to hate reading.

A teacher-centred approach was also used for teaching numeracy; counting was done without using concrete objects, except for one participant who remembered using stones for counting, which shows that her teacher was creative enough to think of this strategy. The group members shared that we remembered our teachers punishing us for failing to count correctly. We were asked to count repeatedly from 1 up to 100 every day without using any concrete objects to assist us. Our shared experiences were similar to those highlighted by Kunene (2009) in her discussion of how drill work, memorisation, and repetition were common methods of teaching numeracy and literacy in black African primary schools during the apartheid era.

What also emerged through our discussion was that when we became teachers ourselves, we did not use any new methods that we were taught at the teacher training colleges; instead, we taught in the way in which we had been taught while in primary school. We agreed that the training we received at the colleges did not prepare us for realities of classroom life in which there are often more than 70 learners in each class, classrooms are overcrowded, and there is a lack of space, suitable furniture, and equipment.

Additionally, in our discussion we acknowledged that we felt that we were not creative enough in our teaching. The memory drawing activity helped us to remember that creativity was not often encouraged when we were learners ourselves. Therefore, we felt that we would benefit from guidance on creative teaching and learning methods, and materials development.

My Professional and Personal Learning
For me, our discussion revealed how and why, despite curriculum policy changes, teachers often resort to teaching the same way in which they were taught at school. Having done my own memory-work and having come to understand why I often still do things in the way in which I was taught, I fully understand why teachers are still teaching the same way they were taught. My self-study helped me to accept and comprehend this. I have realised that, as a subject advisor, it is important for me to work with teachers to reflect on how their past experiences might influence their teaching and on how they can work with their memories to improve on their practice.

Personally, I have realised how powerful memory-work is. It is not only about remembering your past; it is about appreciating and recalling what you have gone through, either good or bad and getting time to heal. It is indeed about healing because the untold stories get to be told through memory-work. It is also about the braveness

Picturing a More Hopeful Future: Teacher-Researchers Drawing ...

you show when sharing with the audience your inner feelings and the things that you have never talked about, whether you felt they were less important or you felt ashamed to talk about them.

In conclusion, remembering the past experiences in our lives can contribute to understanding who we are as teachers and what shaped us to do things the way we do. As teachers and those who support teachers, memory drawing can become a mirror that helps us reflect back to our past to understand and deal with the future. This will help us carry out the task ahead of us, that of teaching and learning, when we have acknowledged our origins and the experiences we have gone through.

5 Graham Downing's Use of Memory Drawing

Graham Downing's master's research (Downing 2014) focused on investigating and exploring his teaching and learning philosophy and his role as a teaching and learning facilitator of visual communications in a private tertiary institution in South Africa. In his self-study research, Graham's use of memory drawing prompted memories of how, when, and what educational influences shaped and framed his early personal educational history as a white boy in apartheid South Africa. For Graham, memory drawing allowed him to communicate a particular situation or context in a way that was aligned to his professional expertise in visual communications.

Picturing the Remembered Self Through Drawing
by Graham Downing

Introduction
Currently, I am a senior lecturer at a private tertiary institution. I have been involved with teaching and the development of the Visual Communications module for the past 12 years. Prior to 2006, I had trained and worked as a graphic designer. I had no formal training as a teacher before my transition from working as a graphic designer in the advertising industry, to teaching at tertiary institution.

The central motivation prompting my undertaking of a Master of Education degree was to formally conduct a self-study research enquiry (Samaras 2011) that identified, confronted, embraced, and renewed my understanding of my teaching and learning philosophy and practice in order to be a more effective teacher. In my study I utilised the structure and format of a narrative enquiry (Hamilton et al. 2008), using personal history self-study (Samaras et al. 2004) as a research approach to identify and scrutinise my significant educational experiences in order to appreciate and grasp the influence they have had in framing my thinking and perception of my practice.

In this mosaic piece, I demonstrate how I made use of memory drawing to prompt my memory and focus my thinking (Pithouse 2011) in the form of a narrative enquiry.

The Framing of My Early Educational Experiences
I begin my personal history narrative by describing my first few years in primary

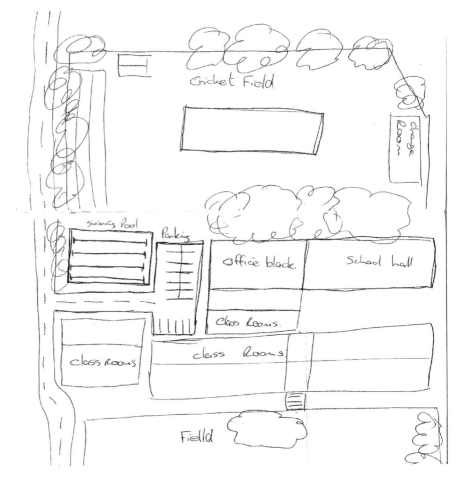

Fig. 2 Welcome to school (Drawing, Graham Downing, with permission)

school and the facilities that the schools provided. After which, I discuss how certain teachers' behaviour and their classroom management impacted on my educational development. I do this by recounting significant moments through the use of memory drawings in my primary school years.

Primary School: The Move
In 1984, I started primary school. The school was situated close to home in a popular white South African middle-class suburb near Durban. It was close enough to walk home after school in the afternoons. It was considered to be a well-respected school with more than adequate facilities for teaching and learning. It had two large fields for sport activities such as soccer and cricket, and a swimming pool. This can be seen in my memory drawing (Fig. 2). During our breaks, the learners were allowed to relax, run around on the field playing soccer, or chase the girls for entertainment!

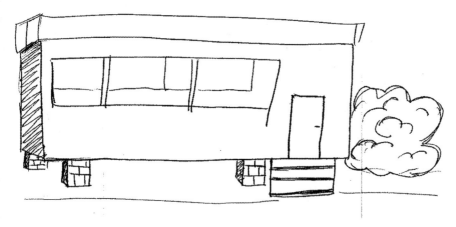

Fig. 3 The new school (Drawing, Graham Downing, with permission)

Change rooms and toilets were also available, with running water and flushing toilets. The structure was built with brick and allowed for classrooms to be built one above each other: a ground floor and a first floor. Every classroom was equipped with the appropriate size and number of desks and chairs for each of the learners and teachers, as well as chalkboards. In terms of the demographics, all the classes were made up of mixed-gender white South Africans. The teaching staff consisted of mostly white female South Africans, with a white male headmaster.

After my first year at primary school (Grade 2), my father accepted a job transfer to a small coastal town in northern Zululand to work as a resident engineer on a construction project for two years. I had never heard of the town we would be moving to, nor did I fully comprehend the consequence of moving to a new town and school. It was only after the two years we spent in Zululand that the repercussions of the move on my education was realised. I started Grade 2 at a small school that catered mostly for the white South African sugarcane farming community. As shown in my memory drawing (Fig. 3), the school's physical structure consisted mostly of prefabricated buildings that reminded me of the temporary site offices my father worked in.

However, the main office block of the school was a more permanent structure made of brick. There was also a noticeable difference in the number of classrooms to that of my previous primary school. This was due to the size of the local community. Every classroom was equipped with desks and chairs, in much the same fashion as that of my previous school. However, a significant difference at this particular school was the organisation and management of classrooms. Each classroom consisted of two grades sharing the same class space. A single teacher gave instruction simultaneously to both the grades in the same space.

Fig. 4 Toothbrush (Drawing, Graham Downing, with permission)

The consequence of this setup seemed to result in the divided attention of the teacher, and confusion and misunderstanding on my part. However, in the initial few months of my schooling at the new school, my teacher communicated to my parents that I was simply lazy, uninterested, and distracted. A notion further emphasised by my parents. It was only later that my parents expressed their concerns that my poor spelling and math competency was a direct result of this particular classroom design.

There also seemed to be a lack of compromise and empathy expressed by one or more of my teachers. We were given notices at the end of each day to be handed to our parents. One such notice required a signature by one of my guardians in order to partake in a class dental hygiene activity. By my mother's own regretful admission, she neglected to sign the receipt and hand it back. This resulted in my being excluded from the class activity.

Each learner in the class received a small coloured cup and a toothbrush to use in the activity. However, I and another learner could only watch as the class participated in the task of learning how to brush one's teeth. I remember sitting on the mat in front of the class with the other learners feeling surprised, embarrassed, and segregated from the class. I reflected on this memory drawing (Fig. 4) in my journal:

> The teacher didn't seem particularly interested in explaining or even understanding the situation. I felt like I didn't have a say. All I wanted was to be part of the activity. Why didn't my teacher try and provide a temporary solution? It's as if she didn't care. (Graham, memory journal, February 2, 2013)

After the first day or two, my mother suggested that I ask the teacher if I could bring my own cup and toothbrush to class to take part in the class activity. The teacher agreed to my mother's suggestion and said I could partake in the class exercise if I came to class equipped with my own cup and toothbrush. When I got home that afternoon, I told my mother the news that my teacher had agreed to her suggestion. My mother was a stay-at-home mom, even though she was a qualified and medically trained nurse. She did her best to raise and provide for us as a family as we grew up. Although she was quite strict, she had a lot of patience and always tried to fix a bad situation. She didn't waste time in getting us ready to go toothbrush shopping because it wasn't long before the shops would close for the day. I remember being excited and happy as my mom drove us on that sunny afternoon to the local pharmacy and grocery stores in search of a small cup and toothbrush.

We tried to find ones that matched those the rest of the class had, but without luck. I had to settle for the closest matching toothbrush and cup we could find. Despite not being able to find the exact same toothbrush and cup, I was still glad to be able to participate in the class activity. The next day I proudly showed my teacher the toothbrush and cup and, as agreed, I was able to join the class in the dental hygiene activity, and no longer be excluded. For some reason, I still felt a sense of separation and exclusion because I didn't have the same cup and toothbrush as the other learners, but this feeling was short lived once the activity began. It was early on in life that I realised that if you lacked understanding or battled to grasp a concept, you were considered unintelligent and, as a result, not appreciated or valued. These feelings of exclusion and difference seemed to reoccur in varying degrees throughout my early education. I often felt alone and ill equipped to deal with the emotions I felt and experienced at school. I always felt it was me who had the issues, and that I was a problem child.

Conclusion

In this mosaic piece, I have shown how memory drawings proved to be beneficial in eliciting rich and fertile memories on which I based my personal history narrative of my educational experiences. I think the first two drawings (Figs. 2 and 3) were less emotionally stimulated than the third drawing. The drawings of the two schools speak more to the geographic contexts and differences of the infrastructures. However, they were helpful triggers in trying to identify the significant teaching and learning experiences attached to these places. The third drawing (Fig. 4) was quite emotional for me; I felt really saddened and hurt. This was the first time I had really tried to make sense of why this emotive memory was so significant to me. By reflecting on these feelings of exclusion and isolation through my memory drawing, I have come to realise how influential the unintentional actions and behaviours of teachers can be, and it certainly made me more aware of the effect my teaching behaviour can have on students' educational development.

6 Nontuthuko Phewa's Use of Memory Drawing

Nontuthuko Phewa is an early career foundation phase teacher. The focus of her master's research (Phewa 2016) was on supportive relationships between teachers and learners. Through her self-study research, she aimed to better understand and evaluate her relationships with her Grade 1 learners. She sought to improve her teaching practice by cultivating supportive relationships with her learners. Nontuthuko used memory drawing as a self-study research practice to help her to make visible, and reflect on, her own experiences as a young black African schoolgirl at the time of South African's transition from the apartheid era to democracy.

Creating Drawings to Help Me Remember and Make Visible My Past Experiences
by Nontuthuko Phewa

The Context of My Research

I am a Grade 1 teacher and I have been teaching for 5 years. I anticipated that applying a self-study methodology in my research would allow me to study my personal history and my relationships with my learners with the aim of thinking deeply and improving my teaching practice.

I teach in a primary school that is located in a semi-urban area. Most learners who attend the school come from low socioeconomic backgrounds, with either one or both parents unemployed. The stress of social challenges that are endured by parents and families, such as poverty, can have a negative emotional and social impact on children. Teachers can play a significant role in ensuring that these learners are emotionally and socially supported. In relation to my own teaching, I felt that maybe some of my learners might not be doing well because they might have experienced a lack of support from me. I was concerned that they might not feel comfortable with me as their teacher or they might not feel safe and supported in our school or classroom environment.

Retracing My Personal History

The first question that guided my research was: "What can I learn from my personal history about supportive relationships?" This question helped me to look back on my past relationships inside and outside of school. As Samaras et al. (2004) clarified, personal history self-study is a process whereby a teacher reconstructs meaningful events in her life history to make sense of her professional learning with the aim of transforming and improving her teaching practice.

To prompt memories of my primary school days, I had conversations with a primary school friend with whom I still have contact. She went to the neighbouring school to mine, and her school was very much like my school in terms of resources and the school location. Through our conversations, we reflected together on our past school experiences.

As part of the process of retracing my personal history, I created memory drawings to help me remember and make visible experiences of supportive and unsupportive relationships during my primary school years. In this mosaic piece, I present and discuss two memory drawings.

Primary School Memories

I started school in 1991 in a neighbourhood primary school. The school was located in a rural area. Learners who attended this school mainly came from underprivileged family backgrounds. Most learners' parents were struggling to pay school fees, to buy the full school uniform, and to buy school stationery. The school was under resourced, and classes were overcrowded because there was only one classroom for each grade. Due to a shortage of school furniture, some learners had to write with their books on their knees because there was not enough space for five or six learners to write on one desk or table.

Like most children, when I started primary school, I was excited to start school. However, my first years of schooling were difficult because I had to adapt to a new environment and see less of my parents and my family. Teachers were taking the place of my parents and I expected that they would be there to guide us, protect us, comfort us, and take care of us. Yet, not everything was according to how I supposed it would be. My primary school memory drawings portray mainly negative memories. These memory drawings show that school often felt cold, unwelcoming, and not safe for me as a child.

We Would Hide to Not Be Seen by Our Teachers

Figure 5 is a memory drawing that represents a learner hiding under a school desk, which was one of the tricks to escape punishment. We were overcrowded in our classrooms and each class had, maybe, 60–65 learners. Because the classrooms were tiny, it was easy to get under a desk to hide. The teacher would not see you, and no one would tell the teacher because everyone knew that it might be her or him doing the same trick next time. We did this not because of fun, but because we were scared of the consequences of not having a pencil or some other wrongdoing. For me, this drawing suggests that the teachers seemed to have had little understanding of us as learners—they probably had no idea about, or ignored, how we were hurt, and the fear we had towards them.

I showed my former primary school friend this memory drawing to trigger her memory of what she remembered about hiding under a desk in school. With some anger and sadness in her facial expression, she whispered, "One thing that made me hide was not having a full uniform." When my friend reminded me of this, I remembered how the principal would come in the morning to our classrooms to check if we all had school jerseys. If you were not wearing the regulation jersey, the principal would take your jersey and keep it until end of the term, which meant that you would be cold at school. However, my friend and I agreed that this kind of behaviour was probably not because our teachers were cruel but, rather, because they wanted to maintain high standards and also make learners and parents aware of the importance of the school uniform.

Fig. 5 A learner hiding under the desk (Drawing, Nontuthuko Phewa, with permission)

Almost Every Teacher in Our School Carried a Stick

Figure 6 represents the stick that was used at school. When I drew teachers carrying sticks, it evoked haunting memories of my primary school experiences. I think almost all teachers in our school carried sticks, even if they were just walking around the school corridors. Whenever they walked to a class, they would be carrying a stick and a book. I still remember the fear we had when we saw the teacher with the stick. Even if we were not doing anything wrong, we would still be scared because the teacher might find fault with whatever we were doing.

The stick was the enemy of every learner at school. Most teachers seemed to think it was the only solution to maintain discipline in school. I remember how, in my Grade 1 class on the first day of school, we went to the assembly for morning prayer. The principal was leading the assembly. She was carrying a stick and some teachers who were standing behind learners were also carrying sticks. Therefore, I think they were passing a message to every new learner that they were going to use the stick to make sure that we learners obeyed their rules. I think most of the learners were scared of being beaten because most learners tried their best not to upset teachers—they knew the consequences. I soon learned that to avoid being beaten, I had to try to stay in the good books of all teachers. Doing my homework and performing well in my tests kept me safe from trouble. That was the remarkable thing; learners' academic performance decided if they were safe or not.

I think that our teachers knew that many parents in our community beat their children to discipline them. Furthermore, the teachers themselves were probably raised in that manner. So they held on to what they believed would work better to build children's futures. However, as my school friend mentioned, "Even though at

Fig. 6 Teachers carrying sticks (Drawing, Nontuthuko Phewa, with permission)

home parents disciplined us by using a stick, we never got used to it." I can say that it made most learners feel uncomfortable. For instance, if you had forgotten or did not get a chance to do your homework, you would think of any possible excuse not to go to school that day because of the fear of punishment. I think corporal punishment somehow made it difficult for most learners to develop supportive relationships with their teachers. I for one found that it was very difficult for me to approach a teacher with any problems that I encountered outside school, even if those problems affected my academic performance.

Learning from Memory Drawing as a Research Tool
As Pithouse (2011) explained, drawing can make unclear memories vivid with details of an event and emotions associated with the experience. Memory drawing can bring the past to the present and unblock forgotten memories. In particular, the use of drawings in my study helped me to bring past emotions to the present. This allowed me to write in detail of how punishment alienated many learners from teachers. It also helped me to become aware of the consequences of this. For instance, I remembered how most learners were scared to be called on by a teacher, even if they knew they had done nothing wrong. From the drawings, I saw how this was a result of pain, and how punishment hurt us as learners emotionally and physically. I saw how, in my primary school days, many teachers seemed to distance themselves from learners' social and emotional wellbeing. Hence, I realised that when my classmates dropped out of school or repeated the same grade several times, it might not have been because they were empty minded but, rather, because they lacked social and emotional support at school.

Drawing as a research tool helped me to learn that, as a teacher, I should try not to repeat mistakes that were committed by my former teachers. Retracing and reflecting on my personal history through memory drawing reminded me that learners often experience problems inside and outside of school, and they need support and empathy from teachers. Therefore, it is important that we teachers learn to develop our capacity for listening and empathising (Jairam 2009). This could assist us in developing understanding of learners' problems or concerns. It might also help learners to feel respected, loved, and understood. This could help to cultivate supportive relationships between teachers and learners and create a more favourable environment for learning. By eliminating the element of fear, and allowing my learners to have a voice, I can create a warm, comfortable classroom environment and enhance learners' engagement in their schoolwork.

Memory drawing enriched my study because it allowed me to tell personal stories. Hence, I think memory drawing is a vital tool for teachers because it can assist them to engage with their own experiences. In so doing, it can encourage them to try to avoid negative practices that made them as learners feel hurt or isolated and, rather, try to promote what would help learners to feel loved, understood, and comfortable. Memory drawing can encourage teachers not to just teach the way they were taught, but to rather try out teaching strategies that can improve teaching and learning—therefore, it can promote teacher self-development.

7 A Poetic Response

In working with the three mosaic pieces by Mawi, Graham, and Nontuthuko, Kathleen was struck anew by how "drawing can be a way for self-study researchers to portray and engage with the emotions that give life to personal [and professional] experience and yet are frequently overlooked or downplayed in public accounts of social research" (Pithouse 2011, p. 43). The emotionality of the pieces inspired Kathleen to compose a poem using the French Malaysian pantoum poem format with "its repetitive lines [that allow] for the repetition of salient or emotionally evocative themes" (Furman et al. 2006, p. 28). Kathleen read and reread the mosaic pieces to highlight and extract lines that spoke to the emotional experience and impact of teachers' memory drawings. As she read, she copied and pasted these lines into a new composite text, which then became a source for creating a poem (Pithouse-Morgan 2016). The poem brings together the voices of Mawi, Graham, Nontuthuko, and of Kathleen, who selected the words and arranged them in the pantoum format. *Memory Drawing* illuminates the value and impact of memory drawing as an emotional entry point for teachers' future-oriented remembering.

> **Memory Drawing**
>
> We created drawings
> To remember in detail
> Rich and fertile memories
> To make visible the past
>
> To remember in detail
> For teacher self-development
> To make visible the past
> From which to tell our stories
>
> For teacher self-development
> To trigger emotions
> From which to tell our stories
> To reinvent the future
>
> To trigger emotions
> Rich and fertile memories
> To reinvent the future
> We created drawings

8 Picturing New and More Hopeful Stories for the Future

In the mosaic pieces that are juxtaposed in this chapter, the three individual teacher-researchers' drawings of early memories of school and accompanying written reflections offer access to a variety of stories of the past, with a core moral purpose of generating new and more hopeful stories for the future. This individual and collective pedagogy of reinvention offers a critical counterweight to historical and contemporary forces of social fragmentation. The montage of drawings and reflections presented in this chapter serve as an invitation to ask ourselves as teachers and educational researchers: "What would we hope that children and young people might portray in their future memory drawings of our schools and classrooms?"

Acknowledgement We are grateful to our peer reviewer, Dorothy Jean Stuart (University of KwaZulu-Natal, South Africa), for her encouraging and insightful feedback on this chapter.

References

Christie, P. (1991). *The right to learn: The struggle for education in South Africa* (2nd ed.). Braamfontein: Ravan Press and Sached Trust.

Clark, N. L., & Worger, W. H. (2016). *South Africa: The rise and fall of apartheid* (3rd ed.). Abingdon: Routledge.

Derry, C. (2005). Drawings as a research tool for self-study: An embodied method of exploring memories of childhood bullying. In C. Mitchell, S. Weber, & K. O'Reilly-Scanlon (Eds.), *Just who do we think we are? Methodologies for autobiography and self-study in teaching* (pp. 34–46). London: RoutledgeFalmer.

Downing, G. (2014). *Facilitating ownership in visual communications learning: A lecturer's self-study* (Unpublished master's thesis). University of KwaZulu-Natal, South Africa. Retrieved from http://researchspace.ukzn.ac.za/handle/10413/12651.

Furman, R., Lietz, C. A., & Langer, C. L. (2006). The research poem in international social work: Innovations in qualitative methodology. *International Journal of Qualitative Methods, 5*(3), 24–34. Retrieved from http://www.ualberta.ca/~iiqm/backissues/5_3/PDF/furman.pdf.

Hamilton, M. L., Smith, L., & Worthington, K. (2008). Fitting the methodology with the research: An exploration of narrative, self-study and auto-ethnography. *Studying Teacher Education, 4*(1), 17–28.

Jairam, V. L. (2009). "I am not a trained counsellor but I know I have to do something": Basic counselling strategies for teachers. In C. Mitchell & K. Pithouse (Eds.), *Teaching and HIV & AIDS* (pp. 125–137). Johannesburg: Macmillan.

Kunene, A. (2009). Learner-centeredness in practice: Reflections from a curriculum education specialist. In K. Pithouse, C. Mitchell, & R. Moletsane (Eds.), *Making connections: Self-study & social action* (pp. 139–152). New York: Peter Lang.

Makhanya, H. (2010). *Preparing for the implementation of Foundations for Learning: A self-study of a subject advisor* (Unpublished master's thesis). University of KwaZulu-Natal, South Africa. Retrieved from http://researchspace.ukzn.ac.za/xmlui/handle/10413/6202.

Mitchell, C. (2011). *Doing visual research*. London: SAGE.

Mitchell, C. (2017). Object as subject: Productive entanglements with everyday objects in educational research. In D. Pillay, K. Pithouse-Morgan, & I. Naicker (Eds.), *Object medleys: Interpretive possibilities for educational research* (pp. 11–28). Rotterdam: Sense Publishers.

Mitchell, C., Theron, L., Smith, A., & Stuart, J. (2011a). Picturing research: An introduction. In L. Theron, C. Mitchell, A. Smith, & J. Stuart (Eds.), *Picturing research: Drawings as visual methodology* (pp. 1–16). Rotterdam: Sense Publishers.

Mitchell, C., Theron, L., Stuart, J., Smith, A., & Campbell, Z. (2011b). Drawings as research method. In L. Theron, C. Mitchell, A. Smith, & J. Stuart (Eds.), *Picturing research: Drawings as visual methodology* (pp. 1–16). Rotterdam: Sense Publishers.

Mitchell, C., & Weber, S. (1998). The usable past: Teachers (re)playing school. *Changing English, 5*(1), 45–56.

Mitchell, C., & Weber, S. (1999). *Reinventing ourselves as teachers: Beyond nostalgia*. London: Falmer Press.

Nkomo, M. O. (Ed.). (1990). *Pedagogy of domination: Toward a democratic education in South Africa*. Trenton: Africa World Press.

Onyx, J., & Small, J. (2001). Memory-work: The method. *Qualitative Inquiry, 7*(6), 773–786.

Phewa, Q. N. (2016). *Cultivating supportive teacher-learner relationships in a Grade 1 classroom: A teacher's self-study* (Unpublished master's thesis). University of KwaZulu-Natal, South Africa.

Pillay, D., & Pithouse-Morgan, K. (2016). A self-study of connecting through aesthetic memory-work. In J. Kitchen, D. Tidwell, & L. Fitzgerald (Eds.), *Self-study and diversity II: Inclusive teacher education for a diverse world* (Vol. 2, pp. 121–136). Rotterdam: Sense Publishers.

Pithouse, K. (2011). Picturing the self: Drawing as a method for self-study. In L. Theron, C. Mitchell, & J. Stuart (Eds.), *Picturing research: Drawings as visual methodology* (pp. 37–48). Rotterdam: Sense Publishers.

Pithouse-Morgan, K. (2016). Finding my self in a new place: Exploring professional learning through found poetry. *Teacher Learning and Professional Development, 1*(1), 1–18. Retrieved from http://journals.sfu.ca/tlpd/index.php/tlpd/article/view/1.

Pithouse-Morgan, K., & Samaras, A. P. (2015). The power of "we" for professional learning. In K. Pithouse-Morgan & A. P. Samaras (Eds.), *Polyvocal professional learning through self-study research* (pp. 1–20). Rotterdam: Sense Publishers.

Samaras, A. P. (2011). *Self-study teacher research: Improving your practice through collaborative inquiry*. Thousand Oaks: SAGE.

Samaras, A. P., Hicks, M. A., & Berger, J. G. (2004). Self-study through personal history. In J. J. Loughran, M. L. Hamilton, V. K. LaBoskey, & T. Russell (Eds.), *International handbook of self-study of teaching and teacher education practices* (Vol. 2, pp. 905–942). Dordrecht: Kluwer.

Weber, S. (2008). Visual images in research. In J. G. Knowles & A. L. Cole (Eds.), *Handbook of the arts in qualitative research* (pp. 40–53). Thousand Oaks: SAGE.

Weber, S., & Mitchell, C. (1995). *That's funny, you don't look like a teacher!: Interrogating images and identity in popular culture*. London: Falmer Press.

Weber, S., & Mitchell, C. (1996). Drawing ourselves into teaching: Studying the images that shape and distort teacher education. *Teaching and Teacher Education, 12*(3), 303–313.

Collaging Memories: Reimagining Teacher-Researcher Identities and Perspectives

Daisy Pillay, Reena Ramkelewan and Anita Hiralaal

> The possibilities of using collage to address a variety of issues are endless. (Gersh-Nesic 2017, para. 15)

Abstract In "Collaging Memories: Reimagining Teacher-Researcher Identities and Perspectives," Daisy Pillay, Reena Ramkelewan, and Anita Hiralaal explore teacher-researcher identities and perspectives through the piecing together of lived experience and practice using collage. The exemplars are drawn from ongoing doctoral research by two emerging South African scholars, Reena and Anita. Reena's mosaic piece reveals how collage making assisted her in recognising the multiple and layered selves that constitute her life and work as a teacher-researcher in a public primary school. Anita's piece shows how creating a collage portrait helped her bring together memories of critical experiences and significant people who influenced her in becoming a certain type of teacher educator. Together, Reena's and Anita's accounts of collaging memories show how collage making can reinvigorate critical moments of the past for new perspectives to inform teacher-researchers' selves and practices.

Keywords Collage · Memory-work · South Africa · Teacher professional learning Teacher-researcher identities

---

D. Pillay (✉) · R. Ramkelewan · A. Hiralaal
School of Education, University of KwaZulu-Natal, Durban, South Africa
e-mail: pillaygv@ukzn.ac.za

R. Ramkelewan
e-mail: reena.ramkelewan@gmail.com

A. Hiralaal
e-mail: anitah@dut.ac.za

A. Hiralaal
School of Education, Durban University of Technology, Pietermaritzburg, South Africa

© Springer Nature Switzerland AG 2019
K. Pithouse-Morgan et al. (eds.), *Memory Mosaics: Researching Teacher Professional Learning Through Artful Memory-work*, Studies in Arts-Based Educational Research 2, https://doi.org/10.1007/978-3-319-97106-3_5

1 Introduction

This chapter offers glimpses into using collage to explore teacher-researcher identities and perspectives. It draws on ongoing doctoral research by two emerging South African scholars, Reena Ramkelewan and Anita Hiralaal. Anita is a teacher educator at a university of technology and Reena is a primary school teacher. Anita and Reena share a growing interest in collage making as an arts-based method in qualitative research. Their initial exposure to collage as research happened through research support and workshops offered by their doctoral research supervisors, working specifically to create a space for different types of arts-based methods that "engage [doctoral students] directly and personally as 'makers' and 'doers'" (Norris et al. 2007) in educational research. Daisy Pillay, who is Reena's doctoral supervisor in the specialisation of teacher development studies, serves as a coordinator and facilitator in these research support activities. Daisy is interested in supporting the work of new and emerging researchers inspired by using the arts to inform their scholarly work and its potential for personal and social change (Pillay et al. 2017).

In leading the writing of this memory mosaic chapter, Daisy assembled Anita's and Reena's two seemingly unrelated mosaic pieces—portraying different individuals, places, contexts, experiences, practices, and life-worlds—into purposeful juxtaposition (Allen 1995) for multiple elements to be placed within new connections to one another (Tuck and Yang 2012). The chapter is organised in three sections. The first section presents a brief introduction to collage as art making and as research. This is followed by Reena's first-person mosaic piece, which focuses on research dilemmas she experienced as an emerging doctoral scholar using narrative inquiry methodology. Next, is Anita's first person piece, which is drawn from her self-study research exploring her everyday accounting teaching practices with undergraduate students. Thereafter, all three authors' voices (Daisy, Reena, and Anita) come together to convey their shared learning. The chapter concludes with a final assemblage of interpretations of collaging memory for scholarly learning and identity construction as teacher-researchers.

2 Collage

2.1 Collage as Art Making

Collage describes both the technique and the resulting work of art, in which a variety of materials such as magazine cuttings, pieces of fabric, or found objects are glued onto a flat surface and integrated into a visual arrangement (Gersh-Nesic 2017). The process of collage is often simple, yet creative. The hands-on activity of collaging is accessible enough to allow anyone to participate, regardless of perceived artistic ability. Collage is seen everywhere—for instance, in newspapers, billboards, and quilts—where different visual and tactile pieces mingle "to seduce, to convince, to persuade, to charm, to explain, and to critique" (Norris et al. 2007, p. 481). The materials used in collage compositions tend to be commonplace, and the inspiration is often found in everyday life, but the final work produced is expressive and rich with meaning.

Artists have been experimenting with and using collage techniques for many years. Collage gained popularity in Europe in the 20th century with Spanish artist, Pablo Picasso, and French artist, Georges Braque, as forerunners of a new genre that was called "synthetic" art because of the introduction of tangible materials (Israel 2014). Through a synthesis, or an assemblage of disparate elements and symbols, found materials and objects from the real world were playfully composed into a new, coherent whole (Arnason 1986). The composition was created through the mixing of everyday life with art to challenge traditional art practices (Arnason 1986; Israel 2014). The created imagery in the collage compositions of Picasso and Braque were illustrated an alternate story, in which they rebuilt the artist's view of the world as arbitrary and unfixed, and the properties of things as transitory (Arnason 1986). This very accessible and playful art form also opened up opportunities for visual artists to add commentary using newspaper clippings, photographs, and printed words to blend the visual and the written (Gersh-Nesic 2017).

In her early professional life as an art teacher working with children, Daisy found that collage provided endless opportunities for learners' self-expression. Even in the most dislocated and poorly resourced schools where she worked, all that was needed was glue and contact paper for learners to stick their different found materials together. They could collage on paper, cardboard, or even on three-dimensional objects such as broken unused chairs and tables that had been discarded. As a classroom teacher, Daisy learned that collage can be a democratic practice (Norris et al. 2007), allowing every child the creative space to find a voice, regardless of seeming talent, and a wonderful place to start developing flexibility, choice, and uniqueness through play. Getting children to engage in collage making and creating enabled Daisy to apply her knowledge of Vygotsky's (1998) theory that children must be actively involved in the teaching–learning interaction, and to draw on what each "individual [brings] to the interaction" (Tudge and Scrimsher 2003, p. 293). She found that the created reality through collage making drew on children's own cultural contexts and unlocked a storytelling response.

2.2 Collage as Research

Collage as research has been used in a range of fields including psychology, behavioural science, and education (Butler-Kisber and Podma 2010; Kostera 2006). The use of collage as inquiry is a promising area within arts-based educational research (Butler-Kisber 2008; Butler-Kisber et al. 2003; Finley 2001) because of its potential to make the everyday a critical site for exploring, and opening up, the personal-professional connectedness in everyday practice. As a representational form, collage is made up of piecing together fragmented image pieces of different texture, colour, and shape—and these fragments, juxtaposed, have the imaginative power to unlock embedded meanings in different and multiple ways for knowing as ambiguous, complex, and contradictory (Butler-Kisber 2008).

3 Reena's Memory Mosaic Piece: Collage as Reflection

Reena Ramkelawan, an emerging scholar and teacher-researcher, undertook memory-work to recollect and reflect on her lived educational experiences, past and present, to explore who she is as a teacher and what constitutes her work as a teacher working in a public school in South Africa. Collaging memory helped her to recognise the need for her to explore and understand the multiple layers or selves that constituted her life and work as a teacher-researcher in a public primary school as complex, changing, and dynamic.

Context

My day of reflection and change was a momentous day in December 2014. It took place away from the hustle and bustle of a normal day at school because I was invited to attend a doctoral support group workshop at a local conference venue in a very beautiful and tranquil setting. Initially, I was a bit undecided about whether to attend because it was the last day of school for the term and I would not see my colleagues from school before the summer vacation commenced. However, because it was my initial foray into this adventure called doctoral studies, I decided to forgo the end of year function at school, accept the challenge into this exciting phase of my life, and attend the workshop.

I had met with my doctoral supervisors a few days prior to the workshop, and had been requested to look for a "gap" in the research literature on teachers' work that I could base my research on. Now, for those looking for the gap, it can be a daunting task. Although looking for a gap was frightening to say the least, the one assurance I had was the methodology I was going to use. Using narrative inquiry (Clandinin and Connelly 2000) as a research methodology for my doctoral study had its origins way back in 2010 when I was engaged with my master's studies.

Prior to actually commencing with my master's and deciding on an appropriate methodology, I was required to do a piece of self-narrative writing for my supervisor on my various experiences on this journey called life, and my educational experiences as a teacher. This piece of writing allowed me freedom to express all that I felt as an Indian female, as a mother, as a daughter, as a wife, and as a teacher. Recounting my life story opened doors that had been shut to my memory for so long. The unfolding of my life story assisted in helping me understand how my personal views and experiences have impacted on my teaching and ways of thinking. My reflection on what it means to be a teacher, especially, revealed aspects of my life that I knew I could not talk to anyone about because I felt there was no one willing to listen. So, I put it down on paper for my supervisor to read the retold, relived story of my life as a mother, wife, and daughter and, also importantly, as a teacher. I then decided that narrative inquiry was going to be the methodology for my master's study.

Therefore, when the opportunity arose for me to engage in doctoral studies, I decided once again to draw on narrative inquiry methodology to give ear to the voices and lives of other teachers. As a teacher in the present climate of change, added responsibility, uncertainty, and high attrition rates, I felt that other teachers too needed to tell their stories and have someone take heed of what was being said. What better way to unearth and understand lived experiences and educational challenges than through story form? Hence, narrative inquiry was my choice to elicit and understand teachers' experiences.

Finding a Quiet Space to Engage in the Process

On arrival at the workshop, I must admit I was a bit apprehensive about my own level of competence because the group consisted of students who were well on their way on the doctoral journey. However, on entering the room I relaxed a bit when I saw some familiar faces. My supervisor requested we look at our individual topics and then each compose a collage that would represent our thoughts and feelings about our research ideas. She explained that the aim of the workshop was to enable us to play with a research idea using collage inquiry as a way to come to a research focus for our doctoral study.

Our supervisor presented us with sheets of paper, scissors, glue, and a box of magazines. She then requested we each find a quiet spot and space for engaging in the creative process of composing the collage. For now, things were going a little more smoothly. The tranquillity of the surroundings added to the ambiance. Relaxing and having fun cutting and pasting pictures and words took some time getting used to because it was not something I did very often as a teacher. Being instructed to find a place to relax and play with my research ideas and express them soon became a welcome reprieve from my hectic schedule of the teacher's life. What a calming and enjoyable exercise this became—just to look at magazines and be captivated by certain pictures that evoked memories of critical moments and incidents from my current teaching context as well as my past schooling experiences as a learner.

I was transported back in time to my childhood days as a carefree, creative child. The excitement of finding words and pictures enveloped me. I felt like a child opening a birthday present. The exercise made me feel alive and excited and, soon, the anxiety of finding a research topic faded away. I remember another student asking if she could borrow a few magazines to check through, and my selfish response to her was, "No I am not yet finished." It was as if the magazines with their pictures and words held the content of my life that I still needed to discover, and giving them away would prevent me from discovering me, the person. I needed to find those pictures that evoked memories of experiences of a life I had pushed to the margins.

The process of cutting and pasting the pictures and words was therapeutic. It meant zoning in on what I deemed important as well as pleasing to the eye in the way I moved the pieces around before fixing each. The process made me acutely aware of how the pictures and words started to speak to my inner feelings and thoughts. On reflection, I subconsciously selected pictures and words that revealed how fixed

Fig. 1 Reena's collage: The cabbage-head (Collage, Reena Ramkelawan, with permission)

and enclosed I have become in expressing who I am as a teacher—locked in the dark corners of my mind and soul. I became aware that in all the years I have been teaching, I failed to verbalise or acknowledge who I am and wanted to be as a teacher. The piecing together of the pictures became the story of my life in picture form, experienced like a silent movie.

The collage process started me thinking about my work as a teacher in the schooling context that I currently work in. I found myself expressing frustration with my role as teacher, feeling like a person trapped—a "teacher robot." I saw how, like a mechanical being, I followed instructions from powers that be because I felt as if there was a gun held to my head. As I remembered those emotions, my head swirled with confusion, uncertainty, and utter despair. I pasted an image of a cabbage to show my feeling of being a "cabbage-head" teacher—in a vegetative state (see Fig. 1).

However, making the collage gave me a sense of peace and, as I stepped back to reflect on my creation, little flickers of hope emerged from the folds of the cabbage leaves—in-between spaces that revealed the love I have for my learners at school.

This initial task of compiling a collage was important for inspiring and expressing a written narrative of memorable lived experiences (van Schalkwyk 2010). The written narrative, complemented by the collage, provided a canvas to think deeply and in a more alive and connected way about what was driving my curiosity as an emerging scholar. The collage allowed for words and pictures to come to life. Thus, from the entire collage, one picture struck a chord for me—the cabbage-head. Juxtaposing the swirly layers and folds enabled me to think about my life as a teacher as less of a linear, fixed experience. Inwardly, I was embarrassed that I saw my life as a cabbage and myself as some brain-dead person in a vegetative state. But putting on my researcher lens forced me to question the metaphor I had chosen (subconsciously or not) to depict my teacher life. Undertaking this exercise compelled me to wrestle with the meanings I have come to associate with cabbage-head, forgetting all the hidden parts that lie folded in between. So, who is the real me? who is the real teacher-self?

My Learning: Collage Inquiry as a Pondering Process

The act of composing a collage helped me to step back and ponder on my feelings about being a teacher. As Davis (2008) explained, collage inquiry is a strategy for the exploration of memory, imagination, and experiential reflection. Doing collage opened up a space to reconsider my position as a teacher-researcher. As an imaginative act of cutting and assembling the "imagery of others" (Allen 1995, p. 5) from magazines, I developed a new awareness about myself, and the richness of possibility in my life as a teacher-researcher. Making my collage shifted my focus from the responsibilities of school to me—the person in the teacher in a particular time and context. I became central in the act of creating a collage.

Composing the collage of my research focus developed into something more through the power of reimagination of my disembodied, disconnected teacher self. Shifting from an inner dialogue to focus on one image—the cabbagehead—helped me to feel relaxed and experience a sense of peace within myself (Allen 1995; Butler-Kisber 2008). Feeling replenished through this imaginative act, I was able to, from my position as teacher-researcher, "produce associations and connections [about the inner and outer me] that might otherwise remain unconscious" (Butler-Kisber 2008, p. 270). Acknowledging the inextricable link between the personal-professional (Richie and Wilson 2000), like the swirly uneven layers of the cabbage, drives my curiosity as researcher to develop into something more my understanding of the complexity of teachers' lives relational to public schooling realities in South Africa.

4 Anita's Memory Mosaic Piece: Collaging Memory as Connecting–Conceptualising Process

Anita is a teacher educator in a South African university of technology who teaches accounting education to student teachers. Having been an educator at schools and in higher education for approximately 18 years, Anita was curious about learning how to develop as a more productive role model to her students. In her research, she chose to draw on metaphors and artefacts from her everyday teaching practices and her personal history to explore and better understand her role modelling as a teacher educator.

Context

I have been a teacher educator at a university of technology in South Africa since 2008. I teach accounting education to student teachers completing a 4 year Bachelor of Education degree. I identified a "living contradiction" (Whitehead 1989, p. 42) in my practice when students informed me that they teach as I taught them. Whitehead explained that a living contradiction occurs when the educational values you subscribe to are not evident in your teaching activities. My students made me aware of such a contradiction between my espoused values and my pedagogic practice during discussions I had with them on the negative comments they had received from their mentor teachers at school during their teaching practicum.

Russell (as cited in Pinnegar and Hamilton 2009) drew my attention to how teacher educators role model behaviours and actions in their classes that students are acutely aware of in their search for messages about how to teach. Hence, I realised I needed to explore what I was role modelling for my students in the classroom, and how I could develop as a more productive role model. Consequently, I embarked on a self-study of my practice (Samaras 2011). As I oriented myself to self-study research, I became aware that not only did I need to I explore myself in relation to my practice, but that a key requirement of my research would be going back into my personal history to explore how these lived experiences could have moulded and shaped the way I experience the world in the present (Samaras et al. 2004).

I selected the novel, *The Secret Garden,* by Frances Hodgson Burnett (1969) as a personal history artefact because it had had special significance for me as a child. Apart from being my favourite storybook, the storyline had a magical quality to it and I would immerse myself into its fantasy world to escape the harsh realities of my tragic young life. I related the fictional life experiences of the novel's protagonist, Mary Lennox, to my own real-life experiences. Mary sought refuge in a secret garden to heal emotionally and physically after losing both her parents to cholera in her birthplace, India. Mary had to leave the country of her birth, and all that was familiar to her, and travel across the world to England to live with her hunchback uncle where she discovered a secret, locked garden. The secret garden had belonged to her uncle's wife who tragically fell from a tree in the garden and died. So distraught was her uncle that he locked the garden and threw away the key. Mary found the key and revived the garden, an act that helped bring life back to her uncle, her uncle's son Colin, the house, and the other occupants of the house who had been in mourning for 10 years.

I identified with Mary Lennox because, after the death of my father when I was two years old, we were forced to leave our home and move to another town to live with my grandparents. My mother had to leave me and my sister, who was just 19 days old, in the care of my maternal grandparents to seek employment to support us financially. The initial sadness and desolation of Mary's fictional life experiences resonated aptly with my own real, lived experiences and acted as an enabler for me to engage in the process of reconstructing my personal history narrative (Cheney 2001).

Deciding to Develop My Collage Portrait

I wanted to represent my learning about my personal history in a way that was captivating, "evocative, provocative and at best arresting" (Eisner 2008, p. 23). When reading Hamilton and Pinnegar (2009), I saw how creating a collage, the "juxtaposition of image and word" (p. 161) could help me create a visual image of my internal feelings, and illuminate my examination of my first research question: "What could have influenced my role modelling as a teacher educator of accounting pedagogy?"

I was intrigued by collage and, to make more sense of what I wanted to do, I read an article on collage portraits as a "blending of the arts-based research methods and artistic genres of collage and portraiture" (Gerstenblatt 2013, p. 12). Gerstenblatt explained that collage portraits can be made through a process of "cutting and pasting" (p. 12) pieces of texts, photographs, artefacts, drawings, and other images together on a chart or canvas. When the different pieces are connected, they represent a portrait of someone—or a story you are trying to tell about someone. I was intrigued by this and decided to use personally meaningful images and photographs to create a collage portrait to illustrate my learning from exploring my personal history.

The Process of Cutting and Pasting

I was advised by an artist relative that I should not work on the final collage portrait immediately but should rather play around and plan it on ordinary chart paper. Once I was sure of what I wanted to do, then I should work on the final artist's canvas I had chosen. I made a number of copies of the photographs and images I wanted to use so that I could play around, and first used Prestik (a temporary adhesive) to glue the images because I wanted the freedom to move them around.

In the centre of the chart paper, I placed the image of *The Secret Garden*, which I believed was the central object of my story. As I placed the image of the novel on the paper, I experienced a very strange feeling. It was as if the image were talking to me. I was initially alarmed and thought something was wrong with me, but then I realised the image was awakening memories and emotions of my childhood within me. As I scrutinised my collage portrait, I realised I had placed the image of *The Secret Garden* in the centre because, whatever happened in my life, this novel was my safety net—my cocoon that sheltered me from the outside world.

When I was finally convinced of what I wanted the collage portrait to look like, I began the final process of setting the photographs, images, and text on the chart paper. For example, I wrote words such as "dark," "dismal," and "desolate" in black on the paper where I had represented sad unhappy phases of my life. I used green for writing key words such as "comfort" and "independent" in the part containing photographs of *The Secret Garden* and my mother. Both the novel and my mother represented the encouraging and inspirational phases in my life. For me, green represents growth and life.

On my collage portrait (Fig. 2), I also pasted a photograph of my maternal grandparents' home, which my mother, sister, and I were forced to live in after my father had died. But then, my mother had to move to another town and live away from us because she found employment as a private nurse caring for an aged patient in the patient's home. Seeing the photograph on the collage portrait created mixed

Fig. 2 Anita's collage portrait: Exciting connections (Collage, Anita Hiralaal, with permission)

emotions for me. Whilst I still remembered the smell of tasty fresh food being cooked every morning by my grandmother on her old coal stove and the stories she told us on cold winter nights around the fire next to the coal stove, I also remembered my grandfather telling me that I was the ugly duckling. I was awarded a book prize, *The Ugly Duckling*, for coming first in Grade 2 but my grandfather played a cruel joke on me when he explained that I was given the book because I had come last in class and that the teachers felt sorry for me. Being young and naïve, I believed him. I was teased as being an ugly duckling by the whole family and developed a negative self-image. This impacted on my performance and behaviour and the manner in which my teachers treated me. The photograph of my primary school that I pasted on the collage portrait reminded of this time when I had no confidence and the teachers had no confidence in me and treated me dreadfully. I was called a "dirty pig" because I had an untidy vocabulary book, and was made to kneel on the floor with my hands on my ears.

The photograph of my father that I pasted on my collage portrait is the only photograph I have of him. I cried when I saw the photograph. Only after pasting this photograph of my father on the collage portrait, did I get closure. I finally accepted that my father did exist and that my resemblance to him was not a figment of my imagination.

I placed the photograph of my father next to the only photograph I have of myself as a young child (Fig. 3). After my father died, no one ever bothered to take photographs of my sister or me as children growing up. I never knew this until I began searching for photographs in old albums to use on my collage portrait. I was

Fig. 3 Anita's only photograph of herself as a young child (Photographer, Roy Ramjewan, with permission)

very disturbed when I found the photograph of myself, tattered and torn like the story of my life. My family had always told me I resembled my father but I never realised how much so until I really looked at this photograph of him next to the tattered and torn photograph of me as a child.

The photograph of my mother in her work attire as a nurse reminded me that, despite the many adversities and challenges she faced in her life, she became an independent, secure, and motivated woman who inspires others. She is a role model for me because, despite all the hardships she faced in her life, she never succumbed to them. However, I also realised that this might have influenced me to become the teacher educator that my students pointed out to me. I always wanted to be like my mother—always in control of every situation. I became aware that I felt in charge as the deliverer of the content while the students listened.

Relational Ethics

Ellis (2007) referred to the ethical responsibility we have to close others who we include in our work about ourselves as relational ethics. According to Ellis, relational ethics requires us pay careful attention to the relationship between the researcher and the person or persons who are implicated in the research. Asking my family for old photographs and engaging them in discussions about my childhood posed a few ethical dilemmas for me. Initially, when I explained to my family about writing my thesis, they were excited and went out of their way to send me old photographs. However, at family gatherings during my data generation process, some family members asked casually if I was going to write "anything bad" about them adding, seriously, that they would be upset if I did. I reassured them that once the thesis was complete, they would all be welcome to read it. As Ellis (2007) had noted, she was keeping the memory of people alive by writing about them. I also informed my family that writing about them in my thesis would keep their memories alive and maybe, years from now, the younger children in the family would read my thesis and learn more about the family.

My Learning: Collaging as a Connecting Process

The living contradiction in my practice became more visible to me as I pieced together my memories of critical moments, memorable experiences, and significant people who influenced me and moulded me to become a certain type of teacher educator. Creating my collage portrait helped to reassemble and create a new and embodied image of myself as teacher educator and opened up a different reality of who I could be.

The collage portrait represents the different phases in my past history which I believe influenced how I role modelled. As a young child, after my father died, I was thrown into circumstances that were out of my control. My father's untimely demise itself influenced the identity I moulded for myself—a lost, desolate, and abandoned child. Every child seeks protection and security from her or his parents. Unfortunately, I did not get this security or protection that I so desired. I did not get to know my father and after he died, my mother had a difficult time coping with his loss and having to care for two young children. Her situation was exacerbated by the fact she was removed from her home and had no source of income. As young as I was then, I see now that this impacted on me heavily. I have come to realise that I literally burdened myself with the responsibility of caring for my sister and myself.

I did not realise at that time because I was too young to analyse my childhood but now it has dawned on me that wanting to take charge of our lives and protect us was a burden that I carried with me throughout my life. This manifested itself in the teacher educator I became because I always wanted to be in control of every situation. In my class with my students, I always took charge and controlled their every action. Students commented that I was very rigid in the way I approached my teaching—everything had to be in order and presented in an orderly fashion.

I realise now that although I qualified as an English teacher, when I was asked to teach accounting, it appealed to me. Accounting is a very procedural subject and I took this as a cue that I should teach in a very disciplined manner. I took much joy in ruling straight columns and entering figures and, when the figures balanced, I got a secret thrill that everything was okay in my organised world. I never allowed my students to transgress in any way. If their work was not presented in an organised manner, I deducted marks. When a student presented a lesson, I was absolutely rigid in how I wanted them to present the lesson. If they did anything that was out of the ordinary, I would severely penalise them.

In creating my collage portrait, I could immerse myself into an imaginative space. Playing around with copies of the photographs and images made me feel like a true artist. The juxtapositioning process of piecing and arranging words and images helped me realise that I had the choice to rearrange my life, and the perspectives I adopt as a teacher, in less controlling ways. Intuitively selecting, arranging, and rearranging the images, words, and photographs was a way of confronting myself and getting to know the practices that needed changing in order to be a different kind of teacher educator and role model to my students. Deepening my awareness of my engrained habits of being a controlling teacher helped me to open up my interpretations and imagine exciting synergies between the personal and professional fragments of my life.

As a teacher-researcher, I learned that "occupying my hands, freeing my mind" (Vaughan 2005, p. 11) enabled the unravelling of my experiences in deep, rich, and evocative ways that writing alone could not do. The collage portrait gave me access to complex feelings and ideas from my past. More importantly, I was able to practise freeing myself from these feelings and habits that were unconsciously inhibiting my pedagogy. The collage portrait became a tool for me to interpret and reinterpret those unspoken thoughts and feelings and free me to reimage myself as more open-minded, less controlling, and as a more productive role model for my students.

5 Assembling Our Ideas and Voices as Lessons to Convey Our Learning

In this section, Daisy, Reena, and Anita share some of the lessons learned from their collaging memory inquiries as teacher-researchers. Drawing on selected conversation pieces from a 2-hour face-to-face meeting held in Daisy's office, and on follow-up e-mail chats, Daisy further reflected on the shared discussion and selected phrases and words to create a free verse poem, "View Yourself from a Fresher Perspective." This poem provided further movement for crystallising understandings, and to communicate shared scholarly perspectives on collaging memory as teacher-researchers.

> **View yourself from a fresher perspective**
>
> An enabler to peel away the layers
> To reveal you, your being
> A metaphor for your identity
> To see yourself
> To see yourself in the world

5.1 Collage as a Way to Open up Teacher-Researcher Self Through Play

We agree with Vinz (1997, p. 139) that becoming scholarly, "requires continuous reformulations" of the teacher-researcher self. Collage making offers an opportunity for us as teacher-researchers to theorise the situated self (Vaughan 2005, p. 13) and peel away the layers to reveal our inner being as provisional and contingent. Through play, collage, as an act of the imagination, offers a space for teacher-researchers to dwell on who we are as teachers and on the embedded beliefs and perspectives behind our everyday practices. As Anita explained in our discussions, "I was advised by an artist relative that I should not work on the final collage immediately but rather play around and then plan my collage portrait." Imagining what is possible through the creation of self as meaning maker may provide creative ways of thinking and feeling about the teacher-researcher self in the future. Reena highlighted this hope when she added: "While I acknowledge my 'stressed' state as a teacher, [making the collage] opens up other realities where I acknowledge that I am still a teacher with hope and care."

5.2 Collage as a Metaphor for Transforming Teacher-Researcher Self Through Pondering

Collage as rearranging and reconfiguring new synergies and regenerating different meanings and perspectives was expressed vividly by Anita in our conversations, "I was not aware of any faults in my teaching until my students brought this to my notice and, for the first time in my teaching career, I looked to myself for answers. This is what led to me exploring my teaching practice." This "un-knowing or giving up" (Vinz 1997, p. 139), of fixed and essentialised constructions of self makes collaging a potent, chaotic space for discovering a multiplicity of meanings and identities trapped in the unconscious (Butler-Kisber 2008)—imaginatively evolving and transforming as we make sense of our lives as teacher-researchers and the world from a fresher perspective. Reena articulated her empowering experience of imagining her transformation when she explained how "the collage enabled me to reflect on my acceptance of my troubled overwhelmed state of being as a teacher. The collage was initially there to represent my state of feeling disillusioned but it developed into something much more when I began to ponder on it."

5.3 Collage as a Space for Supporting Teacher-Researchers' Well-Being in the Everyday Through Practising

According to Vaughan (2005, p. 13), "the individuality and handmade-ness of an art product begins the process of situating its creator at a particular moment, a location, an identity." Collaging memories of critical moments and experiences of everyday lives brings the teacher-researcher back into the "immediacy of situations" from the past (Vinz 1995, p. 203). In this imagined spaced, these critical incidents serve as sites for reflection on the dilemmas and the multiple forces that one needs to negotiate in everyday situations. Making collage is where "disparate voices cohere" (Finley 2001) and new and different choices and positions can be taken up. As a creative act, collage becomes a relaxing space for envisioning emotional well-being. As Reena said, "I still cling to the metaphor of the cabbage because I still experience the 'troubled' state of school and certain things are entrenched and I will take time to change. I think I want to be delicious as a teacher but hardy to deal with the challenges of school." As a teacher educator, Anita finds comfort and joy in collage making because it offers her a space to be a creator, doing something artistic. Contrary to her everyday teaching practices as a lecturer, where, as she described, "I took control to a different level because I did not even give my students an opportunity to ask questions, and if I did ask a question, I would answer my own questions because I wanted to be in charge, I wanted to be the expert in the class," the creative space helped her feel alive and less controlling. Anita described how this sense of freedom and movement made the "collage my fantasy world for feeling mentally and emotionally alive."

6 The Final Assemblage: Opening Pathways to Play, Ponder, and Practise Ambiguity, Complexity, and Multiplicity

Collaging memories, for opening up teacher-researcher identities and perspectives, is imbued with power to reimagine and reinvigorate critical moments of the past as embodied and empowering experiences. As Butler-Kisber (2008, p. 268) explained, the ambiguity exhibited in collage provides "a way of expressing the said and the unsaid, and allows for multiple avenues of interpretation and accessibility" to not-knowing and un-knowing the self (Vinz 1995) as a site for potential change. Collaging teacher-researcher selves can become an act of identity (Goffman 1979), and the act serves as an occasion for opening up a multitude of ways for thinking and interpreting the complexity and contradictions of everyday practices. Mosaic-ing collage practices from Reena and Anita's different worlds into a single, unifying composition, invites a way to make sense of multiple truths and experiences, and offers a potential transforming knowledge production and aesthetic scholarship (Brockelman 2001). The sense of discovery that the juxtapositionings of collage make available can authorise teacher-researchers to look to themselves as funds for new and fresher perspectives and identity positionings.

Acknowledgements We thank our peer reviewer, Devarakshanam Govinden (University of KwaZulu-Natal, South Africa), for her helpful advice on how to strengthen the chapter.

References

Allen, P. (1995). *Art is a way of knowing: A guide to self-knowledge and spiritual fulfilment through creativity*. London: Shambhala.

Arnason, H. H. (1986). *History of modern art: Painting, sculpture, architecture, photography* (3rd ed.). Upper Saddle River: Prentice Hall College Div.

Brockelman, T. P. (2001). *The frame and the mirror: On collage and the postmodern*. Evanston: Northwestern University Press.

Burnett, F. H. (1969). *The Secret Garden*. London: Harper Collins.

Butler-Kisber, L. (2008). Collage as inquiry. In J. G. Knowles & A. L. Cole (Eds.), *Handbook of the arts in qualitative research: Perspectives, methodologies, examples, and issues*. SAGE: Thousand Oaks.

Butler-Kisber, L., Allnutt, S., Furlini, L., Kronish, N., Markus, P., Poldma, T., et al. (2003). Insight and voice: Artful analysis in qualitative inquiry. *Insight and Voice, 19*(1), 127–164.

Butler-Kisber, L., & Poldma, T. (2010). The power of visual approaches in qualitative inquiry: The use of collage making and concept mapping in experiential research. *Journal of Research Practice, 6*(2). Retrieved from http://jrp.icaap.org/index.php/jrp/article/view/197/196.

Cheney, T. A. R. (2001). *Writing creative non-fiction: Fiction techniques for grafting great non-fiction*. Berkeley: Ten Speed Press.

Clandinin, D. J., & Connelly, F. M. (2000). *Narrative inquiry: Experience and story in qualitative research*. San Francisco: Jossey-Bass.

Davis, D. (2008). Collage inquiry: Creative and particular applications. *LEARNing Landscapes, 2*(1), 245–265.

Eisner, E. W. (2008). Art and knowledge. In J. G. Knowles & A. L. Cole (Eds.), *Handbook of the arts in qualitative research* (pp. 3–12). Thousand Oaks: SAGE.

Ellis, C. (2007). Telling secrets, revealing lives: Relational ethics in research with intimate others. *Qualitative Inquiry, 13*(1), 3–29.

Finley, S. (2001). Painting life histories. *Journal of Curriculum Theorising, 17*(2), 13–26.

Gersh-Nesic, B. (2017, July 6). How Is Collage Used in Art? *ThoughtCo*. Retrieved from https://www.thoughtco.com/art-history-definition-collage-183196.

Gerstenblatt, P. (2013). Collage portraits as a method of analysis in qualitative research. *International Journal of Qualitative Methods, 12*, 294–309.

Goffman, E. (1979). *Gender advertisements: Studies in the anthropology of visual communication*. New York: Harper & Row.

Hamilton, M. L., & Pinnegar, S. (2009). Creating representations: Using collage in self-study. In D. Tidwell, M. Heston, & L. Fitzgerald (Eds.), *Research methods for the self-study of practice* (pp. 155–170). Dordrecht: Springer.

Israel, M. (2014, February 6). The birth of collage and mixed-media. *Artsy*. https://www.artsy.net/article/matthew-the-birth-of-collage-and-mixed-media.

Kostera, M. (2006). The narrative collage as research method. *Storytelling, Self, Society, 2*(2), 5–27.

Norris, G., Mbokazi, T., Rorke, F., Goba, S., & Mitchell, C. (2007). Where do we start? Using collage to explore very young adolescents' knowledge about HIV and AIDS in four senior primary classrooms in KwaZulu-Natal. *International Journal of Inclusive Education, 11*(4), 481–499.

Pillay, D., Pithouse-Morgan, K., & Naicker, I. (2017). Composing object medleys. In D. Pillay, K. Pithouse-Morgan, & I. Naicker (Eds.), *Object medleys: Interpretive possibilities for educational research* (pp. 1–8). Rotterdam: Sense Publishers.

Pinnegar, S., & Hamilton, M. L. (2009). *Self-study of practice as a genre of qualitative research: Theory, methodology, and practice*. Dordrecht: Springer.

Ritchie, J. S., & Wilson, D. E. (2000). *Teacher narrative as critical inquiry: Rewriting the script*. New York: Teachers College Press.

Samaras, A. P. (2011). *Self-study teacher research: Improving your practice through collaborative inquiry*. Thousand Oaks: SAGE.

Samaras, A. P., Hicks, M. A., & Berger, J. G. (2004). Self-study through personal history. In J. J. Loughran, M. L. Hamilton, V. K. LaBoskey, & T. Russell (Eds.), *International handbook of self-study of teaching and teacher education practices* (Vol. 2, pp. 905–942). Dordrecht: Kluwer.

Tuck, E., & Yang, K. W. (2012). Decolonisation is not a metaphor. Decolonisation: Indigeneity. *Education & Society, 1*(1), 1–40.

Tudge, J., & Scrimsher, S. (2003). The teaching/learning relationship in the first years of school: Some revolutionary implications of Vygotsky's theory. *Early Education and Development, 14*(3), 293–312.

Van Schalkwyk, G. J. (2010). Collage Life Story Elicitation Technique: A representational technique for scaffolding autobiographical memories. *The Qualitative Report, 15*(3), 675–695.

Vaughan, K. (2005). Pieced together: Collage as an artist's method for interdisciplinary research. *International Journal of Qualitative Methods, 4*(1), 27–52.

Vinz, R. (1995). Opening moves: Reflections on the first year of teaching. *English Education, 3*(27), 158–207.

Vinz, R. (1997). Capturing a moving form: "Becoming" as teachers. *English Education., 29*(2), 137–146.

Vygotsky, L. (1998). *The collected works of L. S. Vygotsky: Child psychology* (Vol. 5). New York: Plenum Press.

Whitehead, J. (1989). Creating a living educational theory from questions of the kind, "How do I improve my practice?". *Cambridge journal of education, 19*(1), 41–52.

Seeing Through Television and Film: The Teacher's Gaze in Professional Learning

Claudia Mitchell, Bridget Campbell, Stephanie Pizzuto and Brian Andrew Benoit

Abstract "Seeing Through Television and Film: The Teacher's Gaze in Professional Learning" by Claudia Mitchell, Bridget Campbell, Stephanie Pizzuto, and Brian Andrew Benoit draws together three exemplars for using film and television in teachers' professional learning. Bridget Campbell, working at a South African university, embarked on the use of two teacher films, *Freedom Writers* and *Dead Poets Society*, to enrich her understanding of her work with the preservice teachers in her class. Then Stephanie Pizzuto, as a master's student at a Canadian university, used a popular television series from her childhood, *Boy Meets World,* to deepen an understanding of the teacher she now wants to become. Brian Benoit, also at a Canadian university, explored the way he used repeated viewings of a local television series he remembered from an earlier time, *Les Bougon*, to engage in memory-work and critical autoethnography in relation to class structures.

Keywords Canada · Critical autoethnography · Film · Memory-work
Narrative self-study · South africa · Teacher professional learning · Television

This chapter draws attention to the ways in which film and television episodes can be central to artful memory-work. The chapter builds on exemplars that highlight the use of various media forms to both remember and re-vision the future in professional development. In the chapter, we consider two types of visual texts: teacher films

---

C. Mitchell (✉)
Department of Integrated Studies in Education, McGill University, Montreal, Canada
e-mail: Claudia.mitchell@mcgill.ca

C. Mitchell · B. Campbell
School of Education, University of KwaZulu-Natal, Durban, South Africa
e-mail: campbell@ukzn.ac.za

S. Pizzuto · B. A. Benoit
Department of Integrated Studies in Education, Faculty of Education, McGill University, Montreal, Canada
e-mail: Stephanie.pizzuto@mail.mcgill.ca

B. A. Benoit
e-mail: Brian.benoit@mail.mcgill.ca

© Springer Nature Switzerland AG 2019
K. Pithouse-Morgan et al. (eds.), *Memory Mosaics: Researching Teacher Professional Learning Through Artful Memory-work*, Studies in Arts-Based Educational Research 2, https://doi.org/10.1007/978-3-319-97106-3_6

as a genre of film that highlights a teacher as protagonist, and films and television episodes that teachers find provocative as memory prompts and as prompts for self-study (Samaras 2011) and autoethnography (Mitchell 2016).

As highlighted in *That's Funny You Don't Look Like a Teacher* (Weber and Mitchell 1995), along with numerous other publications such as Dalton's (1999) *The Hollywood Curriculum: Teachers in the Movies*, the teacher film has occupied a long history in film studies as a particular genre. Teachers of various subject or disciplinary areas are represented in these films (see for example Mr. Escalante in *Stand and Deliver*) with history teachers well represented (see for example, *The Prime of Miss Jean Brodie* and *Sarafina*). However, it seems that Hollywood is particularly in love with the English teacher and over several decades has produced numerous blockbusters such as *Dead Poets Society, Dangerous Minds, Blackboard Jungle, Renaissance Man, To Sir with Love, Bad Teacher, Teachers*, and *Freedom Writers*. Viewing, reflecting on, discussion and writing about these films can offer an engaging form of self-study (Mitchell and Weber 1999; Butler 2000). As noted by Weber and Mitchell (1995)

> Critical interrogations of the popular images of teaching may lead in surprising directions. For one, we may discover images of hope that please in the most unlikely of places. . . . By clarifying and displaying those images that we do like, by articulating and sharing those that resonate deeply, we breathe new life into them, and their power increases. The project that grows out of a close reading is to imagine and realize other possibilities, ways to get beneath the stereotypes, sometimes, paradoxically, by embracing them. The *post–reading project* [emphasis added] becomes a writing project, one that creates new images. (pp. 139–140)

But, the process of teachers and teacher educators engaging with films and television episodes relevant to self-study and autoethnography is not limited to working with teacher movies. Building on the idea of viewing and reflection as proposed by Hallam and Marchment (1995), Motalingoane-Khau (2007) described the ways that films such as *Coming to America, Lambada, The Forbidden Dance*, and *Dirty Dancing* all made ideal prompts in her study of collective viewing with teachers in Lesotho looking back at their own memories in relation to their current work with youth and sexuality education. Mitchell and Pithouse-Morgan (2014) in referencing this work noted how other films such as the *Toy Story* films might similarly be valuable in studying childhood, a theme that would equally be valuable to teachers' professional learning through memory-work and offer a set of guidelines for conducting a collective viewing session

A more recent innovation in teachers' use of film in professional development looks at the ways in which teachers making their own film productions can also be a form of self-study. With easy access to cell phones and other devices for filming, film production becomes relatively easy as highlighted in work, for example with teachers in rural KwaZulu-Natal and the Eastern Cape in South Africa producing their own cellphilms about sexuality education (Mitchell and de Lange 2013; Mitchell et al. 2014, 2016, 2017). Termed *poetry in a pocket* (Mitchell et al. 2017), these productions draw attention to the significance of aesthetics in the everyday world of teachers and, also, the significance of "disrupting" the everyday. For Ashley DeMartini, for example, "seeing" is done through digital storytelling and video production using cellphilms in her doctoral work with preservice teachers at a university in Canada. She asked, "How do non-Indigenous teachers represent their histories in relation to dealing with colonial pasts?" In particular, she was interested in ways of deepening intercultural understandings and developing a sense of responsibility towards the shared stories that Indigenous and non-Indigenous peoples to North America have to land in Canada. As she observed:

> I asked pre-service teachers to create cellphilms that examined the role of reconciliation (as outlined by the TRC[1]) in their own lives, to determine what such a process looks like. Many of their stories revealed students struggling with dominant narratives about who they are in relation to the past and present. In another assignment, I asked students to create digital stories that examined their relationships or connections with land (this latter assignment becoming the foundation for my doctoral project). For both assignments, the visual and oral narratives revealed how students struggled to come to terms with (or not) their own investments with Canada's foundational myths in relation to their connections with land. What I find interesting is how students' stories about Canadian–Indigenous relations varied in their scope, structure, and content as a result of the different modes of storytelling within participatory visual methodologies. Each mode reveals a different way of seeing, unique to each genre's production parameters (cellphilm 60–90 s; digital storytelling 3–5 min). I think a dimension worth exploring within the field of participatory visual methodologies is how media converges across devices—blurring the notion of genre yet, at the same time, the mode of production shapes how, and in what way, a multimodal story might unfold. (cited in Mitchell et al. 2017, Chap. 3: Speaking Back as Method)

Each of these approaches can be done either individually or collectively. Self-selecting images that provoke reflection and memory-work, and taking hold of the camera or cell phone and creating the images, has unique features in relation to professional development. What cuts across them, as we see in the mosaic pieces below, is the central role of cinematic images and narrative to evoke the personal, and the significance of deep engagement with story. Here we (Claudia Mitchell, Bridget Campbell, Stephanie Pizzuto, and Brian Benoit) offer three exemplars for working with film and television

We start with Bridget Campbell's mosaic piece, "I Am an English teacher," in which she highlights the ways in which she has used two teacher films, *Freedom Writers* and *Dead Poets Society*, in her own narrative self-study in a South African university classroom (Campbell 2017). The second exemplar, written by Stephanie Pizzuto, comes out of a "Bad Teacher" prompt (inspired by the film, *Bad Teacher*) regularly used by Claudia in a master's level course she teaches on secondary language arts teaching at a Canadian university. In response to the prompt "Choose a Hollywood English teacher," Stephanie looks back into her childhood and recalls watching the *Boy Meets World* television series

The third exemplar is written by Brian Benoit, based on his doctoral research at a Canadian university (Benoit 2016) looking at the significance of memory-work in critical autoethnography and teaching. Like Motalingoane-Khau's (2007) work noted

---

[1] The TRC (Truth and Reconciliation Commission) in Canada was part of a holistic and comprehensive response to the abuse inflicted on Indigenous peoples through the Indian residential school system, and the harmful legacy of those institutions. The Commission was officially established on June 2, 2008, and was completed in December 2015.

above, it highlights the significance of viewing films that are not specifically teacher films but which are, nonetheless, evocative in relation to memory-work, self-study, and autoethnography.

1 I Am an English Teacher

by Bridget Campbell

I am an English teacher educator at a university in South Africa. When I embarked on my doctoral research *Influences on, and Possibilities for, My English Pedagogy* (Campbell 2017), it was with the intention of researching what would be useful to myself, my students, teachers of English in secondary schools, and to fellow English teacher educators. I also wanted to use my disciplinary knowledge of working with literary and cinematic texts in my research

The Process

The first draft of my personal history narrative, which was in response to the research question, "What has influenced my pedagogy?" merely told a story which I found to be trite and lacking in depth and complexity. My initial literary analysis of this personal history narrative took the narrative elements of characterisation, plot, and setting (Coulter and Smith 2009) into consideration but revealed very little to me—which confirmed my reservations as to the lack of depth and complexity of my story. I then worked on a second layer of analysis wherein my personal history narrative was juxtaposed with events and characters from Dickens' novel, *Hard Times* (1854/1973). The juxtaposition of my personal history narrative with a literary "proof text" (Nash 2004, p. 65) created a rich tapestry through which my story then came alive. Through this juxtaposition, I created spatial distance (Coulter and Smith 2009) as I stood back from my personal narrative. This also enabled me to see how my narrative might resonate with other lives and contexts because personal narrative writing is meant to "benefit readers, touch readers' lives by informing their experiences, by transforming the meanings of events and delivering "wisdom" (Nash 2004, p. 28)

In writing a further version of my response to this research question, I developed a third layer of analysis, which was juxtaposed with two films: *Dead Poets Society* and *Freedom Writers*. I chose these two films because I teach them and know them well and, also, because they both revolve around teaching English using innovative pedagogical practices. *Dead Poets Society* (Weir 1989) is a film about an old established American school, Welton Academy, steeped in tradition and to which parents send their sons in order that they can be prepared to embark upon careers as professionals. As is the case in the school featured in *Hard Times*, there is no place for fancy or imagination in this school, and it is all about learning the facts on which to build a career. Mr. Keating, who is an alumnus of Welton Academy, is appointed as an English teacher and his innovative pedagogy deviates from the traditional methods deemed suitable and encouraged within the school. Mr. Keating's motto is "Carpe diem," which means, "Seize the day." He encourages his charges not to take anything at face value but, rather, to be critical in their thinking. His teaching methods are viewed as unorthodox and frowned upon by the authorities at Welton.

The second film which I chose to focus on is *Freedom Writers* (LaGravense 2007), which is a film based on actual events. It is set in a school that is in sharp contrast to Welton Academy. The setting is Woodrow Wilson High in Long Beach, United States of America. A first-year teacher, Ms. Gruwell, is appointed at the school which, like Welton in *Freedom Writers,* is proud of its high academic standards and achievements. An integration programme had been introduced into the school two years prior to Ms. Gruwell's appointment and the school is now open to anybody wishing to apply. This means that many learners from marginalised communities have enrolled. Following the introduction of this programme, the academic results dropped dramatically and it is no longer a given that all of the learners will graduate. The school is fraught with social problems and racial tensions, with ethnic groups sticking together and gangs fighting both in the school and on the streets

In contrast to the awe in which the boys at Welton hold Mr. Keating, Ms. Gruwell is unpopular when she first arrives at Wilson High School. Her class of "at risk" learners cannot relate to her in any way. It is only when she asks them to keep journals that she begins to understand their world as she reads their life stories. By asking learners for their personal stories, she is making it clear that she wants to know the learners as individuals rather than categorising them all according to societal stereotypes. She gets a glimpse of the personal experiences that learners bring to the class and, thus, has a better understanding of the social issues influencing their behaviour. This exercise allows her to get to know learners as individuals rather than as a group. As Ms. Gruwell gets to know and understand her learners, she changes her attitude and the way in which she responds to them. She adjusts her pedagogy to make it more relevant to the needs and concerns of her learners—which is what I was hoping to achieve in determining possibilities for my pedagogy

Juxtaposing my personal history narrative with cinematic and fictional literature assisted me by taking some of the focus off myself as I attempted to bridge the gap between my personal history narrative, which revealed the influences on, and possibilities for my pedagogy, and my current pedagogy. It helped to make the writing richer and more complex as I connected beyond myself and "tried to tell a good story" (Nash 2004, p. 62)

This was a complex process in which I was constantly going backwards, forwards, inwards, and outwards (Clandinin and Connelly 2000). I experienced many moments of uncertainty and anxiety and constantly analysed my pedagogy and my lecture reflections. I also analysed my students' lecture reflections, their evaluations of my lectures, and their circumstances inside and outside of the university through the process of multilayered pedagogic reflection in which the voices of critical friends (Samaras 2011) were also important

This creative analytical practice added to the depth and complexity of the analysis. It also added to going beyond the particularity of my own personal history (Nash 2004; van Manen 1990). The possibilities that were revealed through this layering were rich, and more purposeful pedagogies evolved from these. According to Samaras (2011), "pedagogical strategies generated from your noticing" in a self-study project can be understood as "purposeful pedagogies" (p. 137). She advised that when practising purposeful pedagogies, a clear rationale should be evident but what one must realise is that this is not binding and may change as learning progresses. This is because pedagogy is not a linear process but is fluid and constantly changing and teachers need to reflect and be open to effecting changes in order to be responsive to what is happening inside and outside the classroom

In this mosaic piece, which presents my use of creative analytic practice (Richardson 2001) through layering, a second research question—"How can awareness of these influences offer possibilities for my pedagogy?"—was at the forefront of my mind. I was questioning the pedagogic impact of the influences on my pedagogy and began a process of developing possibilities for a pedagogy that is relevant within the current context in which I practise as an English teacher educator.

Turn on a Small Light in a Dark Room: Possibilities for Purposeful Pedagogies for My Undergraduate Modules
The heading for this section—Turn on a Light in a Small Dark Room—has been borrowed from what Ms. Giep tells Ms. Gruwell's students when she addresses them in *Freedom Writers* (LaGravense 2007, 34:37). Ms. Gruwell was practicing purposeful pedagogies that are culturally responsive and designed to empower her students when she requests that Ms. Giep, a survivor of the holocaust, address her students. In my case, the light is being turned on to improve my pedagogy and, in turn, benefit my students.

In 2015, I selected the novel, *Dog Eat Dog* by Niq Mhlongo (2004), as the South African text to be studied by the third-year English Major students. I read four South African novels before making the selection and settled on *Dog Eat Dog* because the novel is centred on university students in post-apartheid South Africa. The protagonist is a university student who comes from a poor family and who has not been awarded a bursary. Amongst other issues, it revolves around the anger and frustration of the situation and the ways in which the student found to deal with the problem. Themes include student life and relationships as well as poverty. Many of the students whom I teach face the same battles as the characters in the novel and, in discussions around the potential of fiction as a pedagogical tool, Leavy (2016) made the point that when learning is relevant to people's lives it is more likely to engage them. What became clear in my personal history narrative, which I had written at the start of my doctoral journey, is that the only time that I recall teaching and learning at school being relevant to my life was in my English classes wherein my Grade 11 teacher, Mr. BP, linked literature to our everyday lives. It was this aspect of his pedagogy that I attempted to model when I first started teaching. My personal history narrative also revealed that Mr. BP was the only teacher who ever showed learners a glimpse of his private life, and who encouraged us to connect with the characters in our prescribed novels, and this must have made an impact on me. However, this narrative self-study, which revealed the influences on my pedagogy, has brought me to the realisation that I did not have a clue as to how to go about encouraging my students to make the connections between the novel and their own lives and that I could not simply copy Mr. BP's way of teaching. I needed to spend time reflecting on the possibilities for my pedagogy that were revealed in this study

When I selected *Dog Eat Dog*, I was very aware that I had to be wary of offending the students—as illustrated in the following incident from *Freedom Writers* (LaGravense 2007, 53:36) where Mr. Gilford, who teaches the high achievers, is introducing a novel entitled *The Color Purple* written by Alice Walker (1982).

> **Mr. Gilford**: So, you have all summer to read and consider this book and you know, I thought it would be most valuable to begin with Victoria to ummmmmm, give us the black perspective
>
> **Victoria [thinks]**: Do I have a stamp on my forehead that says I am the national spokesperson for black people? How the hell should I know the perspective of the black people of *The Color Purple*? That's it! If I don't change classes, I'm gonna hurt this fool. Teachers treat me like I'm some sort of Rosetta Stone for African Americans. What? Black people learn to read and we all miraculously come to the same conclusions?!
>
> **Victoria [says]**: At that point I decided to check out my friend Brandy's English class

I knew that in introducing *Dog Eat Dog* I could not risk alienating my students as Mr. Gilford does by offending Victoria because I would then run the risk of losing the students for the duration of the course

The process of writing and analysing my personal history brought me to the realisation that in the past I had not known the students' contexts and that I had made assumptions about the extent to which the students understood what I was teaching. It had also become clear that, as in *Hard Times* wherein the students accepted what was taught without questioning, my students were expected to accept that I was the authority in the room. I could not risk making my students anxious and I knew from what had been revealed in the analysis of my personal story that I needed to build on the students' experiences and to understand their sociohistorical contexts. I thus spent time getting to know my students in the same way as Ms. Gruwell in *Freedom Writers* gets to know the contexts of her students. I started the lectures by asking that students respond to questions about their school and home contexts and amongst the questions was how many of them had bursaries and how those who had not secured financial assistance managed to pay their university fees. This enabled me to make the link between the content of the novel and the students' sociocultural contexts even though the group was large. At the end of every lecture, the students were asked to reflect on what they had learned.

Clarke (2011) observed that when one is teaching large groups, a way in which to engage the students in reflecting on what has been taught is to get them to verbalise their ideas. I would add another step to this process wherein after students have reflected on what the lecturer has delivered, and explained their understanding to their peers in small groups, they are given the opportunity to ask questions about what is not clear to them. This is in contrast to my school experiences, the experiences of the learners in *Hard Times,* and the way in which many of the older teachers in *Dead Poets Society* teach, wherein the class members were seated in rows and expected to listen quietly as the teacher spoke. In delivering the content and then allowing students to make sense of it, one is working from the known to the unknown and from the simple to the complex, which is in line with constructivist pedagogy (Vygotsky 1978). The variable nature of constructivism means that learners will construct knowledge differently as they acquire and organise information in making sense of it (Adams 2006). There is not one way of knowledge construction. As learning is happening in the classroom, it is not done in isolation and there are both personal and interpersonal components in constructing knowledge. Whilst individuals construct knowledge using their own learning styles and what is already known, they should engage in discussion because interaction is important in the development of understanding (von Glasersfeld 1995).

When I lectured in this manner and the students were working in their small groups in discussing what they understood, they were engaging in cooperative learning and because I was walking around engaging with the groups, I was practising what van Amerom (2005) referred to as coordinating collaborative activities. What I tended to do in the large group tutorials was divide the group up by means of lecture rows and give every third row a different question on which to work. The students were permitted to engage with anybody seated in their three rows. The feedback session thereafter encouraged discussion about the responses to questions. As in *Freedom Writers*, the students were working from the known because the questions related to what I knew of the students' contexts, as well as to what was lectured in the session before, and constructivist teaching was thus evident.

To build on the session that has gone before is an important aspect of pedagogy that I have identified through this study because in reading my journal reflections, I usually spent time planning a lecture and was happy with what I intended doing. However, my reflections after the session often stated that I did not account for something such as the group dynamics or the fact that the students did not have the necessary background and I had not scaffolded the lecture content adequately.

Conclusion

This mosaic piece illustrates that responding to my research questions—"What has influenced my pedagogy?" and "How can awareness of these influences offer possibilities for my pedagogy?"—was not a simple linear process. Rather, it was a complicated multilayered process as I wrote my personal life history narrative and analysed it through layering, reflected, analysed my reflections, asked that the students reflected, analysed their reflections, engaged with students about their lives and their responses to my pedagogy, and drew comparisons between what they had said and what I had said. Using the films in my multilayered analysis allowed me to apply my disciplinary knowledge to the study and enabled me to avoid two-dimensional and predictable writing (Coulter and Smith 2009).

What emerged from the writing of my personal history, and the juxtaposition of the analysis with films and novels, was an ongoing and ever evolving multilayered reflective process in which I was constantly looking inwards and outwards and going backwards and forwards (Clandinin and Connelly 2000) as I sought to turn on that light in a small dark room to benefit myself and the students as my pedagogic learning developed.

2 Bad Teacher/Best Teacher: Reading Popular Images of English Teachers as English Teachers

by Stephanie Pizzuto

Introduction

While completing a master's at a university in Canada, my cohort of novice English teachers was asked to participate in an Images of English Teachers roundtable. This required each of us to present an English teacher from popular culture and to consider the extent to which this image informs both our students' expectations and our own expectations of ourselves as English teachers. When first asked to engage with the "bad teacher" prompt, I was admittedly skeptical of its value as professional development. However, as I reflect below, drawing on my memories of my chosen teacher, Mr. Turner of *Boy Meets World* (Jacobs 1993–2000), as well as the recollections of some of my peers, this prompt enabled me to locate and contextualize my emerging identity as a teacher.

In "The Decay of Lying," Oscar Wilde subverted the longstanding, Aristotelian understanding of art as mimesis by proposing that "Life imitates art far more than art imitates life" (1889/1997, p. 943). This anti-mimesis is reflected in the profound influence that popular culture has on the dynamics of student–teacher relationships. In *That's Funny, You Don't Look Like a Teacher!* Weber and Mitchell noted that popular culture informs student expectations and that these expectations, in turn, influence teacher behaviours (1995, p. 3). Beyond this, my own experiences, as well as those reported by my peers, suggest that popular culture can also shape a teacher's professional identity and educational philosophy. In particular, mediated representations of teachers can serve as "a kind of informal curriculum" for those who wish to become teachers (Mitchell and Weber 1999, p. 170).

Boy Meets World

From 1993 to 2000, I was a devoted viewer of the television series *Boy Meets World*. I followed the show's young protagonists, Cory Matthews, Shawn Hunter and Topanga Lawrence, from Jefferson Elementary to John Adams High to Pennbrook University and internalized many of their life lessons as my own. Although I had always been aware of the series' lasting imprint on my psyche, I had never truly considered the extent of its influence until I embarked upon this bad teacher activity. I have always considered myself somewhat of a modern culture aficionado—not in a master of trivia sort of way, but rather in my profound belief that the construction and organization of words and images provides valuable insight into the society that produced them. This passion has had a significant impact on much my academic career and has ultimately come to shape my professional aspirations—to teach literature by appealing to its lasting influence on popular culture. In retrospect, these defining aspects of who I am can be traced to my childhood fascination with Jonathan Turner: an English teacher at John Adams High.

Mr. Turner boasts neither the mainstream popularity nor the cultural cachet of his colleague, Mr. Feeny; however, he is an important member of the *Boy Meets*

World family and an influential teacher in his own right. Mr. Turner is young, laid back, wisecracking, and hip to pop culture—qualities, which tend to result in interactive, culturally relevant lectures that are usually delivered while sitting on a desk. The latter is consistent with Weber and Mitchell's (1995) assertions that teachers who are romanticized in popular culture tend to "distinguish themselves from ordinary classroom teachers through innovative pedagogy and curriculum" (1995, p. 88). This is certainly true of Mr. Turner, whose approach to English language arts surmises that the classics are only as important as their lasting relevance. To this end, Mr. Turner repeatedly acknowledges the importance of popular culture and characteristically grounds the classics within their contemporary legacies. In "Wake Up, Little Cory" (Merzer and Trainer 1994), for instance, Mr. Turner explores the thematic underpinnings of Shakespeare's *Much Ado About Nothing* by equipping students with video cameras and instructing them to film documentaries about their friends' perspectives on sex and love. Whether he is defending his own participatory video assignment or Cory and Shawn's right to host a lunchtime radio show, Mr. Turner always strives to uphold student interests—even if it means butting heads with his superior, Mr. Feeny. Taken together, Mr. Turner's approach to the curriculum and persona establish him as the quintessential cool teacher. In fact, Mr. Turner actually rides a motorcycle to work, wears jeans and a black leather jacket, and can often be seen carrying his helmet to and from class.

Mr. Turner serves as a character foil for the more traditional Mr. Feeny who customarily wears Harris tweeds and sweater vests, and delivers inspirational lectures peppered with garden metaphors. Considered on a grander scale, Mr. Turner seemingly offers a stereotypical depiction of what many high school students believe is the "ideal" teacher. Having asked students to draw their ideal teachers, Weber and Mitchell (1995) noted, "the ideal teacher for teenagers is a young and stylish person who shares or empathizes with the popular culture of adolescence" (p. 68). Interestingly, they further identified a marked preference for black leather, ripped jeans, and "avant-garde versions of the latest trend" (p. 68), most of which Mr. Turner embraces as his signature look.

While students may have a predisposition to be more receptive to this physical presentation, it does elicit a certain set of expectations. In particular, students expect such a teacher to be laid back, approachable, and not very strict. As such, these teachers may be viewed more as buddies than authority figures—a misconception that, left unchecked, can be deeply problematic. In her presentation on our bad teacher reflections, one of my peers, Clarissa, explored the teaching style of Hannah Horvath—the protagonist of HBO's *Girls* (Dunham 2012–2017). Twenty something years old and an aspiring writer, Hannah positions herself as the students' peer and quickly establishes a connection with her students that is neither professional nor appropriate. As far-fetched as the premise may seem, Clarissa recalled her own high school experience with a young teacher with whom she attended a concert shortly after graduation—an outing that, in retrospect, she describes now as definitely "weird." A similar trend was also identified by Mike, another of my peers, in his presentation about *Californication's* (Duchovny et al. 2007–2014) Hank Moody. Much like Ms. Horvath, Mr. Moody is an aspiring writer and seems to perceive his position in the classroom as transient. As such, he repeatedly blurs the boundaries between teacher and student—sometimes even frequenting the strip club where one of his (college) students moonlights.

The expectation of camaraderie with a cool teacher is one that is addressed early on in *Boy Meets World*. In their first meeting with Mr. Turner, Cory Matthews and his peers assume that they finally have a cool teacher because he assigns X-Men. When Cory quickly realizes that his cool teacher is nonetheless authoritative and demanding of hard work, he dubs Mr. Turner, "Feeny with an earring" (Kendall and Trainer 1994, 9:26). This is an important moment because it highlights Mr. Turner's obligation to navigate student expectations and depicts the resistance that teachers may sometimes meet in the classroom. Although Mr. Turner develops close bonds with his students, these require consistent renegotiation because the students can still fall back into a sense of comfort.[2]

Conclusion

Ultimately, Mr. Turner's authenticity and dedication permit him to establish a student–teacher relationship centred on mutual respect and understanding. This dynamic is one that I hope to achieve in my own teaching practices. Moreover, I also wish to emulate his classroom management style, which relies heavily on sarcasm and wit. While this sort of thinking is consistent with Robertson's (2013) suggestion that images of teaching from film and other forms of popular media help to shape the thinking and learning of beginning teachers, this teaching style is one that I feel is genuinely well suited to my own personality and that I naturally fall into when teaching. It is also a teaching style that I have gravitated towards as a student because it allows one to maintain an air of approachability and relevance without ever being "warm and fuzzy."

What difference did it make for me (and for our group of a dozen new teachers) to watch, reflect on, present, and discuss these fictional teachers? Individually, it positioned us to produce a critical autoethnography through which we would come to better understand our professional motivations, expectations, and identities. Collectively, it offered us an opportunity to share our aspirations and confront our anxieties, as it quickly became clear that the teachers we selected were alternatively, who we hoped to be and who we feared we would become.

3 Looking in the Mirror: Reflections

by Brian Andrew Benoit

Television not only entertains, it can educate; equally, it can misinform. In looking at the role of television in framing issues of class and the idea of the working class as a particular group in North America, and reinforcing negative stereotypes about it, Leistyna et al. (2005) observed that viewing popular television programs through

---

[2]Because *Boy Meets World* is not overly concerned with realism, Mr. Turner does actually become the legal guardian of one of his students: Shawn Hunter.

a critical lens can encourage the development of a critical cultural literacy. In line with this, Mitchell and Weber (1999) argued that because stereotypes are so often caricatures, popular images "left unexamined can be dangerous" (p. 172). We need to take into account that what a particular set of images can mean or represent is often tainted by the perspective of the person doing the viewing, and by the context in which the event is occurring (Weber 2008). A researcher is encouraged to be cognizant of his or her role as a researcher and, also, to recognize that researchers cannot place themselves "above or beyond what they study" (Ellis and Bochner 1996, p. 19). As Ellis and Bochner (1996, p. 28) asked, can critical autoethnography allow for the researcher to reflect on his or her own experience, "enhancing [the]... capacity to cope with life's contingencies?" In my doctoral dissertation, *Understanding the Teacher Self: Learning Through Critical AutoEthography* (Benoit 2016), I was interested in exploring, through memory-work, experiences that have shaped me into the researcher and educator I have become. One way to do this was to engage in personal viewing and close reading of a television series, *Les Bougon* (Larouche 2004–2006).

Les Bougon

Les Bougon tells the story of a family that inhabits a working class neighborhood in Montreal. The family consists of Paul Bougon (father), Rita (mother), Junior (son), Dolorès (daughter), Mao (adopted daughter), Frederic (uncle), and Leo (grandfather). Paul is a former dockworker who, after losing his job, decides to fight against the injustices of society by getting back at the system. Rather than work, the family decides to participate in various schemes that enable them to get "back at the man." My examination of this television series provided the necessary platform from which I could begin to draw upon autobiography, autoethnography, and memory-work in order to develop and examine my identity as a teacher. In essence I have attempted to use the series and my initial analysis of it as well as the memories these prompted in order to begin to unravel the assumptions I have (and have had) as an individual and as a teacher in order to better understand myself as a teacher.

To use this television series in my critical autoethography, I went through a number of steps. First, I used my initial analysis of the series as well as the memories that these prompted in order to unravel the assumptions I have as an individual and as a teacher in order to better understand myself and my identity as a teacher. I also discussed which aspects of the series resonated with my experience. I then looked into the specifics related to the closeness I felt with the show. My study drew on my initial analysis of the series, as well as the memories they prompted, in order to unravel my assumptions—in order to be better prepared for the future. I began my study by watching the 51 episodes of the three seasons over a period of a week. During the first viewing, I did not take any notes in order to emulate how I would have watched the show under normal circumstances. I then spent the next three weekends watching each season separately. During this viewing, I took notes regarding issues and questions that I had. I also noted where I laughed as well as where I felt uneasy. Once I had watched the entire series a third time, I chose one episode from each season that had made me feel uneasy and watched them again with a friend.

Reproducing and Reinforcing Class Structures

There are three ideas that seem to me to be at the heart of *Les Bougon* and that strike me as being at the heart of informing my own teaching. The first idea is the fatalism of the characters in *Les Bougon*; their lack of concern with the world only reinforces the long-established prejudices regarding class that they have inherited. Essentially, in this series, any path that is chosen will lead to the same fatalistic end. How can I as a teacher effectively work towards providing my students with the tools to succeed when the message they receive through such shows is that success is related only to how hard you work. Are there not other factors as well that determine success? The Bougon family fight against the reality they are dealt but are, in fact, only held hostage to the rules that they claim they are above obeying. For example, although the Bougons claim to be able to make a living without having to play by the rules of the system, they are in fact not self-sufficient in that they often call on other characters in the series for help, such as Rita's wealthy parents. As a teacher, I must go beyond these simplistic portrayals of reality to provide myself and my students with the tools to deconstruct this reality so that we can reformulate our own. In other words, trying to present things in simplistic ways does nothing to prepare my students for the changing realities we all face.

The second idea from *Les Bougon* that informs my teaching is the awareness that popular texts play a critical role in the formation of our identity. The role of technology is evolving and increasing in the classroom and, therefore, we must be increasingly critical of the information we receive. Studying *Les Bougon* using critical autoethnography helped create the basis for being able to identify and construct a challenge to my worldview. It essentially provided me with the language I could use to articulate what I was feeling but not expressing. Studying the series made the unfamiliar familiar (Hirsch 1997). For example, why did watching this series make me reformulate my relationship with Hugo (pseudonym), my childhood best friend?

Another idea relates to the way that we can see that positivism as a form of research that values scientific inquiry over all else, is not dead but is, rather, presented in another form that is more subversively distributed. The television series is presented as a lighthearted depiction of a family that remains together no matter what difficulties they live through (Krauss 2004). Despite the claim to the contrary in the media by the creators of the show (Cauchon 2004), the Bougon clan can expect to die in the isolation and darkness that Paul's father experienced; Leo was left alone in a corner until his death. Junior and his sister are not able to make any meaningful connections with anybody. Not long after the pilot episode aired, as I have already mentioned, mainstream media began using the term "Bougon" to identify the type of person who lives off society. A new reality was constructed around a fictional portrayal of one family's reality.

Dolorès

Dolorès is the Bougons' 30-year-old daughter. She is an exotic dancer and does sex work in the family home. Every episode begins with her exiting her room with a client. In every case, she is portrayed as the person in control of the situation. She chooses to have sex with people for money. In some ways, ironically enough, she is a strong symbol of various women's rights movements because she continually pushes the boundaries of what is considered decent in society. Her family members watch her both recruit and satisfy her clients. In one episode, she is actually seen engaging in intercourse. I found myself wondering if this dehumanizes sex by presenting it as just a means to attaining income. Is the message here that humans are all interchangeable? As a teacher, I sometimes have to deal with students who are in some way affected by substance abuse. How have my views on issues such as sex work changed? How have I been affected by this investigation? How has the issue of Dolorès's characterization worked in relation to my own teacher identity and practice?

My response to the depiction of sex work and drug addiction was that they are dealt with in a simplistic manner, and that this creates, in the show, the idea that both are choices that one can make to improve one's own agency. When I discussed Dolorès with a colleague, she asked why I felt that she was doing anything wrong by engaging in sex work. My colleague pointed out that her conducting her business in her family's apartment might be a smart move in order to ensure her own safety and security. I replied that it was not the fact that she was generating income from the selling of sexual services that I was objecting to but that she had to do it in order to make money for her father who controlled the family funds. What does this say about my development into the teacher that I have become? Is the fact that I was always trying to be accepted a reason why I take students' concerns regarding fitting in more seriously? Do I allow students with single parents more sympathy as a result of my encounters with memories associated with those who have inhabited my past? Do I have a sensitive spot for children who have two full-time working parents because of my own experiences?

How did my conservative views regarding Dolorès shift during my study of the show and how had this affected my teacher identity? Upon initial contact with the character, I was disgusted with the fact that she was selling her body in the family home. Although I could accept that she should be allowed to choose the means that she wanted of producing income I felt that her use of sex for money dehumanized love. Why did I think this? Seeing Dolorès made me think of the mothers in the neighborhoods that I lived in and the fact that some of them had to do the same thing. Perhaps my views had been formulated as a protective device to block out what I saw? As a teacher I undoubtedly shared these beliefs through my lessons without even realizing it. In a sex education class I taught, I can remember making remarks during my teaching regarding sex workers, or as I thought of them then, prostitutes, without really analyzing what I was saying. I am now more cognizant of the need to deal differently with issues such as these.

Les Bougon and My Teacher Identity

A central part of teaching involves preparing students for their place in the world. As a child, my parents reminded me that hard work leads to success. The school also reinforced this idea which, on the surface, makes sense. The Bougons are continually working but they are not able to get out of the poverty in which they live. It is as if the show's creators are equating poverty to a type of personality. In one sense, the Bougons are doing everything they can to move up in society but they are never really able to do it. As a teacher I used to equate hard work with results but upon further examination I realize more than ever that other elements come into play. Now, I make sure that my students know that there is more to success than hard work and that they have to be aware that elements such as social and economic barriers exist.

Viewing *Les Bougon* prompted memories, which, when I studied them, taught me about my teacher identity and practice. Seeing how the patriarch of the series, Paul Bougon, relentlessly fights the system without ever really getting anywhere highlights how the concept of power and who holds it operates. This must feed into my teaching. As a teacher I am responsible for ensuring that my students are not provided with false hope but, rather, given the opportunity to identify the barriers that are holding them back. Paul does not fight to change the system; he just allows it to govern how his family will act. Popular texts such as *Les Bougon* play a role in disseminating misinformation and views of the world that, without further study, can lead to the reinforcement of stereotypes. Teacher-researchers can use these underlying themes in order to uncover their own assumptions so that they may begin to make the necessary corrections required to become more humane teachers.

4 Reflecting Forward: The Affective Lens

Feminist bell hooks (1996) noted that

> trying to teach complicated feminist theory to students. .. often led me to begin such discussion by talking about a particular film. Suddenly students would be engaged in an animated discussion deploying the very theoretical concepts that they had previously claimed they just did not understand (p. 3).

While it is beyond the scope of this final section to provide a comprehensive argument for why "film works" in professional development studies, we can look to several key areas for further exploration as supported by these three exemplars. First of all, there is clearly a need to look more closely at what Rose (2012) termed, *audiencing*. While film viewing is a significant area of audiencing, the notion of *how* teachers view teacher films (or how doctors view doctor films or lawyers view lawyer films) remains understudied. At a second level then we might think of how various researchers in cultural studies and film studies have drawn attention to the affective potential of film to engage the emotions of the viewer and, especially, as Sinnerbrink (2016) noted to be empathetic. The examples make it clear that while empathy is complex, there is clearly a need for the viewer to "feel for" (even if it is to dislike) certain characters in a film or television series. At a third level, Sara Ahmed's (2017) work on the affective may help us understand what she described as *coming undone*. At the risk of over simplifying Ahmed's idea of coming undone, we might think about the ways in which film narratives can provoke something that we didn't necessarily know was there. All three mosaics give a sense of this, and suggest that teachers' professional development studies would do well to draw on these cinematic narratives.

At the same time, each mosaic pieces draws attention to some of the reasons why viewing these film and television narratives can be so compelling in teachers' professional learning through memory-work. Bridget's idea, for example, that writing about the films "assisted me by taking some of the focus off myself" offers an important nuance to empathy and feeling. Work in self-study and autoethnography in professional development is sometimes criticized for being too self oriented but, clearly, as Bridget points out, such a comment does not do justice to what it means to take the focus off one's self. For Brian, it may be that the opposite is true. In engaging with his repeated viewings of *Les Bougon*, he tries to determine what it is in his personal life that compels him to write about these characters in relation to his teaching. For Stephanie, she focuses on what she regards as aspects of her teacher identity that were already there but are affirmed in her consideration of Mr. Turner. Each of these positions can be true and, in so doing, confirms the importance of the Hollywood (or Quebec) curriculum to professional learning—particularly as seen through the gaze of the teacher.

Acknowledgements We are very grateful to Naydene de Lange (Nelson Mandela University, South Africa) who served as the peer reviewer for this chapter.

References

Adams, P. (2006). Exploring social constructivism: Theories and practicalities. *Education, 3*(13), 243–257. https://doi.org/10.1080/03004270600898893.

Ahmed, S. (2017). *Living a feminist life*. Durham: Duke University Press.

Benoit, B. (2016). *Understanding the teacher self: Learning through critical autoethnography (Unpublished doctoral dissertation)*. Canada: McGill University.

Butler, F. (2000). *Hollywood films, reflective practice and social change in teacher education: A Bahamian illustration (Unpublished doctoral dissertation)*. Canada: McGill University.

Campbell, B. (2017). *Influences on, and possibilities for, my English pedagogy: A narrative self-study (Unpublished doctoral dissertation)*. South Africa: University of KwaZulu-Natal.

Cauchon, P. (2004, January 17). Médias: Bourgonner autour des Bougons. *La Presse*. Retrieved from http://www.ledevoir.com/societe/medias/45198/medias-bougonner-autour-des-bougon.

Clandinin, D., & Connelly, F. (2000). *Narrative inquiry: Experience and story in qualitative research*. San Francisco: Jossey-Bass.

Clarke, M. (2011). Promoting a culture of reflection in teacher education: The challenge of large lecture settings. *Teacher Development, 15*(4), 517–531.

Coulter, C., & Smith, M. (2009). The construction zone: Literary elements in narrative research. *Educational Researcher, 38*(8), 577–590.

Dalton, M. (1999). *The Hollywood curriculum: Teachers in the movies*. New York: Peter Lang.

Dickens, C. (1973). *Hard times*. London: Penguin (Original work published 1854).

Duchovny, D., Kapinos, T., Paolillo, M. (Executive producers). (2007–2014). *Californication* [Television series]. New York: Showtime.

Dunham, L. (Executive producer). (2012–2017). *Girls* [Television series]. New York: Home Box Office.

Ellis, C., & Bochner, P. (Eds.). (1996). *Composing ethnography: Alternative forms of qualitative writing*. Walnut Creek: AltaMira Press.

Hallam, J., & Marchment, M. (1995). Questioning the ordinary woman: *Oranges are not the only fruit*, text and viewer. In B. Skeggs (Ed.), *Feminist cultural theory: Process and production* (pp. 169–189). Manchester: Manchester University Press.

Hirsch, M. (1997). *Family frames: Photography and postmemory*. Cambridge: Harvard University Press.

Hooks, B. (1996). *Reel to real: Race, sex, and class at the movies*. New York: Routledge.

Jacobs, M. (Executive producer). (1993–2000). *Boy meets world* [Television series]. New York: American Broadcasting Company.

Kendall, D. (Writer), & Trainer, D. (Director). (1994). Back 2 school [Television series episode]. In M. Jacobs (Producer) (Eds.), *Boy meets world*. New York: American Broadcasting Company.

Krauss, C. (2004, December 27). A twisted sitcom makes the Simpsons look like saints. *The New York Times*. Retrieved from http://www.nytimes.com/2004/12/27/international/americas/27montreal.html?_r=0.

LaGravense, R. (Director). (2007). *Freedom Writers* [Motion Picture]. US: Paramount.

Larouche, F. (Producer). (2004). *Les Bougon c'est aussi ça la vie!* [Television series]. Montreal: Radio-Canada Télé.

Leavy, P. (2016). Fiction as a transformative tool. *LEARNing Landscapes, 9*(2), 29–33. Retrieved from http://www.learninglandscapes.ca/index.php/learnland/article/view/Commentary-Fiction-as-a-Transformative-Tool/761.

Leistyna, P., Alper, L., Asner, E., & Foundation, Media Education. (2005). *Class dismissed: How TV frames the working class*. Northampton: Media Education Foundation.

Merzer, G. (Writer), & Trainer, D. (Director). (1994, November 4). Wake up, little Cory [Television series episode]. In M. Jacobs (Producer), *Boy meets world*. New York: American Broadcasting Company.

Mhlongo, N. (2004). *Dog eat dog*. Cape Town: Kwela Books.

Mitchell, C. (2016). Autoethnography as a wide-angle lens on looking (inward and outward): What difference can this make to our teaching? In D. Pillay, I. Naicker, & K. Pithouse-Morgan (Eds.), *Academic autoethnographies: Inside teaching in higher education* (pp. 175–189). Rotterdam: Sense Publishers.

Mitchell, C., & de Lange, N. (2013). What can a teacher do with a cellphone? Using participatory visual research to speak back in addressing HIV&AIDS. *South African Journal of Education, 33*(4), 1–13.

Mitchell, C., de Lange, N., & Moletsane, R. (2014). Me and my cellphone: Constructing change from the inside through cellphilms and participatory video in a rural community. *Area, 48*(4), 435–441. https://doi.org/10.1111/area.12142.

Mitchell, C., de Lange, N., & Moletsane, R. (2016). Poetry in a pocket: The cellphilms of South African rural women teachers and the poetics of the everyday. In K. MacEntee, C. Burkholder, & J. Schwab-Cartas (Eds.), *What's a cellphilm?* (pp. 19–34). Rotterdam: Sense Publishers.

Mitchell, C., de Lange, N., & Moletsane, R. (2017). *Participatory visual methodologies: Social change, community and policy*. London: Sage.

Mitchell, C., & Pithouse-Morgan, K. (2014). Expanding the memory catalogue: Southern African women's contributions to memory-work writing as a feminist methodology. *Agenda, 28*(1), 92–103. https://doi.org/10.1080/10130950.2014.883704.

Mitchell, C., & Weber, S. (1999). *Reinventing ourselves as teachers: Beyond nostalgia*. London: Falmer Press.

Motalingoane-Khau, M. (2007). *Understanding adolescent sexuality in the memories of four female Basotho teachers: An auto/biographical study (Unpublished doctoral dissertation)*. South Africa: University of KwaZulu-Natal.

Nash, R. (2004). *Liberating scholarly writing: The power of personal narrative*. New York: Teachers College Press.

Richardson, L. (2001). Getting personal: Writing stories. *International Journal of Qualitative Studies in Education, 14*(1), 33–38.

Robertson, J. P. (2013). Fantasy's confines: Popular culture and the education of the primary school teacher. In S. Todd (Ed.), *Learning desire: Perspectives on pedagogy, culture, and the unsaid* (pp. 75–96). New York: Routledge.

Rose, G. (2012). *Visual methodologies*. London: SAGE.

Samaras, A. (2011). *Self-study teacher research: Improving your practice through collaborative inquiry*. Thousand Oaks: Sage.

Sinnerbrink, R. (2016). *Cinematic ethics: Exploring ethical experiences through film*. New York: Routledge.

Van Amerom, W. P. C. (2005). Active/interactive learning facilitation in large classes. *Journal for New Generation Sciences, 3*(2), 116–124.

Van Manen, M. (1990). *Researching lived experience: Human science for an action sensitive pedagogy*. Ontario: Althouse Press.

Von Glasersfeld, E. (1995). *Radical constructivism: A way of knowing in learning*. London: Falmer Press.

Vygotsky, L. (1978). *Mind in society: The development of higher psychological processes*. Cambridge: Harvard University Press.

Walker, A. (1982). *The color purple*. San Diego: Harcourt.

Weber, S. (2008). Visual images in research. In G. Knowles & A. Cole (Eds.), *Handbook of the arts in qualitative research* (pp. 41–54). Los Angeles: SAGE.

Weber, S., & Mitchell, C. (1995). *That's funny you don't look like a teacher: Interrogating images of identity in popular culture*. London: Falmer Press.

Weir, P. (Director). (1989). Dead poets society [Motion picture]. USA: Touchstone.

Wilde, O. (1997). *The collected works of Oscar Wilde*. Hertfordshire: Wordsworth (Original work published 1889).

Creative Nonfiction Narratives and Memory-Work: Pathways for Women Teacher-Researchers' Scholarship of Ambiguity and Openings

Daisy Pillay, Mary Cullinan and Leighandri Moodley

Abstract "Creative Nonfiction Narratives and Memory-Work: Pathways for Women Teacher-Researchers' Scholarship of Ambiguity and Openings" by Daisy Pillay, Mary Cullinan, and Leighandri Moodley, draws on exemplars of memory-work and creative nonfiction narratives presented by two teacher-researchers from their graduate studies. Mary, a Canadian teacher and late-entry doctoral student, used personal photos and metaphorical images to evoke memories of how women saw their journey as late-entry doctoral students in order to come to a closer understanding of her life and place in academia. Leighandri shares two creative narratives she composed with South African women novice teachers in her master's study to bring her to a deeper understanding of her own story as a novice teacher. The mosaic pieces illustrate ways in which memory-work and creative nonfiction narratives can facilitate new understandings of both past and present, generating new narratives of women teachers that can activate change for the future.

Keywords Artefacts · Creative nonfiction · Doctoral students · Memory-work
Novice teachers · Photographs · South Africa · Teacher professional learning

---

D. Pillay (✉) · L. Moodley
School of Education, University of KwaZulu-Natal, Durban, South Africa
e-mail: pillaygv@ukzn.ac.za

L. Moodley
e-mail: lpmoodley26@gmail.com

M. Cullinan
Faculty of Education, McGill University, Montreal, Canada
e-mail: mary.cullinan@mail.mcgill.ca

© Springer Nature Switzerland AG 2019
K. Pithouse-Morgan et al. (eds.), *Memory Mosaics: Researching Teacher Professional Learning Through Artful Memory-work*, Studies in Arts-Based Educational Research 2, https://doi.org/10.1007/978-3-319-97106-3_7

1 Creative Nonfiction Narratives and Memory-Work in Educational Research

Polkinghorne (1988) proposed that social researchers should "change their voices from logicians to story-tellers" (Banks 2008, p. 158) to bring to light narrativity in research experience. As Witherell and Noddings (1991, p. 1) explained, "stories and narrative, whether personal or fictional, provide meaning and belonging to our lives." To a certain extent, these stories can attach us to others and to our very own histories by "providing a tapestry rich with threads of time, place, character, and even advice on what we might do with our lives" (Witherell and Noddings 1991, p. 1). Selfhood and identity are grounded in narrative because "narrative gives life its figuration and each individual's life its figure... its uniqueness, and coherence over time" (Banks 2008, p. 159). To understand persons as unique, and constituted relationally with or through the human and nonhuman, narrative becomes fundamental to human understanding, selfhood, and sociality.

Memories leave their trace on everyone (Heikkillä et al. 2012) and narrative social researchers create stories of these traces using the methodological tools at their disposal—"rediscovering what people once were told [and experienced] and need to be (re)told again" (Postman 1992, p. 151). Memory-work as "deliberate remembering" (Kuhn 1996, pp. 146–161) provides meaningful information necessary "for our constructions of ourselves or to deconstruct our notions of ourselves to gain insight into how a certain meaning and sense of the world [is] produced" (Haug 2008, p. 540). In this way, "personal and social narrative" (Mitchell 2011, p. 44) become critical instruments for naming, revising, and revisioning lived lives in social contexts (Richie and Wilson 2000).

Educational researchers who compose creative narrative texts give recognition and acknowledgement to texts that celebrate ambiguity in which social researchers "dance in what is seen like a fiesta of textual possibilities... qualified as creative, classified as non-fictional" (Barone 2008, pp. 113–114). Interweaving different textual realities offers glimpses into the nuanced, textured understanding of "what people are and of what people can be" (Banks 2008, p. 162). Capturing and expressing the interiority of the persons (Coles 1989) through unique art elements and stories fashioned out of selected real and imagined happenings and experiences (Banks 2008) for scholarly research is useful for social researchers privileging voices and lives of participants, and for including the expressive–emotional dimensions of the researcher–participant research relationship.

The work of Geertz (1983), "a self-described anthropologist/storyteller" (Barone 2008, p. 107), is recognised for the notion of genre blurring, which advances the story telling and poetic qualities in ethnographic work and other fields of human sciences. Eisner (1979) and Barone (1979) coined the term *arts-based research* to refer to research that integrates a range of aesthetic design elements (Barone 2008). Eisner (2008, p. 19) argued that art provides an evocative approach for representation and knowing not "expressible in ordinary discourse" and the potential to enable the researcher to "walk in the shoes of another" (2008, pp. 6–7). Including these artistic design elements in nonfictional stories can promote imagination, ambiguity, and creativity (Barone 2008). Evoking researchers' awareness and understandings "through aesthetic pleasure" (Banks 2008, p. 161) derived from the subjective memories and experiences of participants enables a scholarship of openness rather than singularity to interpretations, and where details of both "fact and emotion, structural and emotional complexity, is emphasised" (Bochner 2000, p. 271). This form of genre blurring research, often labelled as creative nonfiction (Barone 2008), is burgeoning in various fields and disciplines, including educational research. The work being done takes on varied literary and artistic forms including, but not limited to, life stories, life histories, autoethnographies, nonfictional stories, films and videos, ethnographies (Barone 2008), as well as "creative analytical practices" Richardson's (2000, p. 930) such as polyvocal texts, visual presentations, layered accounts, writing stories, and mixed genres (Barone 2008, p. 108).

This chapter builds on this developing scholarship, drawing specifically on the use of memory-work and creative nonfiction narratives for enabling scholarship of ambiguity and openings. The chapter showcases how two women teacher-researchers, Mary Cullinan and Leighandri Moodley (née Pillay), chose to integrate aesthetic (visual and artefactual) elements as alternate expressive and representational strategies for evoking and eliciting stories of "'a life' lived—what actually happens" (Bruner 1984, p. 7) and life experienced—"consisting of images, feelings, sentiments desires, thoughts, and meanings known to the person whose life it is" (Bruner 1984, p. 7). Life story narratives provided a "plausible and integrative framework" (van Schalkwyk 2010, p. 676) for Mary and Leighandri's educational research and the study of different forms of positioning in the study of teacher-researcher dialogical self (Hermans 2001). Expressive spaces for autobiographical remembering that involves the cognitive, motivational, and affective aspects, became a necessary part of the collaborative co-construction between these two narrative inquirers and the women research participants with whom they worked.

2 Crafting Creative Nonfiction Narratives as Mosaics of Teacher-Researcher Learning

This chapter is composed from different creative nonfiction narratives reconstructed by Mary and Leighandri and is pieced together by Daisy Pillay, a teacher educator, researcher, and graduate supervisor who works in different graduate communities to support doctoral and master's students' research learning. Daisy has, in her own work, explored arts-based research and aesthetic memory-work for teacher development and teacher identity studies (Pillay and Pithouse-Morgan 2016; Pillay et al. 2017).

To develop this chapter, Daisy invited Leighandri, a novice South African teacher and graduate student and Mary, a Canadian teacher and late-entry doctoral student, to develop short mosaic pieces from their respective master's and doctoral theses. The two exemplars of individual memory-work and creative nonfiction narrative in this chapter are presented as two different mosaic pieces: (1) individual memory-work and visual imagery, and (2) artefactual storytelling.

These exemplars contribute to a transnational dialogue of creative nonfiction modes of inquiry and representation that evoke aesthetic, intuitive pleasure, an enhancement of emotional resources and relationships, new ideas, and insights necessary for tackling critical socially just women teacher–researcher's learning practices and discourses. Inspired by their own personal histories and childhood memories, both Mary and Leighandri worked over a 6 month period to write about and reflect on the values and priorities that shaped their research interests and perspectives. Daisy, Mary, and Leighandri continued their conversations via e-mail and Skype to deepen and expand how their employment of memory-work and creative nonfiction narrative modes opened up relationships for passionate, critical engagement with many voices and perspectives shaping women teacher-researchers' lived educational experiences. Their work together responded to the call for social researchers to "engage in passionate criticism... full of passionate conviction, where knowledge and art and caring are intertwined" (Bateson 1984, p. 216).

The chapter is organised in three sections. The first section below presents a brief introduction to Mary Cullinan, and is followed by her creative nonfiction narrative exemplar—composed from narrative writing and visual imagery. This is followed by Leighandri's creative nonfiction narrative exemplar—composed of narrative and artefactual memory-work. Thereafter, all three authors' voices (Daisy, Mary, and Leighandri) are woven together as unifying lines of continuity to create the mosaic composition.

3 Mary Cullinan's Narrative Inquiry

Mary worked as a teacher before and after her children were born and, in her 50s, took up doctoral studies at a university in Canada. As a late-entry woman student, Mary experienced different forms of invisibility and marginalisation at university. In her narrative inquiry doctoral study, she focused on studying the lives of 39 late-entry doctoral women students across Canada who chose to further their studies and return to school later in life, as a way to change and challenge the world of academia. Co-constructing stories of late-entry women and making connections with so many like-minded women—who supported her and each other as they shared their life challenges while pursuing their degrees—was reminiscent of the kinds of support received from the "girls" her mother invited for tea many years ago. A photograph of teatime (Fig. 1) evoked childhood memories as well as a visual expression of the camaraderie and laughter she experienced in the doctoral study that "warmed [her] mind and fed [her] intellect" (Cullinan 2015, p. 229). Sharing these voices and these stories in her doctoral dissertation, *Echoes of Late-Entry Women in Academia: A Narrative Inquiry* (Cullinan 2015), became a way of making a place for exploring her own memories of talking and listening, and a space to recognise and to see some connections to the women in her past—and those others to come.

Fig. 1 Teatime meant support to my mother's friends (Photographer, Mary Cullinan, with permission)

Mary selected from a range of personal photos (including childhood photos) and metaphorical images that evoked memories and experiences of how the women saw their educational journey. Through these unique stories fashioned out of selected real and imagined happenings and experiences (Banks 2008), she seeks to privilege the voices and lives of the women participants as a well as the expressive–emotional dimensions of the relationship she shared and through which she is able to free herself from self-closure and "engage in passionate criticism" Bateson (1984, p. 216) of the oppressive and traditional challenges of academia.

Mary Cullinan's Mosaic Piece: Individual Memory-Work and Visual Imagery

I am Mary Cullinan and I was born in a traditional family, the fourth of five children. Academia was not on my parents' agenda. It was not considered a necessary stepping-stone in life, certainly not for a girl. As I made my way through university, this fact was never far from my mind. At 53 years old, I returned to university to pursue doctoral studies. I was mystified to see that, still, years later, there were still some people who didn't understand why I (or other older women) was there. Perhaps my contribution here will illuminate why.

As a child, I was interested in listening to women talk about their lives. My mother used to invite the "girls" (her friends) over for tea. Once a month, these neighbourhood women would meet to talk about their lives, their struggles. When they met at our house, I would listen to their lively conversation, enjoying the loud laughter and friendships they had formed. It was energising, even to the young girl I was. Little did I know that one day I would find inspiration from those gatherings for my dissertation! From an early age, I knew that women find strength, encouragement, and solace from their conversations with other women. And so, it was with confidence that I turned to listening to and learning from late-entry women's voices as they pursued their doctoral studies.

Beginning my doctoral journey at 53 years of age, I soon realised that older women regularly seemed to feel (or be told) that they did not belong on the demanding, sometimes turbulent, doctoral voyage. Often struck by comments others freely made about my age and what possible reason I might have to embark on such a journey at a later stage in life, I began to ask myself, "Why embark on this journey at my age?" I soon found many other women were weary of the constant need to defend or explain reasons for returning to school later in life. Fortunately, for many, these feelings were often tempered by the growing awareness that with age comes recognition that, indeed, we bring years of knowledge and experience that inform our journey. Through my research, I was going to create a place for voice and give power to the stories of the sometimes ignored and undervalued late-entry women in academia.

Methodology

I began my venture into narrative inquiry using a method called photovoice (de Lange et al. 2008; Gubrium 2009; Holm 2008; Koltz et al. 2010; Wang and Burris 1997). Photovoice (Wang 2006) is a participatory action research (PAR) approach that can help groups voice their opinions and be heard. It is based on the theoretical literature on education for critical consciousness—a popular term developed by Brazilian pedagogue and theorist, Freire (1993)—feminist theory, and a community-based approach to documentary photography (Wang et al. as cited in Wang 2006; Wang and Burris, 1997). Inspired to use visual data in my research of late-entry women by my own experience of taking part in a classmate's photovoice project, I was curious to see what sort of images women might use to illustrate their doctoral journey.

Regarding the images, I took what the women said and chose what I felt was a good caption. Always, I asked the women if the caption was acceptable (I have lots more images on my website). In a few cases, I could not use the image they sent; they had taken it off the Internet and I was not sure of the legality of using it in my thesis. So, I bought a similar image through iStock or through the website builder I used called, Wix. I really enjoyed that part of my research—the pictures. I felt the images really embodied the women's feelings. These images helped provide an understanding of how the women saw their journey, and, honouring Dorothy Smith (1989) allowed for some unique understanding, from the women's point of view.

In addition to photovoice, I used other methods of narrative inquiry including a writing workshop and interviews. All these methods provided me with a chance to experience the women's lives in their own words. The images and reflections women provided about their doctoral journey were at times heart wrenching and, frequently, truly inspiring. Maintaining an awareness of my own story, as Clandinin and Connelly (2004) suggested, I felt sure that listening to others would bring me to a closer understanding of my own story. It did. As women reflected on their education, it was as though the opportunity to supply images along with their words brought them to a deeper understanding of their journey.

Fig. 2 Lac La Ronge, Saskatchewan (Photographer, Mary Cullinan's participant, with permission)

Welcoming the Doctorate into Our Lives

While Cole and Gunter (2010) recognised how demanding the technical aspects of the doctoral journey can be, they also note that this challenge is only one part of the story. Busy lives take over at times. As they so aptly and, I feel, poetically wrote:

> The thesis becomes and remains—even after graduation—a member of the family. So while much depends on agency, it is the structures that shape and control our capacity to exercise control that matter, and a doctoral student cannot be successful without being able to juggle a range of demands on their time, not least partners and children who expect to be loved and cuddled. It is a long process that demands a huge amount of commitment from partner and family. (Cole and Gunther 2010, p. 139)

As they made their way through their doctoral (Ph.D.) journey, women in my study found encouragement and wonder all around them, as illustrated in the image (Fig. 2) and words by one of my participants, Bridget (pseudonym). She reflected on her position at the university, and she recalled her time at home with her young son. Drawing a parallel between her life as a mother and a doctoral student, she provided the following:

> My backyard was this lake, my sanctuary of unkempt, messy beauty—poplar trees and swampy willows. This was a time when my solitude was only interrupted by the sound of small planes taking off to fly their American passengers to some northern wilderness camp. I could watch their progress through the trees, but they could not see me... I was hidden

behind this protective wall. I reflect on this moment as a commentary on how my journey towards a PhD has been a somewhat camouflaged process. I do not think the academy would have noticed me had I not simply stood my ground, demanding to be acknowledged. I am older, and as people age I think we become more invisible in society. The academy (even with all their rhetoric of individuality and inclusiveness) has shaped ideas of usefulness in society. On many occasions I've felt my usefulness, by both the academy and society, was questioned. Only when I confronted these mainstream ideas, did I suddenly emerge behind the wall of ignorance and stereotypical rhetoric. Even some of my colleagues found it amusing to comment on my age and usefulness or contribution to academia. This was a painful time for me, and it still stings. Yet when I think about this picture, I am reminded that this wall of trees that hid me also provided a protective barrier, shelter and comfort. It prepared me for what was to come. I could see out, but they could not see me.... I think I was starting my journey towards a higher education long before I set foot on any campus. (Cullinan 2015, p. 44)

Like Bridget, many of the late-entry women I interviewed felt that their usefulness in the academy was not only questioned, but trivialised as well. Images like hers embodied women's isolation. Some women's images and words were truly alarming. Hesitancy to believe in self recurred. Many women talked of how, so many times during their studies, they felt that they couldn't go on—they wanted to quit.

Women often recalled their upbringing, and how very little was expected of them as young women other than the obvious—get married and have children. These memories still resonated, and many recalled parents' words with great clarity.

Most women were highly aware that they were nontraditional learners, different from the other students in their programmes, but just as smart and capable. Many women spoke of the support they enjoyed and where they found inspiration. While some women made reference to their upbringing, and how it affected their thinking today, some spoke with pride about how they have affected their children. Others spoke of the need to reinvent the past. Carol (pseudonym) commented that she didn't do the degree for money; she had already peaked in terms of earnings in the public school system. She was not the slightest bit interested in turning towards an academic career at 60 years old. See and feel her joyousness in her words and image (Fig. 3).

The process of doing this degree has been one almost of getting to know myself better, rewriting early history, showing myself that I could do this in light of the many people in my past who did not support my education attempts (some of them have died but their voices still resound in my ears). I think it was a process of reinventing myself... rewriting script... after all the deep reflection, connecting with my passion for dance in a meaningful way... nurturing from two amazing women who believed in me every step of the way... as senior supervisor and committee member. I definitely came out the other side of the wall of fire knowing myself better, believing in myself more... understanding *duende*... the Spanish flamenco older woman dancer who 'knows what she knows' when she dances... knowing now that I know what I know... in this dance of life... I am duende now.... Yes... I have a few things to say about the process... it was simply one of the most important and best things I could possibly have done in my entire list of life experiences. Cost be damned! (Cullinan 2015, p. 193)

My Learning
As women reflected on their memories of their educational experiences through

Fig. 3 Reinventing myself… rewriting script (Photographer, Mary Cullinan's participant, with permission)

creative narrative constructions, the images along with their words bring them to a deeper understanding of their journey. While they mined their own past, in turn, always, I felt as though I were coming closer to a clearer understanding of my life, my place in academia. I knew that I was not only informing myself on this journey, but also providing an important outlet for the women to share their own stories. In a way, I was connecting with them through their stories. As I shared the women's concerns, I became, in Richardson's (1997) words, someone who was not only witnessing their journey, but also walking with them. In allowing their voices to be heard, I brought forth my own.

Leonard's (2001) suggestion that we might see the stress that is inherent in doing the doctorate as a new expert knowledge seemed to resonate with the stories

I was hearing. She suggested that universities should recognise the real anxiety that women experience as they make their way through their doctoral studies.

Although the subject of my conversations was vastly different from the ones I eavesdropped on in my family home so many years ago, the laughter and camaraderie that surfaced, and how supportive my participants were of me and each other, and how, in many cases, they shared images of their life challenges while pursuing their degrees, was sweetly reminiscent of the kinds of support I could hear from those friends my mom invited for tea many years ago.

4   Leighandri Moodley's Narrative Inquiry

Leighandri Moodley is a practicing Hindu woman and a novice teacher who has worked since 2009 in a private Catholic school in South Africa. In her master's thesis (Pillay 2014), she described how, as a 21 year old and novice teaching in the distinctive private school setting, she felt like a stranger being watched by the older, experienced teachers. Left to her own devices to cope in this strange unfamiliar space, she undertook memory-work and narrative inquiry to recollect and reflect on the lived experiences of three newly qualified women teachers—one Indian and Hindu, and two white and Christian—to better understand what contributions their own memories and past experiences made to their lives as newly qualified teachers in a private Catholic school. In her master's research, *Narratives of Novice Teachers in a Private Catholic School* (Pillay 2014), she composed stories with other three newly qualified teachers. In Leighandri's mosaic piece, she shares two of the creative narratives she composed with women novice teacher participants in her master's study. Through the act of remembering, and the telling stories of self evoked through artefactual inquiry and conversations, stories were shared and relationships were forged with like-minded individuals. Leighandri engages in selective ordering of these experiences to capture and express the voices and lives of novice teachers. Just as importantly, through expressing the interiority of these particular persons, Leighandri was able to bring herself to a closer understanding of her own story as a novice teacher teaching in a private Catholic school.

Leighandri Moodley's Mosaic Piece: Artefactual Memory-Work

I was born in a family of Hindu faith and the eldest of three siblings. We lived in a place called Chatsworth, a typically Indian neighbourhood.[1] Brought up in a typically "Indian home," with mom being a teacher and my dad a tradesman, I remember my two sisters and I spending many weekends and holidays with my granny. I was her

---

[1] The Group Areas Act (1950), which was the cornerstone of apartheid policy, was instituted by the National Party government and greatly polarised the South African community along racial lines. For the South African Indian community, this meant a mass exodus of people from different areas along the Natal coastline to areas such as Phoenix and Chatsworth. Leighandri was 5 years old when a new democracy was ushered in, and people of all races were allowed to live and move freely irrespective of their historical racial categories.

Fig. 4 Leighandri's memory drawing (Drawing, Leighandri Moodley, with permission)

favourite grandchild. As I think back to my earliest memories of wanting to be a teacher, I also remember how I loved being at my granny's home because it made me feel safe, free, and comfortable. I also remember the red polka-dot dress that I wear in my memory drawing (Fig. 4), and remember the love and care that my granny invested into making this garment for me. It is a treasured item that is kept in my mom's old wooden chest. This memory of the trusting and caring relationship that I shared with my granny in the comfort of her home played an instrumental role in my educational journey as a young woman, teacher, and postgraduate student-researcher.

In my honours degree, I was offered the opportunity to introspect and reflect on myself as an individual through the various memory-work activities, one of which one required of us to write or draw about, "My First Memory of Wanting to Be a Teacher."

> As a child I can still remember talking to the furniture and writing on the wall of my granny's veranda. Whenever I put on my red polka dot dress, I imagined myself as a teacher.... I was five years old, it was a hot sunny morning and I was happy and excited to be at my granny's home as I played in the veranda with my toys as the smell of fresh coffee filled the air. I soon got tired of playing with my toys and my colouring book and decided it was time to play my favourite "teacher game," which I loved. The oily smell of the blue wax crayon that I used to write with on the wall still lingers in my memory. I can still hear my granny asking me what I had done and I replied by saying, "I was teaching the children to write." My granny just laughed. (personal journal, September 19, 2011)

As a novice teacher, there are critical moments that I remembered through memory-work and arts-based research in my postgraduate study, which have assisted me in thinking about my life and what I do as a new teacher from a different perspective. When I was employed as a novice teacher, I was the youngest member on the school staff. I had no one to go to with all my questions. I had to find my own way. I did not go through any induction or mentoring process at the school because there wasn't one. As a result, I enrolled for the honours programme and, inside that lecture room with the lecturer and the students, I found my safety net to explore my uneasiness and discomfort.

There were many experiences during my first few years when I had many questions, and not many teachers were willing to assist me. Everything that I learned during my years at campus felt useless at that moment. I remembered feeling like a stranger as a novice and non-Christian in this private Catholic school. Sabar (2004) reminded us that "the beginner teacher is a stranger who is often not familiar with the accepted norms and symbols in the school…. [Novice teachers] seem to resemble immigrants who leave a familiar culture and move into a strange one that is both attractive and repellent" (p. 147), while attempting to make personal sense of "how it should be; whilst at the same time being subjected to the powerful socialising forces of the school culture" (Flores and Day 2006, p. 220).

Being a Woman Novice Teacher-Researcher

Taking up postgraduate studies and registering as a master's student in the teacher development studies specialisation, was the only way out for me to deepen my learning as a novice teacher. Having engaged and experienced memory-work for myself during the honours module, I was aware of the "aesthetic pleasure, understandings derived from narrative coherence and verisimilitude, and the enhancement of emotional resources" (Banks 2008, p. 161) when evoking personal memories and stories. Through this research inquiry process, I was able to connect with three other novice teachers and collaboratively work with them to deepen my understandings of lived truths (Richardson 2000).

Methodology

Reconstructing and recreating novice teacher's stories through memory-work allowed me as the researcher to explore the difficulties, desires, anxieties, practices, interests, and critical moments in the lives of the novice teachers. Through the use of memory-work, a "range of emotions, both positive and negative" (Cole 2011, p. 226) were explored through the use of unstructured interviews, collage, and artefact retrieval strategies to generate the data for my study. For this mosaic chapter, I offer two of the three stories I composed of women novice teacher-research participants.

Kerusha's Artefactual Story

Kerusha (pseudonym) was a first-year teacher, teaching Grade 1 in the foundation phase. She is an Indian woman in her early twenties:

> I was born and raised here in Durban, KwaZulu-Natal. My family and I have recently moved from the residential suburb of Musgrave to Glenwood, in KwaZulu-Natal. My brother is my

Creative Nonfiction Narratives and Memory-Work ...

rock. My brother is so "big" in my life; he is a few years older than me. We bake together, cook together… we have so much fun together. We have an amazing relationship.

Growing up in a Hindu home and attending a Catholic school was normal for me. When you are young and in Grade 00, you don't really know what Christianity or Hinduism is. When I was in the primary school, I can remember the teachers saying, "Go and get a blessing from the priest," even though I could not receive the Holy Communion.

As a novice teacher, I knew that being in a Catholic school I had to partake of certain rituals and I had no problem doing that. I partake of the rituals performed because I believe that all religions teach the same values in different ways. I even teach learners things from my own Hindu spiritual teachings. I believe we should all appreciate each other for who we are.

My most sacred possession is an elephant-headed Ganesh (Fig. 5), which, according to Hinduism, represents the deity who is the remover of obstacles. Statues of Ganesh can be found in most Indian homes and his image is placed where new houses are to be built; and amongst other symbolic gestures, poets traditionally invoke him at the start of a book. Ganesh is also patron of letters and of learning.

This artefact was given to me by a girl learner in my Grade 7 class. Not having much of a relationship with God at that time in my life, and being young and naïve, I accepted this gift without really understanding the meaning it carries. However, over time, my life has changed. My whole focus and outlook on life changed for the better. I believe in God and I'm constantly talking to him. I always keep it on my person. If I do not have pockets, I will find some way of keeping it on me. I have lost it so many times and it has always come back to me. I have learnt that all religions are working towards achieving the same thing and that is to love one another and to do good. This deity, to me, is like a safety blanket. (personal communication, November 2012)

Kerusha grew up in a family that discouraged fixed views about being a girl or boy or of being a practising Catholic or Hindu. This open-mindedness assists her in negotiating her values and perspectives as a woman and novice teacher. From her creative stories, I was also to get into the real values and knowledges (family relationships, her love for diverse food dishes, and being creative) that are inextricably shaping the position she adopts to become the teacher she wants to be—creative, open-minded, and having respect for diversity.

Elizabeth's Artefactual Story

Elizabeth (pseudonym) is a white female in her late twenties, and is a Grade 4 teacher in the intermediate phase:

I was born in the late 80s on a farm in Northern Mpumulanga, in the small town of Commondale. As a small close-knit group of four, my family grew up in comfort. My dad runs a farm called Wit River, and my mum is a teacher in a rural primary school near my home. I was familiar with the black farm labourers and their children, but I never really got a chance to know them. (personal communication, November 2012)

Elizabeth's parents put an end to any interaction she may have had with the "farm kids" when she and her sister were sent off to boarding school in Vryheid.

I went to Stellenbosch straight after school. It was far away from home and I just wanted to experience something new. After qualifying as a teacher a few years ago, I had to leave home once again to start work in Durban at the Holy Convent as a Grade 4 teacher.

Fig. 5 Kerusha's artefact (Photographer, Leighandri Moodley, with permission)

My mum got me this notebook (Fig. 6). Inside the lively pages of this book are memories and praises that my nearest and dearest had written to me. Each person got a page to write something about what I mean to them, with a picture of them and me. At my 21st party, my mum sent the book around for people to write their wishes for me in the book.

This book is so special and valuable to me, it is like my pick-me-up book, better than any glass of wine. When I read the messages, I feel appreciated and loved. I thank God for the people in my life who are there for me. Being so far away from home, when I open up this book, it just takes me back and I feel close to my loved ones. One of my favourite Bible verses is "God has made everything beautiful in its time." Right now, this is where I know I am supposed to be. I feel like I am changing myself through my learners.

The religion teacher is important for me at school. I draw my strength and courage from her. Whenever I'm feeling down or I need to talk, I know that she is always there to listen. She makes us all feel like we are important because we are all God's creation. I feel

Fig. 6 Elizabeth's artefact (Photographer, Leighandri Moodley, with permission)

like a better teacher after her encouraging words. She reminds me of my mother (personal communication, November 2012).

When Elizabeth spoke about her memory book, she became emotional. I was able to pick up from Elizabeth's story that she is a reflective teacher. Relationships are an important part of her life. Elizabeth finds that being a teacher gives her the freedom to interact with people who are different from her. As a teacher in a Catholic school, Elizabeth draws on Catholic teachings and values to form caring relationships with her black learners. As a teacher, Elizabeth tries to be accepting of her learners by learning from, and interacting with, them. Elizabeth uses her classroom space to rework her misconceptions and stereotypes about black people, and to confront and change her prejudices and meanings of race. Through this process, she frees herself as a person and as a teacher.

My Learning
All our stories have their good moments and bad moments. Using arts-based methods that I had learnt and worked with in my honours module allowed me, as a researcher, to bring together layers of nuanced understandings about Kerusha and Elizabeth in a personally meaningful and pleasurable way. Playing with different textual possibilities, I was privy to novice teachers' everyday lives in a private Catholic school in a way such that I was able to develop respectful and supportive relationships. My professional learning was heightened because I was able to create

meanings as my participants shared their most intimate thoughts, feelings, and experiences with me. Through the momentarily caught glimpses of their shifting and multiple identities, I learned about how they were negotiating the private religious school context, and the different relationships they were able to develop with staff and students. Interestingly, through collaborating with like-minded individuals in aesthetically pleasurable ways, I have developed greater awareness of how spiritual teachings and beliefs are the basis for creating loving and caring relationships between teachers and learners irrespective of race, gender, religion, and ethnicity.

5 Our Thoughts that Hold Our Mosaic Pieces in Place

What does a woman teacher-researcher look like in different teaching and learning sites—from school to university academic settings? And what kinds of passionate scholarship can women teacher-researchers offer the field of educational research? The varied personal life experiences that women teacher-researchers bring to their graduate research study most certainly seeps into and informs what their research interests are, and how they choose to engage as educational researchers on their educational journeys through academia.

Mary and Leighandri's evocative stories and evocative visual images collected and generated with women research participants freed them to "inspire imagination, give pause to new possibilities and new meanings, and open new questions and avenues of inquiry" (Bochner and Ellis 2003). Portraying actual women and their real life experiences, the illustrated creative narratives draw on, amongst other devices, vernacular language, inclusion of aesthetic elements combined with story, metaphors, flashbacks and flash forwards, and stories (Barone 2008) and, combined, they move both reader and author—"giving power to ambiguity, emotion, intuition, and relationships in human lives" (Witherell and Noddings 1991, p. 4). As Mary wrote, "Leighandri, the picture you paint of the novice teacher—I felt all of what you described! Sink or swim! Profession that eats its young! Ghastly, but that is just how I felt! A baptism by fire! I started my teaching career in 1980; you started so many years later, yet we experienced such similar emotions."

The power of constructing creative stories that can join the world of thoughts and feelings, and attach us to others and to our very own histories are important for us as women teachers and researchers. Constructing creative stories "frees up spaces for the feminine side of human experience" (Witherell and Noddings 1991, p. 4) but, more than that, it frees up spaces for us to get to know ourselves better as women, as teachers, and as researchers. By listening to our hearts (through art), passion moves us to open our minds to new perspectives, voices, and ideas and to be better able to help others—irrespective of how old or young, how novice or how experienced, Canadian Anglophone or South African Indian. It is about our celebration of working joyfully with imagination and uncertainty that women (and men) will come to know and understand who they are as teachers and how we can contribute to a scholarship of understanding what teachers are, and what teachers can be (Banks 2008).

We can learn from each other's stories. Mitchell et al. (2009) remind us that by opening up and sharing stories or experiences, we allow for engagement and healing that can improve the individual's personal, social, and professional development. Creative nonfiction narratives and memory-work help to ground us and bring others close. In Mary's words, "Isn't it easier to talk about ourselves through our artefacts that we hold dear, than to answer pointed questions? I feel that as we get to know ourselves better, as we listen to our hearts, we are better able to help others. When we open up to our students, we become more real... I think what you are doing, exposing novice teachers and what moves them or makes them tick helps to give them space to understand others, namely, their students."

Scholarship that promotes passionate engagement with ambiguity and uncertainty, using evocative images and creative nonfiction narratives, serves to invite different audiences into experiencing and connecting with the world and work of the researcher. It invites readers to be able to pause for a moment to dwell on the lives of "real characters" (Barone 2008, p. 113), and get to know better these particular individuals, portrayed as possible openings. As Leighandri expressed, "Mary, before I read what was written beneath each image, I tried to look at the image myself and tried to work out what the participant saw in that image and why it was important. I really enjoyed that because as I read what was written it was quite lifelike and apt."

6 Final Thoughts

This mosaic chapter builds on scholarship that illuminates "the interaction of experience and thought in different voices and dialogues" (Gilligan 1982, p. 2). It offers a textual and visual restorying of the ambiguity and complexity of lived experiences marked by relationships of openness, respect, support, and a sense of equality irrespective of age, experience, religious affiliation, race, class, ethnicity, and so on. Emihovich (1994, p. 45) reminds us that opening up through narratives "lies in collaboration, of constantly testing our meaning against that of others, building consensus around shared meaning, and ensuring that as many voices as possible are included." Together, the exemplars presented by Mary and Leighandri illuminate ways in which memory-work and creative nonfiction narratives can create new understandings of both past and present, enabling new narratives that can change the future for both reader and author.

Acknowledgements Permission was received from Kerusha, Elizabeth, Carol, and Bridget for their contributions to be included in publications based on Leighandri and Mary's research.
We are grateful to our peer reviewer, Marie Hyleen Sandra Mariaye (Mauritius Institute of Education, Mauritius), for her reassuring and insightful feedback on this chapter.

References

Banks, S. (2008). Writing as theory: In defence of fiction. In J. G. Knowles & A. L. Cole (Eds.), *Handbook of the arts in qualitative research* (pp. 155–164). Los Angeles: SAGE.

Barone, T. (1979). *Inquiry into classroom experiences: A qualitative holistic approach*. Stanford, CA: Stanford University Press.

Barone, T. (2008). Creative non-fiction and social research. In J. G. Knowles & A. L. Cole (Eds.), *Handbook of the arts in qualitative research* (pp. 105–115). Los Angeles: SAGE.

Bateson, M. C. (1984). *With a daughter's eye*. New York: Washington Square.

Bochner, A. P. (2000). Criteria against ourselves. *Qualitative Inquiry, 6*(2), 266–272.

Bochner, A. P., & Ellis, C. (2003). An introduction to the arts and narrative research: Art as inquiry. *Qualitative Inquiry, 9*(4), 506–514.

Bruner, E. M. (1984). The opening up of anthropology. In E. M. Bruner (Ed.), *Text, play and story: The construction and reconstruction of self and society* (pp. 1–18). Washington: American Ethnological Society.

Clandinin, D. J., & Connelly, F. M. (Eds.). (2004). *Narrative inquiry: Experience and story in qualitative research*. San Francisco: Jossey-Bass.

Cole, A. (2011). Object-memory, embodiment, and teacher formation: A methodological exploration. In C. Mitchell, T. Strong-Wilson, K. Pithouse, & S. Allnutt (Eds.), *Memory and Pedagogy* (pp. 223–238). New York: Routledge.

Cole, B. A., & Gunter, H. (Eds.). (2010). *Changing lives: Women, inclusion and the Ph.D.*. Staffordshire: Trentham.

Coles, R. (1989). *The call of stories*. Boston: Houghton Mifflin.

Cullinan, M. (2015). *Echoes of late-entry women in academia: A narrative inquiry (Unpublished doctoral thesis)*. Canada: McGill University.

De Lange, N., Mitchell, C., & Stuart, J. (Eds.). (2008). *Putting people in the picture: Visual methodologies for social change*. Rotterdam: Sense Publishers.

Eisner, E. W. (1979). *The educational imagination*. New York: Macmillan.

Eisner, E. W. (2008). Persistent tensions in arts-based research. In M. Cahnmann-Taylor & R. Siegesmund (Eds.), *Arts-based research in education: Foundations for practice* (pp. 16–27). London: Routlege.

Emihovich, C. (1994). Distancing passion: Narratives in social science. In J. A. Hatch & R. Wisniewski (Eds.), *Life history and narrative: Qualitative Studies Series 1* (pp. 37–48). London: Falmer.

Flores, M. A., & Day, C. (2006). Contexts which shape and reshape new teachers' identities: A multi-perspective study. *Teaching and Teacher Education, 22*(1), 219–232.

Freire, P. (1993). *Pedagogy of the oppressed* (Revised ed.). New York: Continuum.

Geertz, C. (1983). *Local knowledge: Further essays in interpretive ethnography*. New York: Basic Books.

Gilligan, C. (1982). *In a different voice*. Cambridge: Harvard University Press.

Gubrium, A. (2009). Digital storytelling: An emergent method for health promotion research and practice. *Health Promotion Practice, 10*(2), 186–191. https://doi.org/10.1177/152483990 9332600.

Haug, F. (2008). Memory work. *Australian Feminist Studies, 23*(58), 537–541.

Heikkilä, V., Uuisiatti, S., & Määttä, K. (2012). Teacher students' school memories as a part of the development of their professional identity. *Journal of Studies in Education, 2*(2), 215–229.

Hermans, H. J. (2001). The dialogical self: Toward a theory of personal and cultural positioning. *Culture & Psychology, 7*, 243–281.

Holm, G. (2008). Photography as a performance. *Forum Qualitative Sozialforschung/Forum: Qualitative Social Research, 9*(2). Retrieved from http://www.qualitative-research.net/index.php/fqs/article/view/394/857.

Koltz, R. L., Odegard, M. A., Provost, K. B., Smith, T., & Kleist, D. (2010). Picture perfect: Using photo-voice to explore four doctoral students' comprehensive examination experiences. *Journal of Creativity in Mental Health, 5*(4), 389–411. https://doi.org/10.1080/15401383.2010.527797.

Kuhn, A. (1996). Remembrance. In L. Heron & V. Williams (Eds.), *Illumintions: Women writing on photography from the 1850s to the present* (pp. 146–161). Durham: Duke University Press.

Leonard, D. (2001). *A woman's guide to doctoral studies*. Buckingham: Open University Press.

Mitchell, C. (2011). *Doing visual research*. London: SAGE.

Mitchell, C., Weber, S., & Pithouse, K. (2009). Facing the public: Using photography for self-study and social action. In D. Tidwell, M. Heston, & L. Fitzgerald (Eds.), *Research methods for the self-study of practice* (pp. 119–134). New York: Springer.

Pillay, L. (2014). *Narratives of novice teachers in a private Catholic school (Unpublished master's thesis)*. South Africa: University of KwaZulu-Natal.

Pillay, D., & Pithouse-Morgan, K. (2016). A self-study of connecting through aesthetic memory-work. In J. Kitchen, D. Tidwell, & L. Fitzgerald (Eds.), *Self-study and diversity II: Inclusive teacher education for a diverse world* (pp. 121–136). Rotterdam: Sense Publishers.

Pillay, D., Pithouse-Morgan, K., & Naicker, I. (2017). Self-knowledge creation through collective poetic inquiry: Cultivating productive resistance as university academics. *Cultural Studies-Critical Methodologies, 17*(3), 262–265.

Polkinghorne, E. (1988). *Narrative knowing and the human sciences*. Albany: State University of New York.

Postman, N. (1992). *Technopoly: The surrender of culture to technology*. New York: Knopf.

Richardson, L. (1997). *Fields of play: Constructing an academic life*. New Brunswick: Rutgers University Press.

Richardson, L. (2000). Evaluating ethnography. *Qualitative Inquiry, 6*(2), 253–255.

Richie, J. S., & Wilson, D. E. (2000). Reclaiming and revising personal and professional identities. In J. S. Richie & D. E. Wilson (Eds.), *Teacher narrative as critical inquiry: Rewriting the script* (pp. 74–76). New York: Teacher College Press.

Sabar, N. (2004). From heaven to reality through crisis: Novice teachers as migrants. *Teaching and Teacher Education, 20*(1), 145–161.

Smith, D. E. (1989). *The everyday world as problematic: A feminist sociology*. Boston: Northeastern University Press.

Van Schalkwyk, G. J. (2010). Collage life story elicitation technique: A representational technique for scaffolding autobiographical memories. *The Qualitative Report, 15*(3), 675–695.

Wang, C. (2006). Youth participation in photovoice as a strategy for community change. *Journal of Community Practice, 14*(1–2), 147–161. https://doi.org/10.1300/J125v14n01_09.

Wang, C., & Burris, M. A. (1997). Photovoice: Concept, methodology, and use for participatory needs assessment. *Health Education & Behaviour, 24*(3), 369–387.

Witherell, C., & Noddings, N. (Eds.). (1991). *Stories lives tell: Narrative and Dialogue in Education*. New York: Teachers College Press.

The Promise of Poetry Belongs to Us All: Poetic Professional Learning in Teacher-Researchers' Memory-Work

Kathleen Pithouse-Morgan, S'phiwe Madondo and Edwina Grossi

Abstract "The Promise of Poetry Belongs to Us All: Poetic Professional Learning in Teacher-Researchers' Memory-Work" by Kathleen Pithouse-Morgan, S'phiwe Madondo, and Edwina Grossi builds on the developing scholarship of poetic professional learning in the social sciences by exploring two exemplars of South African teacher-researchers' poetic engagement with memory and pedagogy. The mosaic pieces by S'phiwe Madondo and Edwina Grossi, which exemplify professional learning by way of poetry, offer windows into poetic explorations of these teacher-researchers' own memories and histories in relation to varied educational and socio-cultural contexts and concerns. The pieces illustrate poetic inquiry as a mode of working deliberately and imaginatively with memories to produce evocative insights into teaching and learning. They also offer encouragement to teacher-researchers who might not have a formal background in the literary arts to start to play with composing poems as research data, representations, and interpretations.

Keywords Autoethnography · Memory-work · Poetic inquiry
Poetic professional learning · Poetry · South Africa · Self-study
Teacher professional learning

K. Pithouse-Morgan (✉) · S. Madondo · E. Grossi
School of Education, University of KwaZulu-Natal, Durban, South Africa
e-mail: pithousemorgan@ukzn.ac.za

S. Madondo
e-mail: siphiwemadondo@ymail.com

E. Grossi
e-mail: edwina@letni.co.za

© Springer Nature Switzerland AG 2019
K. Pithouse-Morgan et al. (eds.), *Memory Mosaics: Researching Teacher Professional Learning Through Artful Memory-work*, Studies in Arts-Based Educational Research 2, https://doi.org/10.1007/978-3-319-97106-3_8

1 Poetic Inquiry

Van Manen (1990) explained that poetry can be understood as "a literary form that transforms lived experience into poetic language, the poetic language of verse" (p. 70). The word *verse* has roots in the Middle French *verser*, meaning, "'to turn, revolve' as in meditation" (verse n.d.). Thinking about the poetic language of verse as the language of meditation evokes the musings of the poet as she plays with the transformative possibilities of combinations of words and their lyrical, pictorial, rhythmic, and symbolic qualities.

As Young (1982) described, "poetic writing pleases and surprises—it is a place for play, imaginative thinking, developing personal knowledge" (p. 84). In contrast, research reports are usually written in a propositional style in which "facts are piled on facts, interview quotes are stacked on interview quotes" (Caulley 2008, p. 428). Propositional research writing typically depicts the researcher as an "omniscient narrator" (Richardson 1993, p. 706) who delivers certainty and "permanently nailed down facts" (Eisner 2008, p. 4), while often "[leaving] the reader unmoved" (Richardson 1993, p. 706). Although more conventional research writing continues to serve particular purposes, modes of constructing and communicating qualitative research are evolving as "scholars invent new ways through new means of representing what matters in human affairs" (Eisner 2008, p. 6). Qualitative researchers are increasingly turning to alternative modes such as poetry when they find that their exploratory and nuanced studies "simply [refuse] to be flattened onto a page of scholarly text" (Weber 2008, p. 49). These more creative approaches to research writing can work together with and even enhance modes that are more conventional. For instance, as Young (1982) pointed out, "practice and facility in writing poetically may indeed increase a writer's effectiveness in writing transactionally" (p. 94).

Poetic inquiry emerges in spaces where the meditative and creative possibilities of poetic language and poetic ways of seeing, hearing, and thinking intersect with the mindsets, practices, and products of qualitative research (Leggo 2008). In poetic inquiry, "poetic processes can be used as tools of discovery and a unique mode of reporting research" (Brady 2009, p. xiii). Diverse forms of poetic expression can be used to represent and discern the distinctiveness and multiplicity of the voices of research participants and researchers (Richardson 2003). Furthermore, poetry can be used to not only generate and represent qualitative data, but as a creative means of analysis and interpretation (Lahman et al. 2010).

A critical survey by Prendergast (2009) on the use of poetry in social science qualitative research showed that over the past two decades, poetic inquiry has been gaining momentum within fields such as education (e.g., Leggo 2005), nursing (e.g., Breckenridge 2016), and social work (e.g., Furman et al. 2006). For research that centres on understanding and making a qualitative difference to lived human experience in social contexts, poetic practices of "settling words together in new configurations lets us hear, see and feel the [social] world in new dimensions" (Richardson 2003, p. 516).

2 Poetic Professional Learning

"Poetic professional learning" (Pithouse-Morgan 2017, p. 63) engages the power of poetic inquiry for the purposes of exploring and enriching professional learning (Pithouse-Morgan 2016, 2017). The intentions and practices of poetic professional learning are informed by conceptualisations of professional learning that reposition professionals such as teachers, nurses, and social workers as "self-directed" (Webster-Wright 2009, p. 712) and "*self*-developing" (Easton 2008, p. 756) learners. Essentially, these conceptualisations—which have been described in terms of "authentic professional learning" (Webster-Wright 2009, p. 702) and "powerful professional learning" (Easton 2008, p. 756)—emphasise how professionals, often working in collaboration with colleagues and other interested parties, can gain critical insights into their own professional identities and practices. Significantly, as Webster-Wright (2009) emphasised, "such learning has the potential to not only alter ways of being a professional … but also effect positive social change and improvement" (p. 727).

Scholars in a range of social science fields have explored poetry as a means of professional learning research and practice (e.g., Butler-Kisber 2005; Furman 2014; Short and Grant 2016). Their work reveals how poetic professional learning can heighten self-insight, empathy, and social awareness on the part of professionals such as teachers, social workers, and nurses, as well as offer insights into the individual and collective learning experiences of these professionals. Notably, the focus is not principally on composing poems that demonstrate literary expertise or innate artistic merit; more emphasis is placed on using poetic language and forms of expression for the educative purposes of researching, and enhancing professional learning.

3 Composing This Memory Mosaics Chapter

This chapter builds on, and complements, the developing scholarship of poetic professional learning in the social sciences by exploring two original exemplars of South African teacher-researchers' poetic engagement with memory and pedagogy. The chapter brings into dialogue the perspectives of the two teacher-researchers, S'phiwe Madondo and Edwina Grossi, and Kathleen Pithouse-Morgan—a teacher educator and researcher who works to support teacher-researchers in initiating and directing their own professional learning to enhance their continuing growth. In her scholarship, Kathleen has explored poetry as a literary arts-informed medium for professional learning research (Pithouse-Morgan 2016, 2017).

Kathleen, who was familiar with the poetic aspects of the self-study research conducted by S'phiwe (Madondo 2014) and the autoethnographic research by Edwina (Grossi 2006), invited each of them develop a short mosaic piece for this chapter—in whatever format they preferred. The two very different mosaic pieces, written in the first person, offer glimpses of poetic explorations of S'phiwe's and Edwina's own memories and histories in relation to wider educational and sociocultural concerns. The pieces illustrate the use of poetic inquiry as a means of working consciously and creatively with memories to produce new understandings for acting with and upon lived experiences of teaching and learning.

The chapter was developed over a 6-month period from the two initial mosaic pieces and e-mail conversations between Kathleen, S'phiwe, and Edwina. The process of composing the chapter over this period allowed the three authors time to express and reconsider understandings of working with poetry and memory. Kathleen used the mosaic pieces, together with ideas from the e-mail correspondence, to fashion a first draft of the chapter. She then shared this draft with S'phiwe and Edwina for their responses and revisions. The final version of the chapter was settled through a back-and-forth revision process involving the three authors, the book editors, and a peer reviewer.

The next section of this chapter offers a brief orientation to S'phiwe's self-study research and then presents his first-person mosaic piece. This is followed by an outline of Edwina's autoethnographic research and then her mosaic piece. Thereafter, the voices of Kathleen, S'phiwe, and Edwina are brought together in an elaboration of insights that emerged from the e-mail conversations that were triggered by sharing and responding to the two mosaic pieces. The chapter concludes with a consideration of educative implications of the research and understandings presented.

4 S'phiwe Madondo's Self-study Research

Through self-study research, teachers and other professionals look critically and creatively at themselves with the intention of reimagining their own professional practice to contribute to the wellbeing of others (Pithouse-Morgan and Samaras 2015). Teacher educators who wished to develop self-understanding and professional growth originally developed self-study research methodology in the early 1990s (Samaras and Freese 2009). Subsequently, self-study has continued to develop in new ways in diverse fields and specialisations and across educational contexts (Pithouse-Morgan and Samaras 2015). S'phiwe Madondo's self-study research for his master 's study (2014) focused on nurturing a flair for English written commu-

The Promise of Poetry Belongs to Us All: Poetic Professional ...

nication among isiZulu-speaking primary schoolchildren. He used memory-work as a self-study method to identify negative and positive past experiences as a black African child during apartheid[1] that he could learn from in order to enhance a flair for written communication through his teaching.

The Use of, and the Learning from, Poetry in Memory-Work Self-study by S'phiwe Madondo

Introduction

I am a teacher in a South African English-medium primary school where the majority of learners[2] as well as teachers speak isiZulu as a home language. I had noticed that learners seemed to be struggling to express themselves with confidence, skill, and flair through English written communication. Hence, my aim in undertaking self-study research (Madondo 2014) was to enhance my understanding of what I could do to nurture the development of flair for English written communication among my learners. In my understanding, a flair for written communication means being able to express oneself using written language with creativity and flamboyance. My aim was, therefore, to cultivate flair and to motivate learners to have a love for written communication from a young age.

My methodological approach was self-study of practice. According to Pithouse (2011), self-study pays attention to the researcher's own personal and professional experiences. The self-study methodological component that best suited my study was that of "personal situated inquiry" (Samaras 2011, p. 74) because I drew from my personal experience as a practitioner in a particular classroom context, trying to find out what worked and what did not work by questioning my teaching (Samaras 2011). My study aimed at contributing to the body of professional knowledge on teaching written communication as well as to enhance my understanding of the uniqueness of my teaching within my school context. As a teacher and researcher, I was aiming at improving my pedagogic strategies in my classroom context through investigation of my practice and lived experience.

Interpretive Poetry

In generating data to respond to a key research question in my study, "What can I learn from my past experiences about developing a flair for written communication?" I used a memory-work self-study method, looking at certain episodes in my own life history that were relevant to developing a flair for communication (Samaras 2011).

---

[1] During the apartheid era (1948–1994), the Nationalist government of South Africa legislated and enforced a hierarchy of racialised privilege and oppression. People designated as *white* were deliberately advantaged while those designated as *black African, coloured*, and *Indian* were disenfranchised and dispossessed.

[2] In South Africa, students at schools are referred to as *learners*.

Cole (2011) explained that memory-work lets us investigate a variety of feelings, which could be good or bad, and it plays a significant role in examining teacher beliefs, teacher development, and teacher self. My memory-work data sources included journal entries where I recorded my thoughts and feelings during my research process, as well as artefacts and memory drawings. I drew on these data sources to compose written memory stories of my own past experiences of learning about written communication.

I employed an arts-based method (Samaras 2011) by using interpretive poetry (Furman et al. 2008) to make meaning of my memory stories. Writing interpretive poetry offered me a way to identify significant educational and emotional episodes in my past experiences. As Furman et al. (2007) explained, writing poetry can help researchers to "synthesise, process and make meaning" (p. 304). I reread my memory stories with the aim of selecting words and arranging them in such a way that would capture the gist of the experience in a more compressed poetic form of writing. Through this approach, I used the words and ideas from my memory stories to develop poetic interpretations (Butler-Kisber 2005).

I then used an inductive approach where I "searched for emerging patterns, associations, concepts and explanations" in my interpretive poetry (Nieuwenhuis 2010, p. 107). This helped me to see vital emerging issues. From there, I had to think carefully about each issue's significance and implications for my teaching of written communication. I also had to consult relevant literature to support and enrich the issues identified. While interacting with literature and thinking critically about each issue, I gained insight and deeper understanding of the phenomenon and on how to assist learners to develop a flair for written communication. I also gained different viewpoints during this process by working with a group of fellow teachers who were doing their own self-study research.

In this mosaic piece, I illustrate how using interpretive poetry helped me to distil the essence of remembered episodes of my communicative experience into poetic form. Each interpretive poem was composed to elicit the significant emotions and experiences of each episode of a memory story. First, I present an example of an interpretive poem that I composed, titled, "My Parents' Impact." Thereafter, I identify and discuss the issue of parental involvement that emerged from this interpretive poem as significant to my learning and teaching of written communication. To conclude, I offer personal and professional reflections on the use of and the learning from poetry in memory-work self-study.

> **My Parents' Impact**
>
> Both uneducated
> Both illiterate
> Unable to read and write
> But they were excellent
> Illiterate teachers
>
> Scribing letters for them
> Through dictation
> Taught me to be a good listener
> In order to write meaningful sentences
> Reading and reading to them again
> Taught me to pronounce words
> The way they said in the dictation
>
> Despite their educational level
> They strived and sacrificed
> For my educational exposure
> From the worst situation they
> Brought out the best
>
> (Madondo 2014, pp. 57–58)

Through composing my poem, "My Parent's Impact," I realised the importance of *parental involvement* in children's education. Having illiterate parents could have impacted negatively on my learning of written communication. But instead, my poem shows that this worked positively for me. When I reminisce about those years, I can see how neither my parents nor I knew the effect that those writing exercises such as writing letters on behalf of my parents would have on my educational journey. Although my parents were illiterate, they made sure that I engaged in many writing activities such as writing invitations, short notes, and letters. Significantly, my parents did not only assist me with informal literacy activities, they went even further by giving me motivation and encouraging words. In looking at my poem, it is clear to me that parental involvement can take the form of providing pedagogical care (Grant et al. 2010). Pedagogical care means that my parents went the extra mile to nurture and develop my writing capacity with their limited knowledge.

In my experience with some parents in my school community, it often seems to be assumed to be acceptable for them not to be involved with their children's education. Reasons given by many parents are their low levels of education or their illiteracy and some also give financial reasons. However, through my memory-work, I realised that informal activities and pedagogical care that might go unnoticed could contribute to parental participation in children's learning.

From recalling my past experiences, I have realised how important it is for me as a parent to make time for my own children's educational matters. It has become clear to me that our level of education or socioeconomic status as parents should not deter us from supporting our children's academic development. As Kajee (2011) argued, "by involving parents, family and community members in literacy teaching, and by building existing literacies of the family and community, schools can act as catalysts in a process of the empowerment for children" (p. 435). This means that in my teaching of written communication I am not the only source of knowledge and educational support for learners. I should also consider the significance of the role that can be played by the learners' families and community members.

I believe that parents can involve themselves more if teachers invite them to meetings where they are shown how valuable their knowledge and pedagogical care is. Mncube (2009) concurred that there is a need for schools to address the lack of education for parents on the importance of parental involvement and the roles they can play in their children's education. This demonstrates the need for schools to organise programmes where parents would be empowered on how they can play their part as important partners in their children's learning.

Conclusion

In this mosaic piece, I gave an example of how I reexamined my interpretive poetry to identify and discuss implications that emerged for nurturing a flair for written communication among learners. Through the use of interpretive poetry in my self-study research, I managed to distil significant experiences which also then helped me to go on to develop new strategies to improve my teaching of written communication and to offer ideas to other professional teachers.

The use of interpretive poetry also helped me to understand the practicality of the idea of education as "the preparation of artists" (Eisner 2004, p. 4). In my understanding, by *artists*, Eisner did not automatically mean painters and dancers, poets, and dramatists. He meant persons who have expanded their thoughts, their responsiveness, their abilities, and their imagination to make work that is well balanced, skilfully executed, and imaginative—whatever sphere they are working in. In my view, the highest honour we can bestow upon an individual, whether a bricklayer or a doctor, a chef or a mechanic, a scientist or a teacher, is to call her or him an artist. In relation to my research topic of cultivating a flair for written communication, I understand this as the educational preparation of learners to be able to assemble words to make meaningful sequences in an artistic and skilful manner. As a teacher, I should provide learners with opportunities to develop and to shape their creative minds, thus preparing them for the world beyond school. Consequently, it is important for me to find ways of developing creativity with my learners at an early stage of their schooling.

Before I undertook my self-study research, I did not know that I could express and make meaning of my own experiences through composing poems. The style of language teaching during my own primary school days in the 1980s promoted rote learning. For example, we were expected to read and memorise poems. Assessment was based on how excellent we were in reciting the exact words of the poet. Every morning, before the teacher came into the class, we were expected to recite all the poems we knew. I do not remember any poetry lessons that demanded our creative thinking or writing. The emphasis was not on creative writing but, rather, was on factual recall.

In high school, we were given opportunities to submit original poems and songs on prescribed topics for an annual inter-school cultural competition. However, the writing of these poems and songs was done individually, with no assistance from teachers. I remember that one year I decided to try writing a poem. In writing the poem, I used my limited knowledge and I did not ask anyone for assistance because I wanted it to be my original work. We were writing a once-off piece. The teachers expected us to write our best at our first attempt. It was a delightful and proud moment to be representing the school if your work was chosen. You were respected and praised by teachers and learners. That is what motivated me to enter. However, I was disappointed to find that it was not my poem that had caught the adjudicator's attention. Looking back as a teacher, I now realise that although we were encouraged to take part in creative writing by submitting pieces for the annual competition, this was not fully nurtured and developed in a structured programme or through curriculum activities. Many years later, by bringing poetry into my research process, I was able to learn firsthand about developing a flair for written communication.

5 Edwina Grossi's Autoethnographic Research

Like self-study research, autoethnography brings into focus the self of the researcher. However, while self-study research can usually be recognised by the explicit attention paid by the researcher to the improvement of her own professional practice, this is not necessarily the case in autoethnography. Rather, as explained by Ellis et al. (2011, para. 1), "Autoethnography is an approach to research and writing that seeks to describe and systematically analyse (*graphy*) personal experience (*auto*) in order to understand cultural experience (*ethno*)." Unlike self-study, autoethnography did not originate in the field of education. Nevertheless, it has been taken up by teacher-researchers who embrace "the idea that [their] teaching is meant to be generative and productive and located within social constructions of knowledge" (Mitchell 2016, p. 176) and that autoethnography is one approach that teachers can use to "connect the personal to the cultural, and the cultural back to the personal" (p. 176) in their research and practice. Edwina Grossi's autoethnographic research for her doctoral study (2006) explored her experiences in South African education over a period of 41 years. The autoethnography examined and interpreted important moments and decision points in her personal life and in her career as a Lebanese woman educator and entrepreneur in the context of apartheid and postapartheid South Africa. In her research, she used a range of creative forms including poetic text, art, photographs, documents, and articles as representation, verification, and confirmation of her life story.

Mosaic—Poetry Woven in Autoethnography by Edwina Grossi

Introduction

I am of Lebanese descent and live in South Africa. I am a mother of three, and grandmother of seven wonderful people. My husband and I celebrate our golden wedding anniversary this year. I was in the profession I was called to, and was passionate about, for 47 years. During my career, I was privileged to found a baby care centre, preschool, primary school, high school, and teacher training college. I was always drawn to the child who, like me, did not fit into the system due to their inborn talent and type of intelligence, and usually found them to be creative individuals who did not enjoy being boxed in. So, autoethnography and teacher self-study for a doctorate was right up my alley!

A mosaic can be defined as a piece of art that is made by placing different shapes and sizes of coloured stones together. These are set in place and enhanced by cement, which is poured between the shapes. My autoethnography, *An Ordinary Teacher* (Grossi 2006), can be compared with a mosaic. The literature, art, photographs, newspaper articles, magazine articles, and quotes are the coloured stones, but the verses woven between the chapters and texts, whether in prose, poetry, or song, are the cement that binds the pieces together—"autobiographical poetic representation, where the researcher explores her memories and translates these into poetic form, provides an interesting approach to researcher reflexivity" (Butler-Kisber 2005, p. 4).

When starting my dissertation, memories and pictures, thoughts and feelings were rekindled and were given a voice as they translated into words that fell into verse. I was free to write from the heart not the head! However, at the start I feared my work was too simplistic, too plain, too "rhymey," too childlike, too nonacademic and too below par for a doctoral dissertation. Then Butler-Kisber came to my rescue and I took my cue from her: "Poetic representation is an arts-based vehicle in qualitative research that allows the heart to lead the mind rather than the reverse, and in so doing, elicits new ways of seeing and understanding phenomena" (2005, p. 108).

At the outset, 11 stanzas of the poem, "An Ordinary Teacher," which tells of my life in, and my passion for, the teaching profession set the scene.

An Ordinary Teacher

As a young girl she wanted to teach
So many thousands she needed to reach
But her heart's desire was God's special child
The broken, the lame, the ones meek and mild

(Grossi 2006, p. xii)

Even before I entered the teaching profession, I was passionate about children with barriers to learning and, on reflection whilst writing this piece, I realise that this reality is woven throughout many verses in the dissertation, for example the verses below can be found in the middle of the work, and answer the verse above by speaking of my later discoveries of some of the many barriers to learning that children face.

Barriers

You called me dumb, but I couldn't get to school
No money, no transport, so I'm known as a fool.
Sandy went, she lives next door—15 kilometres—she left at four.
By ten o'clock she could not think
All she needed was food and drink.
For this basic need she'd have to wait
Maybe Mom would bring something home at eight.
Home—dare she call it that—with Dad and that awful cricket bat!
If a drink he could not buy
She knew she would pay with a blackened eye.

Sipho was called names, amongst them "thick"
Couldn't they see he was just very sick?
Medication and advice was really his due
But with no clinic nearby, what does one do?

John was labelled "slow," so slow he became
Were they not aware of the importance of a name?
Excluded from the system, he became uptight
Looking for John?
You'll find him among the gangs that fight.

They called Maria disabled—she had polio you see
And therefore was educated under a tree.
She was born with a high I.Q.
But due to her affliction, no one knew.
Where is Maria today?
Watching little children as they play.

Gladness was slow due to a language barrier,
Is there any chance of a future for her?
Teacher has no time to wait
The curriculum the pace does dictate.

(Grossi 2006, p. 174)

An excerpt from *The Prophet* by the poet, Kahlil Gibran (1883–1931), "Then a ploughman said, 'Speak to us of Work'" (1923/2013, p. 29), gave me the impetus to answer the prophet as I spoke about my lifetime work and compared it with that of a ploughman and his field. Part Two of the dissertation, "Life in the Field," is divided into four chapters, and each chapter is introduced by a verse that speaks of me as the ploughman, and covers a certain time period of my years and experience in the teaching profession. The use of poetry framed the four chapters listed below.

Chapter 1, "Years of Ploughing and Preparing the Soil"—among other nodal points, this period speaks of the preparation for my future career and how others shaped and influenced my vision, and is introduced by the verse below.

> With shielded eyes the ploughman stands
> Viewing his plantings o'er the lands.
> The soil is good, half the job is done.
> The ploughman and his task are one.
>
> (Grossi 2006, p. 29)

Chapter 2, "Years of Sowing," relates, amongst other important facts, my experience as a class teacher and principal, and my first entry into the field of business and entrepreneurship when I founded a preschool. The verse tells of my love for the young child and my belief in the importance of quality education in the early years.

> Sow the seeds in furrows deep
> Through love and care
> Goodness into the soil will seep.
> Now the seed is plump and full
> Bursting with life to do its will.
>
> (Grossi 2006, p. 67)

Chapter 3, "Years of Growing," affords me the opportunity to take a trip down memory lane and visit the flowering of creativity and other ventures, and speaks of the fact that despite many diversions, my passion for the teaching profession never waned.

The Promise of Poetry Belongs to Us All: Poetic Professional ...   145

> Is that a little shoot I see?
> Are the roots firmly planted like a tree?
> Will it be damaged by pests or rot?
> By its purposeful gait, methinks not.
>
> (Grossi 2006, p. 102)

Chapter 4, "Years of Harvesting," covers the years when, amongst significant nodal moments and experiences, I founded another four educational institutions, one of them being Embury Institute for Teacher Education, and was privileged to experience the growth of many wonderful future teachers, thus the reference to *little saplings* and *flowers and fruit* in the verse below.

> Flowers and fruit burst into brilliant form
> And very soon other little saplings are born.
> With shielded eyes the ploughman stands
> Viewing his plantings o'er the land.
>
> (Grossi 2006, p. 135)

Can Prose Be Classed as Poetry?

> The prose poem essentially appears as prose, but reads like poetry... While it lacks the line breaks associated with poetry, the prose poem maintains a poetic quality, often utilizing techniques common to poetry, such as fragmentation, compression, repetition, and rhyme. (Poets.org 2004, paras. 1–2)

Poetry portrays the truth or the imagination, in verse or prose. A poem about a bird in a gilded cage stands at the end of the first section of my dissertation, that is, at the end of all the "academic stuff." On reflection, I now realise why I felt compelled to write this piece because, when revisiting Part One, I relived the same emotions. I felt trapped! I wanted to break free from prescription. I felt like a bird in a gilded cage—the gilded cage being the glory allotted to a conventional dissertation! I had been subjected to following tradition so many times in my life and now, once again, the same feelings resurfaced—I felt boxed in by academia. Nevertheless, I realise that there are many rules one has to conform to.

> How sad for the bird in the gilded cage
> Who is not free to explore his intended purpose of creation.
> He is trapped by humanity—
> Trapped in the midst of the finest riches,
> Trapped because his wings have been clipped by man.
> Even when his cage is opened he will still never be free
> As he is trapped by habit and comfort
> As he returns to what he knows . . .
> He resists change, he is trapped.
> Because of this resistance he misses out on what nature and life provides.
> Does he not know that change will open up a new, more exciting world?
> Will he stay trapped forever?
>
> (Grossi 2006, p. 28)

Can Songs Be Classed as Poetry?

Can songs not be poetry in motion, or poetry being sung? Do they not both usually portray the feelings and emotions penned by the writer?

"The phatic is common to both song lyrics and poetry; music aids the lyric, condemning it to be not quite poetry forever, while poetry is its own music, condemning it to be naked without music forever" (Scarriet 2013, para. 1). In my dissertation, I classify songs as poetry because I employ the songs of others to tell my story. I quote the three verses of the hymn, "In the Morning of My Life" by Frederick Douglass (Grossi 2006, p. 194), to end the three chapters that speak of the early, middle, and later years of my life. The last verse speaks of the evening of my life and precedes my chapter, "Reflections on the Writing."

At this point in the writing, I recognised the looming end of my career and my dissertation and the words of Frederick Douglass drove me to ask and answer the questions: Was I brave and strong and true enough to hold true to my profession? Was I brave and strong and true enough to tackle autoethnography (the first of its kind as far as I am aware in South Africa) and a dissertation that was to come under much scrutiny and may even have not been accepted as research? Was I brave and strong and true enough to stick to the tenets of the genre I had explored and believed in? Was I brave and strong and true enough to weave my simple poetry around the coloured pieces of my dissertation? Was I brave and strong and true enough to withstand the "stripping" by the academic committee?

The Promise of Poetry Belongs to Us All: Poetic Professional ...   147

I took the liberty of writing three verses to end the dissertation. They can be either read as poetry or sung to the tune of "My Way" (Anka et al. 1969). In the first verse, I reflect on the many happy and exciting years the teaching profession afforded me. Whilst writing the autoethnography, the work begged me to give thought to the fact that I was nearing retirement age, and that I needed to hand some of the reins over to my daughter so she, too, could share in my experiences. Autoethnography does this. It provokes one to change, to have new ways of seeing things.

The second verse speaks of the feelings evoked throughout the autoethnography and that in the writing thereof, I had bared myself to public scrutiny. It also speaks of the relationship I enjoyed with my extraordinary supervisor, Naydene de Lange. Although I don't drink, we shared a glass of wine at a supper to celebrate the end of the dissertation, which I loved writing. We had many a good laugh about the long, long road we had walked together as we experienced the many byways of a first-of-its-kind autoethnography.

> Advice? I've this to give
> You have one life
> Just learn to live
> With faith, give it your all
> And very soon you will stand tall.
> And follow your every dream
> Nothing's as hard as it may seem
> And more, much more than this
> Just do it your way.
>
> (Grossi 2006, p. 236)

The last verse speaks of the scarcity of literature in autoethnography. I had to "dive in" by faith and was forced to write the dissertation my way. Autoethnography calls for writing from the heart and poetry is the blood that breathes life into the piece. By analysing my practice through poetry, professional and personal growth was maximised—"Many scholars do not yet realise the richness and depth of the research produced by 'looking inward' and its value to scholarship" (Mitchell and Weber 2005, p. 4).

As I near the completion of this piece, I feel compelled to write this short poem because it sums up, or binds, my feelings about the role poetry can play in autoethnography.

> **Poetry in Autoethnography**
>
> Poetry it appears to me
> Binds the mosaic in autoethnography
> No-one can say it is right or wrong
> If presented in verse, prose or song
>
> Words that come tumbling from the heart
> Knowledge to self and others impart
> Poetry it appears to me
> Binds the mosaic in autoethnography

6 Insights from Conversations Elicited by the Mosaic Pieces

The two mosaic pieces presented in this chapter open a path for other teacher-researchers who may refer to these exemplars for specific guidance on, and illustrations of, poetic inquiry as professional learning. The chapter demonstrates how teacher-researchers who might not necessarily describe themselves as "qualified" poets can start to play with the imaginative possibilities of poetic language to produce relatively simple poems as research data, representations, and interpretations. Poetry can be seen as moving along a continuum (Young 1982, citing Britton). Towards one end of such a continuum might be poetry that can be recognised as satisfying identifiable literary and artistic criteria. Towards the other end, poetic experimentation with language might serve the purpose of creative and imaginative engagement with experience without necessarily producing poems that adhere to formal requirements of particular poetic genres. Even when teacher-researchers' poems do not stand on their own as literary texts, they can bring creativity, emotion, and sensory impact to memory-work and can allow teacher-researchers to distil and make meaning from their past experiences in order to reimagine themselves and their professional learning.

Nonetheless, many teacher-researchers, whether novice or more experienced, might feel apprehensive about poetry. As Shopsin (2017, para. 1) pointed out, "Like classical music, poetry has an unfortunate reputation for requiring special training and education to appreciate, which … makes most of us feel as if we haven't studied enough to read it." To this, we would add that this intimidating reputation also makes many people feel that they are not erudite or qualified enough to compose poetry. However, through the exemplars of the two mosaic pieces in this chapter, others might be encouraged to follow S'phiwe's and Edwina's lead in exploring the power of poetic professional learning.

The Promise of Poetry Belongs to Us All: Poetic Professional ...

In the context of South Africa, many practicing teachers do not have a schooling background or formal academic qualifications in the arts and so they might not see themselves as possessing the necessary artistic sensibility for poetic inquiry (Chiliza 2015; Singh 2007). Regrettably, S'phiwe's constraining exposure to poetry during his schooling in the apartheid era still seems to be quite typical of many encounters with poetry in postapartheid South Africa (Newfield and Maungedzo 2006). To illustrate, recent self-study research by Bridget Campbell (2016), a teacher educator in English education, revealed that when she asked a class of 54 student teachers about their school-based experiences of poetry, the majority characterised these experiences in negative terms, with many using words such as "horrible," "confusing," and even "torture" (p. 10). Most of these student teachers, who would soon themselves be entering schools as English language teachers, described how at school they "were not given the opportunity to explore the poems themselves and to form their own opinions as the teachers' ideas and interpretations were imposed on them" (p. 10).

It is therefore important to consider poetic professional learning in the context of personal and social histories. For many people, their school-based experiences of poetry were unpleasant and even frightening. Poetry was experienced as something very far removed from themselves and their lived realities. Many were forced to learn poems and prescribed interpretations of poetry by heart. Consequently, just the thought of poetry strikes fear into the hearts of many people, which is an injustice because poetic language is the language of the imagination and each of us has an imagination. Of course, poetic inquiry will not necessarily appeal to or suit all teacher-researchers, and it should not be compulsory for anyone. However, the promise of poetry belongs to us all and the two unique mosaic pieces in this chapter demonstrate that. In contexts where lack of access and generative exposure to poetry and other art forms in the actual school curriculum remain a pressing issue of social and cultural injustice, formal qualifications or even practical experience within the literary arts might be more usefully seen as a desirable development rather than as a prerequisite for poetic professional learning.

Poetic inquiry can also expand possibilities for classroom practice in schools and higher education institutions. When teacher-researchers begin to engage in their own poetic professional learning, this can encourage them to work differently with poetry in the classroom by opening up nonthreatening and pleasurable avenues for students to explore reading, writing, and performing poetry in ways that can set their imaginations alight. Altering the mood of the classroom environment can inspire students and show them how poetry can become an integral part of their lives (Ferguson 2017).

7 The Possibilities of Poetic Language and Poetic Ways of Being and Doing

This chapter contributes to the growing scholarship of poetic professional learning in the social sciences. The chapter calls attention to how the meditative and creative possibilities of poetic language and poetic ways of being and doing can be used

150 K. Pithouse-Morgan et al.

in researching and enriching teachers' professional learning through memory-work. The distinctive mosaic pieces by S'phiwe Madondo and Edwina Grossi, which are exemplary of professional learning by way of poetry, offer windows into poetic explorations of these teacher-researchers' own memories and histories in relationship with broader educational and sociocultural contexts and concerns. As Young (1982) explained:

> What poetic language does—both in the reading and the writing—is provide us with a unique perspective on experience, valuable because it allows us to place our personal interpretation in a social and cultural context, and because it allows the dominant social and cultural interpretation to be subject to personal understanding (p. 96).

The mosaic pieces illuminate poetic inquiry as a means of working imaginatively with personal memories to generate new understandings for making a qualitative difference to lived experiences of teaching and learning. Through this chapter, we offer encouragement to teacher-researchers to start to play with poetic inquiry to compose poems as research data, representations, and interpretations. The chapter also highlights how poetic professional learning can be better understood in the context of personal and social histories. When unwelcoming approaches to teaching poetry continue to make people feel that they are not knowledgeable enough to compose or interpret poetry, it is vital to open up invitations to, and occasions for, more nourishing interactions with poetry. Notwithstanding a lack of formal qualifications in poetry as a literary art, composing poems can facilitate imaginative expression and creative analytic lenses to generate personally, professionally, and socially valuable understandings on the part of teacher-researchers and their audiences. Poetic language is the language of reimagination and hope, and also, equally importantly, of expressing and empathising with pain and uncomfortable feelings. Through carefully selecting and arranging words as poems, we can encounter, articulate, and become immersed in thoughts, feelings, and lived experiences that might be difficult to communicate in propositional academic language.

Acknowledgement We are grateful to our peer reviewer, Valerie Mulholland (University of Regina, Canada), for her perceptive and constructive feedback that helped to strengthen this chapter.

References

Anka, P., Francois, C., Thibaut, L., & Revaud, J. (1967/1969). My way [Recorded by Frank Sinatra]. On *My way* [Vinyl record]. Burbank, CA: Reprise Records.
Brady, I. (2009). Foreword. In M. Prendergast, C. Leggo, & P. Sameshima (Eds.), *Poetic inquiry: Vibrant voices in the social sciences* (pp. xi–xvi). Rotterdam: Sense Publishers.
Breckenridge, J. P. (2016). The reflexive role of tanka poetry in domestic abuse research. *Journal of Research in Nursing, 21*(5–6), 447–460.
Butler-Kisber, L. (2005). Inquiry through poetry: The genesis of self-study. In C. Mitchell, S. Weber, & K. O'Reilly-Scanlon (Eds.), *Just who do we think we are? Methodologies for autobiography and self-study in teaching* (pp. 95–110). London: RoutledgeFalmer.

The Promise of Poetry Belongs to Us All: Poetic Professional … 151

Campbell, B. (2016). Rethinking my poetry pedagogy: An autoethnographic self-study. *South African Journal of Higher Education, 30*(1), 42–56. Retrieved from http://www.journals.ac.z a/index.php/sajhe/article/download/556/138.

Caulley, D. N. (2008). Making qualitative research reports less boring. *Qualitative Inquiry, 14*(3), 424–449.

Chiliza, H. Z. (2015). *Facilitating creative arts teaching and learning with foundation phase teachers: A subject advisor's self-study* (Unpublished master's thesis). University of KwaZulu-Natal, South Africa. Retrieved from http://researchspace.ukzn.ac.za/handle/10413/13666.

Cole, A. (2011). Object-memory, embodiment, and teacher formation: A methodological exploration. In C. Mitchell, T. Strong-Wilson, K. Pithouse, & S. Allnutt (Eds.), *Memory and pedagogy* (pp. 223–238). New York: Routledge.

Easton, L. B. (2008). From professional development to professional learning. *Phi Delta Kappan, 89*(10), 755–761.

Eisner, E. W. (2004). What can education learn from the arts about the practice of education? *International Journal of Education and the Arts, 5*(4), 1–14.

Eisner, E. W. (2008). Art and knowledge. In J. G. Knowles & A. L. Cole (Eds.), *Handbook of the arts in qualitative research* (pp. 3–12). Thousand Oaks: SAGE.

Ellis, C., Adams, T. E., & Bochner, A. P. (2011). Autoethnography: An overview. *Forum Qualitative Sozialforschung Forum: Qualitative Social Research, 12*(1). Retrieved from http://nbn-resolvin g.de/urn:nbn:de:0114-fqs1101108.

Ferguson, K. (2017). A poetry coffee house: Creating a cool community of writers. *The Reading Teacher, 71*(2), 209–213. Retrieved from http://onlinelibrary.wiley.com/doi/10.1002/trtr.161 0/full.

Furman, R. (2014). Beyond the literary uses of poetry: A class for university freshmen. *Journal of Poetry Therapy, 27*(4), 205–211.

Furman, R., Coyne, A., & Negi, N. J. (2008). An international experience for social work students: Self-reflection through poetry and journal writing exercises. *Journal of Teaching in Social Work, 28*(1–2), 71–85.

Furman, R., Langer, C. L., Davis, C. S., Gallardo, H. P., & Kulkarni, S. (2007). Expressive, research and reflective poetry as qualitative inquiry: A study of adolescent identity. *Qualitative Research, 7*(3), 301–315.

Furman, R., Lietz, C. A., & Langer, C. L. (2006). The research poem in international social work: Innovations in qualitative methodology. *International Journal of Qualitative Methods, 5*(3), 24–34. Retrieved from http://www.ualberta.ca/~iiqm/backissues/5_3/PDF/furman.pdf.

Gibran, K. (2013). *The prophet.* New York: Random House. (Original work published 1923).

Grant, C., Jasson, A., & Lawrence, G. (2010). Resilient KwaZulu-Natal schools: An ethics of care. *Southern African Review of Education, 16*(2), 81–99.

Grossi, E. (2006). *An ordinary teacher: An autoethnography* (Unpublished doctoral dissertation). University of KwaZulu-Natal, South Africa. Retrieved from http://researchspace.ukzn.ac.za/xm lui/handle/10413/1343.

Kajee, L. (2011). Literacy journeys: Home and family literacy practices in immigrant households and their congruence with schooled literacy. *South African Journal of Education, 31*(3), 434–446. Retrieved from http://www.sajournalofeducation.co.za/index.php/saje/article/view/545/263.

Lahman, M. K. E., Geist, M. R., Rodriguez, K. L., Graglia, P. E., Richard, V. M., & Schendel, R. K. (2010). Poking around poetically: Research, poetry, and trustworthiness. *Qualitative Inquiry, 16*(1), 39–48.

Leggo, C. (2005). The heart of pedagogy: On poetic knowing and living. *Teachers and Teaching: Theory and Practice, 11*(5), 439–455.

Leggo, C. (2008). Astonishing silence: Knowing in poetry. In J. G. Knowles & A. L. Cole (Eds.), *Handbook of the arts in qualitative research* (pp. 165–174). Thousand Oaks: SAGE.

Madondo, S. (2014). *Nurturing learners' flair for written communication: A teacher's self-study* (Unpublished master's thesis). University of KwaZulu-Natal, South Africa. Retrieved from http:// researchspace.ukzn.ac.za/handle/10413/12626.

Mitchell, C. (2016). Autoethnography as a wide-angle lens on looking (inward and outward): What difference can this make to our teaching? In D. Pillay, I. Naicker, & K. Pithouse-Morgan (Eds.), *Academic autoethnographies: Inside teaching in higher education* (pp. 175–189). Rotterdam: Sense Publishers.

Mitchell, C., & Weber, S. (2005). Just who do we think we are … and how do we know this? Re-visioning pedagogical spaces for studying our teaching selves. In C. Mitchell, S. Weber, & K. O'Reilly-Scanlon (Eds.), *Just who do we think we are? Methodologies for autobiography and self-study in teaching* (pp. 1–9). London: RoutledgeFalmer.

Mncube, V. (2009). The perceptions of parents of their role in the democratic governance of schools in South Africa: Are they on board? *South African Journal of Education, 29*(1), 83–103.

Newfield, D., & Maungedzo, R. (2006). Mobilising and modalising poetry in a Soweto classroom. *English Studies in Africa, 49*(1), 71–93.

Nieuwenhuis, J. (2010). Analysing qualitative data. In K. Maree (Ed.), *First steps in research* (pp. 98–122). Pretoria: Van Schaik.

Pithouse, K. (2011). Picturing the self: Drawing as a method for self-study. In L. Theron, C. Mitchell, & J. Stuart (Eds.), *Picturing research: Drawings as visual methodology* (pp. 37–48). Rotterdam: Sense Publishers.

Pithouse-Morgan, K. (2016). Finding my self in a new place: Exploring professional learning through found poetry. *Teacher Learning and Professional Development, 1*(1), 1–18. Retrieved from http://journals.sfu.ca/tlpd/index.php/tlpd/article/view/1.

Pithouse-Morgan, K. (2017). Beginning to unravel a narrative tension in my professional learning about teaching writing. In M. Hayler & J. Moriarty (Eds.), *Self-narrative and pedagogy: Stories of experience within teaching and learning* (pp. 59–82). Rotterdam: Sense Publishers.

Pithouse-Morgan, K., & Samaras, A. P. (2015). The power of "we" for professional learning. In K. Pithouse-Morgan & A. P. Samaras (Eds.), *Polyvocal professional learning through self-study research* (pp. 1–20). Rotterdam: Sense Publishers.

Poets.org. (2004). *Prose poem: Poetic form*. Retrieved from https://www.poets.org/poetsorg/text/prose-poem-poetic-form.

Prendergast, M. (2009). "Poem is what?" Poetic inquiry in qualitative social science research. *International Review of Qualitative Research, 1*(4), 541–568.

Richardson, L. (1993). Poetics, dramatics, and transgressive validity: The case of the skipped line. *The Sociological Quarterly, 34*(4), 695–710.

Richardson, L. (2003). Writing: A method of inquiry. In N. K. Denzin & Y. S. Lincoln (Eds.), *Collecting and interpreting qualitative materials* (2nd ed., pp. 499–541). Thousand Oaks: SAGE.

Samaras, A. P. (2011). *Self-study teacher research: Improving your practice through collaborative inquiry*. Thousand Oaks: SAGE.

Samaras, A., & Freese, A. (2009). Looking back and looking forward: An historical overview of the self-study school. In C. A. Lassonde, S. Galman, & C. Kosnik (Eds.), *Self-study research methodologies for teacher educators* (pp. 3–19). Rotterdam: Sense Publishers.

Scarriet. (2013, November 8). The top one hundred popular song lyrics that work as poetry [Blog post]. Retrieved from https://scarriet.wordpress.com/2013/11/08/the-top-one-hundred-popular-song-lyrics-that-work-as-poetry/.

Shopsin, T. (2017, July 10). Understanding poetry is more straightforward than you think [Review of the book *Why poetry* by M. Zapruder]. *The New York Times*. Retrieved from https://www.nytimes.com/2017/07/10/books/review/understanding-poetry-is-more-straightforward-than-you-think.html?_r=0.

Short, N. P., & Grant, A. (2016). Poetry as hybrid pedagogy in mental health nurse education. *Nurse Education Today, 43*, 60–63.

Singh, L. P. (2007). *Birth and regeneration: The arts and culture curriculum in South Africa, 1997–2006* (Unpublished doctoral dissertation). University of KwaZulu-Natal, South Africa. Retrieved from http://researchspace.ukzn.ac.za/xmlui/handle/10413/863.

Van Manen, M. (1990). *Researching lived experience: Human science for an action sensitive pedagogy*. Albany: State University of New York Press.

Verse. (n.d.). *In Online Etymology Dictionary*. Retrieved from http://www.etymonline.com/index.php?allowed_in_frame=0&search=verse.

Weber, S. (2008). Visual images in research. In J. G. Knowles & A. L. Cole (Eds.), *Handbook of the arts in qualitative research* (pp. 40–53). Thousand Oaks: SAGE.

Webster-Wright, A. (2009). Reframing professional development through understanding authentic professional learning. *Review of Educational Research, 79*(2), 702–739.

Young, A. (1982). Considering values: The poetic function of language. In T. Fulwiler & A. Young (Eds.), *Language connections: Writing and reading across the curriculum* (pp. 77–97). Urbana: National Council of Teachers of English.

Stories Blending, Flowing Out: Connecting Teacher Professional Learning, Re-membering, and Storytelling

Kathleen Pithouse-Morgan, Sandra Owén:nakon Deer-Standup and Thokozani Ndaleni

Abstract "Stories Blending, Flowing Out: Connecting Teacher Professional Learning, Re-membering, and Storytelling" by Kathleen Pithouse-Morgan, Sandra Owén:nakon Deer-Standup, and Thokozani Ndaleni, offers written research accounts of engaging with oral storytelling as an arts-based community and family practice. The chapter brings together mosaic pieces by two teacher-researchers, who, on different continents, have delved into teacher professional learning in relation to re-membering through mythical and personal stories. The mosaic pieces are complemented by a dialogue piece, which portrays how communicating with each other across continents and cultural contexts deepened and extended Sandra and Thokozani's mindfulness of the educative potential of connecting re-membering, storytelling, and teacher professional learning. The chapter reveals how, as teacher-researchers retell their own stories and listen to others' stories, they can make new sense of their past and present learning, and reimagine stories of the future.

Keywords Canada · Memory-work · Oral storytelling · Mythical stories
Personal stories · South Africa · Teacher professional learning

---

K. Pithouse-Morgan (✉) · T. Ndaleni
School of Education, University of KwaZulu-Natal, Durban, South Africa
e-mail: pithousemorgan@ukzn.ac.za

T. Ndaleni
e-mail: Ndalenit@ukzn.ac.za

S. O. Deer-Standup
Department of Integrated Studies in Education, Faculty of Education, McGill University, Montreal, Canada
e-mail: sandra.deer@mail.mcgill.ca; sdeer17@outlook.com

© Springer Nature Switzerland AG 2019
K. Pithouse-Morgan et al. (eds.), *Memory Mosaics: Researching Teacher Professional Learning Through Artful Memory-work*, Studies in Arts-Based Educational Research 2, https://doi.org/10.1007/978-3-319-97106-3_9

1 A Poetic Prologue

Story Circle

by Kathleen Pithouse-Morgan, inspired by the voices of Sandra Owén:nakon Deer-Standup and Thokozani Ndaleni.

Breath	Weave	Words	Grow
Embers	Stories	Blending	Flourish
Smoke rising	Move tighter	Flowing out	Connecting
Flickering flames	We are so close	Like vines toward	Past in present
Voice	Warmth	Space	Time

2 Setting the Scene

Storytelling is often considered a vital part of being human and of understanding what it means or could mean to be human (Badley 2017; Lewis 2011). As Haarhoff (1998) explained, when we "re-member (the opposite to dismember) our stories, we reconstruct and reconnect our lives" (p. 5). From this perspective, storytelling is fundamental to both individual and communal human "remembering and making [and remaking] history" (Iseke 2013, p. 570).

Re-membering as a research practice of recreating, telling, and responding to personal stories of lived experiences can be retraced to Haug's memory-work methodology (1987, 2008, n.d.) in which individual written memory accounts were read aloud and edited by a group. It also has connections with later work in teacher professional learning research, such as that of Mitchell and Weber (1998, 1999), in which teacher participants have written individual memory accounts and read them to a group. The focus in these approaches to memory-work is on engaging orally with the written text of personal stories.

In this chapter, however, the emphasis shifts to written research accounts of engaging with oral storytelling as a traditional community and family practice. In particular, the focus is on engaging with interconnections between two forms of stories, which have been described in research on Indigenous storytelling as "mythical" and "personal" stories (Iseke 2013, p. 559). Mythical stories "teach morals, lessons, or events," and often appear in collected volumes of Indigenous myths and legends (Iseke 2013, p. 565). These stories "can be shaped by the storyteller—drawing on the teller's or the listeners' experiences—but the underlying message of these stories does not change" (Iseke 2013, p. 565). Personal stories differ in that they draw on individual lived experiences of the storyteller or other people; nevertheless, like mythical stories, personal stories are told with an educative purpose (Iseke 2013).

Both mythical and personal stories can be understood as "pedagogical tools for learning about life and as important forms of [individual and communal] witnessing and remembrance" (Iseke 2013, p. 572).

This chapter brings together original work by two teacher-researchers, Sandra Owén:nakon Deer-Standup and Thokozani Ndaleni, who, on different continents, have explored teacher professional learning in connection to re-membering through interweaving mythical and personal stories. Their inquiries can be considered as *storywork*, which Archibald explained as "the educational and research work of making meaning through stories, whether they are traditional or lived experience stories" (2008, p. 373). Archibald's conceptualisation of Indigenous storywork as an arts-based social science research methodology is rooted in "the teachings and experiences of the Coast Salish peoples of British Columbia, in particular the Sto:lo of the Lower Fraser River" (Archibald 2008, p. 371). Her design for storywork as a research methodology is underpinned by four Sto:lo cultural principles: "respect, responsibility, reverence, reciprocity," which she explained as, "traditional values and teachings demonstrated toward the story, toward and by the storyteller and the listener, and practiced in the storywork context" (p. 373).

Sandra Owén:nakon Deer-Standup is a former language and cultural coordinator at an early childhood centre in Kahnawa:ke, Quebec, Canada. Her narrative research (Deer-Standup 2013) revolved around an investigation of legends and storytelling used in early childhood education. Sandra's focus on stories, curriculum, and early childhood education developed through what she described as a journey back into her imagination. Her investigation of the role of legends and storytelling in an early childhood setting in Kahnawa:ke was portrayed through a combination of personal narrative interwoven with research literature, classroom observations, and personal interviews as portraiture, and a discussion based on data generated. In creating her research text, she retold Indigenous oral stories from her memory of how she had heard them over the decades, and she also drew on the memories and artefacts of her research participants. Through her narrative research, Sandra learned that local cultural legends and stories familiar to historical, ceremonial, and spiritual practices can act as a guiding tool for culturally situated teacher professional learning and curriculum development. She also concluded that legends and storytelling are a contextualisation of Indigenous cultural knowledge passed from one generation to the next. As such, it was prior European colonisation.

The aim of Thokozani Ndaleni's self-study master's research (Ndaleni 2013) was to enhance his teaching of English oral communication to isiZulu-speaking secondary-school learners in South Africa. Thokozani employed a personal history self-study method (Samaras et al. 2004) to better understand his lived experiences of learning and teaching oral communication. He revisited memories of past informal and formal educational experiences as a black African, Zulu child in apartheid South Africa. In retracing his memories, Thokozani photographed, described, and analysed artefacts that influenced his learning to communicate orally. His personal history narrative revealed the vital impact of his family on his learning of oral communication. Through his personal history self-study, in particular through the analysis of family storytelling artefacts, Thokozani realised that awareness of local social and cultural contexts is fundamental to the teaching and learning of oral communication.

It is in a spirit of respect, responsibility, reverence, and reciprocity that this chapter brings into dialogue the plurality and commonalities of the voices of Sandra, Thokozani, and Kathleen Pithouse-Morgan—a teacher educator and researcher who works to support teacher-researchers in creative engagement in professional learning. In her scholarship, Kathleen has explored re-membering and storytelling as vital elements of professional learning research (Mitchell and Pithouse-Morgan 2014; Pithouse 2011). Kathleen introduced Sandra and Thokozani to each other via e-mail and invited them to each create a short mosaic piece for this chapter—in whatever format they preferred. The chapter was developed over an 8-month period from the two written pieces and e-mail conversations between Sandra, Thokozani, and Kathleen. During this time, the three authors were able to share the mosaic pieces and their understandings and reflections on re-membering, storytelling, and researching teacher professional learning. Using the mosaic pieces, together with ideas communicated in the e-mail correspondence, Kathleen prepared a preliminary version of the chapter. She sent this draft to Sandra and Thokozani for development and revision. The final rendering of the chapter was developed through interaction between the three authors, the book editors, and a peer reviewer.

The next section of the chapter offers Sandra's first-person mosaic piece. To follow, is Thokozani's mosaic piece. Thereafter, the voices of Sandra and Thokozani are brought together in a dialogue piece to reveal transcontinental, transcultural conversations and musings. A dialogic format was chosen with the aim of showing how teacher-researcher professional learning can occur through interaction and interdependence. This is followed by a poetic response from Kathleen. The chapter closes with a deliberation on generative connotations of connecting teacher professional learning, re-membering, and storytelling.

3   Sandra Owén:nakon Deer-Standup's Mosaic Piece

Indigenous Storytelling in Contemporary Early Childhood Education: The Creation Story of the Haudenosaunee (People of the Longhouse or Six Nations of the Iroquois)
by Sandra Owén:nakon Deer-Standup

My Introduction
My name is Sandra Owén:nakon Deer-Standup, I am of the bear clan among the Kanien'kehá:ka (people of the flint nation), one of the Six Nations of the Iroquois Confederacy or the Haudenosaunee (people of the longhouse). I am a daughter, sister, mother, wife, grandmother, aunt, great aunt, and a teacher. Several years ago, I left early-childhood teaching to pursue a master's degree. Currently, I am writing this piece as a 4th-year doctoral student. My commitment to education has not changed, however, I would classify it as grown or branched out—grown outward like vines

intertwining between a fence trying to avoid all obstruction that could stunt its growth, moving smoothly toward the clear open spaces that allow it to flourish naturally.

As an Indigenous educator, a large part of my career was spent teaching in Kanien'keha (Mohawk language). Students have come into my classrooms as English speakers to learn to speak Kanien'keha. Our language has almost vanished and our ancestral culture with it. A portion of the curriculum I designed and implemented was culturally based, meaning that as a teacher, I would incorporate oral stories, legends, and activities wherever applicable and relevant to the topic. It was a fun way to engage young children in their own culture and language.

Indigenous Storytelling

Prior to European contact, Indigenous nations used storytelling and legends as an educational tool to promote cultural values, knowledge, and identity (Archibald 2001; Kanu 2006; Kirkness 1995). The story or legend was comprised of those values that reflect identity and the relationship with the environment and the animal world (Antone and Córdoba 2005; Duryea LeBaron and Potts 1993; Friesen and Friesen 2007; Lutz and Moritz-Arndt 1995). This form of transference was an important tool specific to the continuity of that nation's culture (Armstrong 1987; Faries 2004; Ho'omanawanui 2010; Kanu 2006). Providing culturally relevant education through storytelling and legends familiar to that nation helps create a connection to their cultural past in the present (Pence et al. 2007).

The creation story of the Haudenosaunee is a significant piece of culture that transfers the origin of the people in relation to a spiritual connection to the universe and all living things. It is a story that holds much meaning. It is a learning tool that one can return at any given moment and, with each visit, more meaning is revealed. For the Haudenosaunee, it is spiritual and symbolic curricula of life and death, caring and respecting, and a form of reinstating your connection with the earth, the natural world and creator.

The Study

The title of my master's thesis is "An Investigation of the Role of Legends and Story-telling in Early Childhood Practices in a Kanien'kehá:ka (Mohawk) Early Childhood Facility." Prior to entering the master's programme, I was employed through the Step by Step Early Childhood and Family Center; the Kanien'keha name is Kahwatsir-ano:ron Tsi Ionterihwaienstah:kwa (meaning, at the place we teach our precious children). I was employed as the cultural language coordinator for several years. Part of my mandate was to develop cultural curricula, and so, I developed curriculum by using our creation story and many legends that coincide with our seasonal celebrations.

My interest in returning for research stemmed from my own curiosity and the strong connection I had developed with the school and its philosophy surrounding cultural language, knowledge, and the importance of building community relationships. I was also curious to know, after being away for a few years, how things had manifest within the classrooms (with respect to stories and legends) and to investigate any change in teaching philosophies relative to cultural awareness, language acquisition, and teachers' and administration's current beliefs regarding cultural stories and legends being implemented in the classrooms. I wanted to know what had changed or further developed, if anything.

Method and Indigenous Methodology

Indigenous methodology is a culmination or gathering of the researcher's world-view, life experiences, prior knowledge, language background, education, and cultural beliefs. I chose a qualitative method called portraiture. Portraiture seemed to echo (for me) an Indigenous methodology allowing my own knowledge, experience, and cultural beliefs to share the same platform as the interviewees. Portraiture allows the author to make assumptions through her own thoughts and insights about how the actor/interviewee or participant has answered the question, or how he or she reacts physically, emotionally, and so on to the questions or the research topic itself. For instance, looking at one's enthusiasm, how does that play into the research, what is it that you witnessed from that person? How do you interpret your participant's reaction through your own observation? And you write from that perspective, allowing the participant's voice to be intertwined along with your own, blending them as one story. Therefore, by using portraiture I weaved my voice through the telling of the data while blending the teacher's voice as storyteller and cultural advocate. Through a qualitative methodological lens, portraits are "the examination of the ways in which the researcher deals with her or his lenses and tools" (Chapman 2005, p. 34). The researcher's voice is heard "through the central themes" of the data being presented (Lawrence-Lightfoot and Davis as cited in Chapman 2005, p. 34). Below, is a portrait of my research (Deer-Standup 2013, pp. 73–74) that speaks volumes, and demonstrates storytelling as an instrumental part of early childhood education in a Kanien'kehá:ka classroom.

A Big Book Story: Tsi Tiotahsawen Tsi Iohontsà:te (The Creation Story)

I entered Classroom 1 during storytelling time. I arrived a bit early because the teacher had asked me not to disturb the flow of the morning routine. The children were somewhat familiar with me because I had visited twice before to speak with the teacher. On one previous visit, I sat with a little girl who was finishing her snack. I said hello to her and she immediately invited me to a party at her house. I gladly accepted and she rushed off to the sink to wash her hands, and discarded her garbage. At the official observation, the routine was similar. I entered and said hello to the children—they were busy cleaning up the remainder of their snacks and readily preparing for circle time. Circle time is the place and time to gather in preparation for the day's routines and to share any pertinent information about guests, events, outings, or personal celebrations and, of course, story time.

On this day, the teacher chose to tell the children the creation story, using a big book that was nicely illustrated and was laminated and bound with yarn. It was evident that the person who put this big book together had some artistic skill. The drawings were done in colourful markers, on large poster boards, and resembled professional animated artwork with an Indigenous artist style (see Fig. 1). The children all sat on the floor in front, facing the teacher, and another teacher sat among the children acting as a second set of hands and eyes and, through my observation, it was obviously

Fig. 1 Big book, creation story: Corn, beans, squash, and strawberries (Photographer, Sandra Owén:nakon Deer-Standup, with permission)

needed to ensure no monkey business was taking place. I sat at the window to create a place for my recorder and a secure surface on which to write my notes.

The story began with the teacher recapping the title of the book (*The Creation Story*), and asking the children what they remembered about the story. One child replied, "Is that the special one?" and the teacher replied, "Yes that's the special one." After reading the first page, the teacher asked, "What do you see?" The children replied by naming the pictures of the fruit. The children were very tentative of the storybook and sat in amazement as though they were hearing it for the first time. The half circle became tighter as the children moved closer to one another; they looked very relaxed and comfortable leaning on one another trying to get the best possible view of the big book. The children were at the age of three years, and one child had recently turned four years old. One little girl was distracted by something on the window ledge, and the teacher engaged her with "Please pay attention," and called out her name. The little girl looked towards the big book and then returned to her distraction, which was now at the edge of her pant leg.

Culturally and historically, elders taught through stories, ceremony, speaking to the children, leading by example, and teaching about relationships. The stories reflected a relationship to earth, land, water, animals, and encompassed the most complex understanding of the universe. Listening to stories taught listening skills and helped deepen one's thoughts about community, identity, respect, and spirituality. It was a natural process of education and is rarely used in today's native societies (Archibald 2001).

As the teacher read on, it was evident that the children knew this story by their eagerness to provide the answers to the questions posed. The story was now at the part where Sky Woman falls through a hole in the sky. The teacher asked, "Where did she go?" Several children raised their hands in the air and waited to be called on to give their answer. A woman falling through a hole in the sky sounds irrational, mythical, and unrealistic. Paula Gunn Allan (1992) stated that "an American Indian myth is a story that relies preeminently on symbol for its articulation" and "it demands the immediate, direct participation of the listener" (p. 105). We arrived in the story where birds and water animals offer assistance to Sky Woman. The teacher asked, "What happened to her?" The children replied, "She's on the turtle's back." She read on and asked the children, "Which animals dove down to the bottom?" Voluntarily, one child shouted, "Otter!" then another child repeated aloud "Otter." The teacher asked, "What other animals helped her?" "The muskrat," one child said. She repeated the question and another child yelled out, "Beaver!" She said thank you and repeated, "The beaver." "What are they looking for?" she asked. The children, in unison, shouted out "Dirt!" The animals were now diving to the bottom of the ocean to retrieve some dirt for Sky Woman. In the story, Sky Woman uses the dirt to create a land base to walk upon, and plants the seeds and roots that she grabbed at before falling through the hole in the sky.

The children were engaged and verbally participated in the story. The circle again became closed in and smaller in radius as they slid towards the big book on the teacher's lap. One boy jumped up from the floor and began to demonstrate how Sky Woman planted her roots and seeds. He started to move his feet side to side in the motion of a windshield wiper blade of a car. He stood in place, moving his feet and telling his teacher, "This is how she planted." As he demonstrated how Sky Woman planted upon the turtle's back, he began naming vegetables in Kanien'keha. He said, "*ó:nenste, ononh'òn:sera* [corn, squash]." The teacher responded to his enthusiasm

Stories Blending, Flowing Out: Connecting Teacher Professional ...   163

with, "Yes that's right," then repeated the vegetables in Kanien'keha. She continued to praise him and added another vegetable, *osahé:ta* [beans].

Conclusion

As I began writing the portrait, I wrote as though I were telling a story to an audience and thought to myself, "How would I really say this?" As the words flowed from my mind to my fingers and onto the computer keys, my memory traced back to each classroom observation. I remembered what teachers said, word for word, and how each demonstrated what storytelling has taught and brought—not only to the children, but also to themselves as teachers. As I recalled their voices in my head, I knew exactly where to retrieve the data that would weave itself in as though all our voices were one in the portrait's central themes. Strong-Wilson (2008) stated that "teachers have a special affinity to story" (p. 5) because stories are used to teach and complement curriculum. They teach children to read, write, answer posed questions, and articulate the morals, values, and connection that story brings. For me, as an Indigenous educator, stories are my life's history, my family's history, my peoples' history.

Today, Indigenous storytelling continues to articulate cultural and spiritual knowledge. "In many places it is as faint as the smoke rising from the embers of last night's fire; in other places, enough flame to ignite another log" (Deer-Standup 2013, p. 3).

4   Thokozani Ndaleni's Mosaic Piece

Remembering how I Learned Oral Communication Through Storytelling with My Family Members
by Thokozani Ndaleni

Introduction

I have practised as an English language teacher in South African secondary schools for more than 28 years. Currently, I am an English language teacher educator working at a South African university. I am pursuing doctoral studies through which I explore English language teacher learning.

My home language is isiZulu. South Africa has 11 official languages, including English, which is a lingua franca. Nine of the 11 official languages are indigenous languages. Besides isiZulu, I only speak one other indigenous language: isiXhosa; however, I struggle when I read or write it. My learning to speak English has its foundations in both rural and township schools in South Africa. All my schoolteachers were black African people whose home language was also isiZulu.

This mosaic piece draws on my master's research (Ndaleni 2013), which I conducted when I was still a secondary school, English language teacher at a school situated in an isiZulu-speaking community. Although the home language of learners and teachers at that school is isiZulu, the school's official language of learning and teaching is English. In the early development stages, known as the foundation phase (Grade R–Grade 3), the learners are taught in isiZulu. However, English takes precedence in the senior primary, and secondary school phases.

I decided to undertake the self-study research (Samaras 2011) for my Master of Education degree because I was aware of many problems when I taught English oral communication. In my teaching experience, the learners that I taught generally did not have much opportunity or impetus to speak English outside of school. Many learners would utter only a few words or remain quiet when urged to speak in English in class. Consequently, this led me to lack self-esteem as an English teacher. I was concerned about how I could encourage learners to engage in an English conversation and how I could teach learners to communicate effectively in English. In addition, I had observed that learners needed to improve their oral communication skills in order to compete for the limited job opportunities when they finished school.

I resolved to conduct a self-study because I wanted to discover activities that could assist me in facilitating interactive oral communication among learners. I was impeded by the unavailability of literature and research directly related to teaching English oral communication to isiZulu-speaking learners. The studies I found were concerned with teaching English as a second language more generally. They also concentrated on universal trends and issues. None of the material was specifically South African. Thus, through this study I intended to make a contribution by exploring a phenomenon that appeared to be under-researched, namely teaching English oral communication to isiZulu-speaking learners.

In this mosaic piece, I demonstrate how my use of a personal history self-study method allowed me to investigate my own lived experience to better understand possibilities for more effective teaching. The mosaic piece illustrates how I explored the contribution of my family's oral storytelling to my early isiZulu oral communication development. In particular, I show how I identified and analysed personal history artefacts (Samaras 2011) that contributed to my learning of oral communication. From engaging with those artefacts, I discovered key ideas I could be mindful of in my teaching of English oral communication.

Learning Oral Communication at Home: The Fireplace Circle

I was born and bred in KwaZulu-Natal, South Africa. My parents' 2-roomed house was (and still is) in a township that was set aside for black South Africans during the apartheid era. As a young person, I had both an urban and a rural upbringing. I was raised in an extended family numbering 26, which means it included my maternal grandmother, my paternal grandfather, mother, father, uncles, aunts, and cousins (boys and girls). In the urban area, our family comprised 19 members (children and adults). I spent my weekdays with my five brothers and my parents in the urban area. Over the weekends, I went to sleep at my maternal grandmother's house in another section of the same urban area where she lived with my two uncles, three aunts, and nine cousins. It was a 4-roomed house with two bedrooms, a dining room, and a kitchen. Two of my aunts slept in the main bedroom with my grandmother, and two uncles slept in the other bedroom. The children slept on the floor in the dining room. The third aunt worked in a white suburb and slept there.

Fig. 2 The *mbawula's* flickering flames (Photographer, Thokozani Ndaleni, with permission)

Usually, I visited my grandmother's house to listen to her captivating fables and folktales. Every evening after supper, we gathered in the kitchen to cherish her stories. Before the telling of stories started, it was a daily routine for the adults to render evening prayers, to thank God for guiding us through the day and plead with the Almighty to safeguard us in our sleep. In addition, it was to solicit God's benediction on the storytelling sessions so that moral lessons could be conveyed to the listeners. An adult storyteller would plead with the Almighty to bless the day's lesson. Thereafter, the children would take turns in reciting, "The Lord's Prayer" or "The Lord is My Shepherd."

Two artefacts formed an integral part of my family's evening storytelling sessions, and it seemed that one could not enjoy a story without either of them. As children, each of us had a duty to ascertain that they were available during storytelling. During the colder days, we sat around a homemade wood and coal heater called an *mbawula* (Fig. 2). This makeshift heater was made out of a 20 l paraffin container perforated on its sides, filled with wood, and lit to keep us warm. I remember its yellow embers and bluish flames.

For me, the mbawula's flickering flames symbolise the ever-existing need for people's oral communication. When we sat around the heater, we were so close to each other and felt each other's breath. As a story was being told, I would pay attention to the tone of the speaker's voice as well as his or her facial expressions and gestures. Sometimes we children would be asked which characters we loved the most and the reasons for this. I can remember that we would favour the characters who dealt justice to others.

Fig. 3 The family bond, the *isithebe* (Photographer, Thokozani Ndaleni, with permission)

Linked to the mbawula is my grandmother's huge *isithebe*, which was one of her wedding presents. Figure 3 is a photograph of an isithebe that is similar to the one that belonged to my grandmother. The isithebe is a traditional wooden platter carved by amaZulu people out of a tree called mangololo that is red inside. A chisel is used to whittle the stem of a tree to form a plate-like inner part. The outside is burnt into ash black in red burning coals. My grandmother's isithebe had two handles, one on the right-hand side and the other one was on the left. It also had four short legs.

Thinking about the isithebe fills me with nostalgia because it reminds me of the evenings I always cherished. The isithebe would be filled with either *amantongomane* [roasted groundnuts] or *izinkobe* [boiled corn kernels]. Whilst listening to narrations of my grandmother's fables, we took turns picking corn or groundnuts from the platter. It is traditional for amaZulu people to eat from one vessel, using bare hands.

While we were eating, my relatives would take turns in relating stories of African warriors' bravery, and of the intelligence of some wild animals. Below is a snippet of one of the stories that I enjoyed very much.

The rabbit and the lion: The rabbit once fooled a lion by getting it stuck in a hole dug in the ground. It told the lion that there was honey in the hole. The rabbit said it would go first and lick the honey. Because of its tiny body, the rabbit emerged on the other side of the hole, dripping juicy honey on its whiskers. Then it was the lion's turn to relish the honey. However, because of its huge body, the lion got stuck halfway through the hole. The head and the forelegs were inside the hole while the hind legs remained outside. Then the rabbit used a red-hot iron to pierce the lion's buttocks. The lion roared loudly in pain but was unable to free itself. The rabbit left the lion stuck there.

The above story taught me that it is risky to accept other people's suggestions at face value.

The ever cunning rabbit, the revengeful elephant, and the stupid guinea-pig kept me amazed. For example, we were once told the story of how the guinea pig (*imbila*) ended up with a vestigial tail. It is said that a group of animals went past this animal and told it that there was a gathering where all animals would be supplied with well-developed tails. The imbila decided to sleep and told other animals to get a tail for it. Through this story, we were taught that one has to stand up and do things on one's own instead of waiting for others to do things on one's behalf. Furthermore, the rabbit stories taught me that although one should live a communal life, one has to be careful of people with destructive tendencies. On the other hand, through the stories of the revengeful elephant, I learned that one must be extra careful of what one says or does to other people. As the amaZulu say: "*umenzi uyakhohlwa, umenziwa akakhohlwa*" (loosely translated: the one who inflicts pain forgets, while the victim does not forget easily). Later in my, life I realised that those stories were used to teach us social values and norms. My memories of the storytelling emphasised for me that in teaching oral communication, I should bring in moral lessons and life skills.

My Family's Role in My Oral Communication: A Give-and-Take Process

My personal history reveals that, from the beginning to the present, my family has had a vital impact on my learning of oral communication. When we have family gatherings, we still reminisce about these storytelling sessions, and discuss how we should allow our children to experience what we enjoyed.

The mbawula and isithebe symbolise my family unit. Looking at these artefacts, I understand that the storytelling sessions were dialogic because they involved communicating with my family members within a cultural context (Mkhize 2004). This formed the vital core of my research—because the most important tenet of oral communication is the sharing of ideas. From the storytelling sessions, I learned that as a human being, I cannot live in isolation from others and I have to respect fellow citizens' emotional, spiritual, and social well-being (Mkhize 2004). The spirit of the Southern African ethical philosophy of ubuntu, which emphasises that "I am because we are," was cultivated. Thus, oral communication embodies the spirit of ubuntu because "the person in African thought is never a finished product; he or she is perpetually in the making" (Mkhize 2004, p. 25) with others and vice versa.

The above-mentioned artefacts also reminded me that listening and speaking to each other helps people to communicate orally. In this way, they become actively involved in the exchange of information and ideas (Rahman 2010). Most of the time in our storytelling sessions, adults told a story and children listened attentively. However, as children we were also required to provide answers to questions. Sometimes we were asked for our opinions about certain characters. These conversational elements seem to support suggestions that oral communication is about two or more people talking to each other (Rahman 2010). Moreover, the narrator of the story would act out the character of the tale. Such active storytelling approaches "[provide] not only sound, but also visual input providing ... more contextual clues" (Janda 2010, p. 89).

For me, sitting around a heater and eating from a communal platter symbolises collaborative and cooperative learning. My memories of sitting around a fire showed me that learners sitting in rows of desks is not good for an interactive discussion (Doyle 2011). Thus, I became of aware of the value of teaching English oral communication across the curriculum by letting learners talk and listen to each other. Moreover, as I remembered the excitement and the feelings of belonging I experienced during the storytelling sessions, I became aware that all types of learning, including the learning of English oral communication, can be better achieved when we pay attention to how emotions and relationships can enhance learning (Burke 2002; Storrs 2012).

Conclusion

In this mosaic piece, I showed how I revisited my early learning experiences to better understand how I could improve my practice as an English teacher. I remembered how I learned oral communication through storytelling with my family members. These reflections and recollections have helped me to learn that I can draw from my personal history, such as my early experiences of oral storytelling, in my quest to improve my teaching of English oral communication.

5 A Dialogue Piece: Transcontinental, Transcultural Conversations and Musings

This dialogue piece demonstrates how sharing and communicating about their mosaic pieces with each other across continents and cultural contexts intensified and expanded Sandra and Thokozani's awareness of the educative potential of connecting re-membering, storytelling, and teacher professional learning.

Kathleen: Sandra and Thokozani, have your ideas changed or developed through reading and responding to each other's mosaic pieces?

Sandra: My ideas have not changed drastically. However, I would describe my current view as learned. I have learned much through my own research about Indigenous cultures and how Indigenous communities are relearning the significance behind oral teachings, and how educators, curriculum developers, researchers, and so on, have begun to or have already unified and implemented storytelling in many educational settings, classrooms, materials, curricula, and also as methodology in research. I now view the whole idea of cultural storytelling as a growing tree, branching out into many directions symbolising the many district Indigenous cultures across the globe.

Thokozani: My ideas have developed instead of changing. In my doctoral thesis, which is mostly being written in English, I have been sceptical when using my home language, isiZulu. When I realised that Sandra, as a Kanien'keha:ka/Mohawk situated in Canada, is also using her culture and legends to underpin her research and teaching, I was encouraged that indigenous languages could have equal status with English and any other language of European origin. I have also noticed that learners need to be assisted in merging their own cultural schemata and language so

Stories Blending, Flowing Out: Connecting Teacher Professional ... 169

that their acquisition of new knowledge can be facilitated. And, I have seen how oral communication is the crux of teaching learners any language aspect, be it listening and speaking, reading and writing, or critical evaluation of knowledge that teachers present to them.

Sandra: By sharing my piece with Thokozani and his piece with me, I have found a new respect and admiration for other cultural knowledges, languages, and situatednesses. I also have a newfound insight into one teacher's experience—a teacher who is half way around the world, yet our stories as teachers are somehow connected through ideologies surrounding teaching and learning through storytelling and cultural knowledge.

Thokozani: Sandra's explanation of how young learners became enthusiastic during story time, reminded me of how invaluable storytelling is in a teaching and learning process. I also saw how storytelling provides opportunities for sharing and collaborative learning. That became evident when learners got closer to each other during circle time. Moreover, I realised that abstract concepts become more concrete when learners see art displays such as the corn, squash, beans, and strawberries. Participatory teaching strategies such as storytelling and the use of visual artefacts can provide learners with opportunities to engage in oral communication.

Sandra: Remembering and storytelling are a significant part of the learning–teaching process. Whether we use storytelling or historical Indigenous practices as a tool for education and research, it is what manifests through this process that is important to all educators and researchers.

Thokozani: As for my doctoral research and professional learning, I have learned that I must implore my research participants to tell their stories that tap into their memories and their sociocultural and indigenous backgrounds. I have realised that my black South African teacher participants can be rich sources of indigenous knowledge that can be used enrich teaching and learning.

Kathleen: How and why could these understandings and reflections matter to educational researchers and teachers?

Thokozani: It will matter because educational researchers and teachers will be aware that indigenous knowledge is a stepping-stone that one can use to gain entrance to participants' and students' worlds. Therefore, all parties can become involved in the research, teaching, and learning. I also think using storytelling and concrete artefacts can help student teachers to start developing strategies that can be beneficial to them as future educational researchers and teachers.

Sandra: It matters that we as educators and researchers bring to light the personal and professional issues that impact our students, communities, and the cultural philosophy of education. As a researcher, it matters that I know what is taking place in the communities and areas I research because if all is left silent then all is lost. Lost, as in, we will never know how or why things are the way they are—and what we could have gained from them.

6 A Poetic Response

The mosaic pieces and conversations with Sandra and Thokozani moved Kathleen to respond by composing a series of short poems. Kathleen read and reread the mosaic pieces and dialogue piece to highlight and extract words that spoke to the lived experiences and impact of the storytelling described by Sandra and Thokozani. These words then became material for creating poetry (Pithouse-Morgan 2016). Inspired by the voices of Sandra and Thokozani, Kathleen arranged her chosen words in a series of short poems titled "Story Circle," using the concise 5-line Japanese lantern[1] poem format (Hittle 2014). In Kathleen's understanding, this string of lantern poems, which can be read vertically and horizontally, illuminates multiple possibilities of storywork for communicating and responding to diverse and similar human memories, knowledges, and understandings in generative ways that can open up new pathways across contexts.

Story Circle

Breath	Weave	Words	Grow
Embers	Stories	Blending	Flourish
Smoke rising	Move tighter	Flowing out	Connecting
Flickering flames	We are so close	Like vines toward	Past in present
Voice	Warmth	Space	Time

7 Opening up New Pathways Across Contexts

Storytelling as an artful research practice "enables the researcher to engage with the stories and histories of families, communities, and cultures and to begin the transformative process of understanding oneself in relation" (Iseke 2013, p. 573). Thus, researching teacher professional learning through storywork is congruent with conceptualisations of learning, teaching, and researching as experiential, developmental processes that take place though relationships and dialogue with others, as well as through interaction with social communities and customs (Bruner 1996; Dewey 1938/1963; Van Manen 1990). From such perspectives, learning, teaching, and researching are intimately connected with the past, present, and future lives of learners, teachers, and researchers who make sense and communicate through stories.

---

[1] The Japanese lantern poem consists of five lines with a composition of one, two, three, four, and one syllables per line. The meaning of the closing line should connect back to the meaning of the opening line. The lantern poem is also a shape poem due to the Japanese lantern-like shape formed when the lines are centred to the middle (Hittle 2014).

The juxtaposition of Sandra Owén:nakon Deer-Standup and Thokozani Ndaleni's mosaic pieces exemplifies a convergence of re-membering and storytelling as professional teacher learning processes through which ideas, knowledges, and understandings can emerge. Also, the mosaic pieces show how re-membering and storytelling can come together as evocative learning resources, through which teacher-researchers and others can engage with personal insights and culturally imbued ways of knowing and being. Mutual respect, reciprocity, and resonances between Sandra Owén:nakon Deer-Standup's and Thokozani Ndaleni's research, conducted on different continents, demonstrate how implicit, intuitive ways of knowing and being—developed over generations through story circles in families, homes, and communities—can be made visible and be revalued. Their dialogue reveals how, as teacher-researchers re-member their own stories and encounter others' stories, they can make new sense of their past and present learning, and reenvision stories of the future.

Acknowledgement We are grateful to our peer reviewer, Monica Taylor (Montclair State University, USA) whose critically constructive response enabled us to strengthen this chapter.

References

Antone, E., & Córdoba, T. (2005). *Re-storying Aboriginal adult literacy: A wholistic approach.* Retrieved from http://www.casae-aceea.ca/~casae/sites/casae/archives/cnf2005/2005onlineProc eedings/CAS2005Pro-Antone.pdf.

Archibald, J. (2001). Editorial: Sharing Aboriginal knowledge and Aboriginal ways of knowing. *Canadian Journal of Native Education, 25*(1), 1–5.

Archibald, J. (2008). An indigenous storywork methodology. In J. G. Knowles & A. L. Cole (Eds.), *Handbook of the arts in qualitative research* (pp. 371–393). Thousand Oaks: SAGE.

Armstrong, J. C. (1987). Traditional Indigenous education: A natural process. *Canadian Journal of Native Education, 14*(3), 14–19.

Badley, G. (2017). "Manifold creatures": A response to the posthumanist challenge. *Qualitative Inquiry.* https://doi.org/10.1177/1077800417729839.

Bruner, J. S. (1996). *The culture of education.* Cambridge: Harvard University Press.

Burke, R. W. (2002). Social and emotional education in the classroom. *Kappa Delta Pi Record, 38*(3), 108–111.

Chapman, T. K. (2005). Expressions of "voice" in portraiture. *Qualitative Inquiry, 11*(1). Retrieved from http://qix.sagepub.com/content/11/1/27.

Deer-Standup, S. (2013). *An investigation of the role of legends and storytelling in a Kanien'kehá:ka (Mohawk) early childhood facility* (Unpublished master's thesis). McGill University, Canada.

Dewey, J. (1963). *Experience and education.* New York: Collier. (Original work published 1938).

Doyle, T. (2011). *Learner-centered teaching: Putting research into practice.* Sterling: Stylus.

Duryea LeBaron, M., & Potts, J. (1993). Story and legend: Powerful tools for conflict resolution. *Mediation Quarterly, 10*(4), 387–395.

Faries, E. (2004). *Research paper on Aboriginal curriculum in Ontario.* Retrieved from http://www.chiefs-of-ontario.org/sites/default/files/files/A%20Research%20Paper%20on%20Aborigi nal%20Curriculum%20in%20Ontario.pdf.

Friesen, J. W., & Friesen, V. L. (2007). *Storytelling makes a comeback: Aboriginal contributions to the teaching/learning process.* Retrieved from https://www.researchgate.net/publication/2674 15797_STORY_TELLING_MAKES_A_COMEBACK_ABORIGINAL_CONTRIBUTIONS_ TO_THE_TEACHINGLEARNING_PROCESS.

Gunn Allan, P. (1992). *The sacred hoop: Recovering the feminine in American Indian traditions.* Boston: Beacon Press.

Haarhoff, D. (1998). *The writer's voice: A workbook for writers in Africa.* Halfway House: Zebra Press.

Haug, F. (n.d.). *Memory-work as a method of social science research: A detailed rendering of memory-work method.* Retrieved from http://www.friggahaug.inkrit.de/documents/memorywor k-researchguidei7.pdf.

Haug, F. (1987). *Female sexualization: A collective work of memory* (E. Carter, Trans.). London: Verso.

Haug, F. (2008). Memory work. *Australian Feminist Studies, 23*(58), 537–541.

Hittle, D. (2014). *Writing a Japanese lantern poem.* Retrieved from http://playfullearning.net/201 4/11/writing-a-japanese-lantern-poem/.

Ho'omanawanui, K. (2010). Mana Wahine, education and nation-building: Lesson from the Epic of Pele and Hi'iaka for Kanaka Maoli Today. *Multicultural Perspectives, 12*(4), 206–212.

Iseke, J. (2013). Indigenous storytelling as research. *International Review of Qualitative Research, 6*(4), 559–577.

Janda, R. C. (2010). *CALL-based instruction: Toward the teaching of speech and oral communication at Angeles University Foundation.* Retrieved from http://www.asian-efl-journal.com/PDF/T he_Asian_EFL_JournalCEBU_conf.pdf.

Kanu, Y. (2006). Reappropriating traditions in the postcolonial curricular imagination. In Y. Kanu (Ed.), *Curriculum as cultural practice: Postcolonial imaginations* (pp. 203–222). Toronto: University of Toronto Press.

Kirkness, V. J. (1995). Aboriginal peoples and tertiary education in Canada: Institutional responses. *The London Journal of Canadian Studies, 11,* 28–40.

Lewis, P. J. (2011). Storytelling as research/research as storytelling. *Qualitative Inquiry, 17*(6), 505–510.

Lutz, H., & Moritz-Arndt, E. (1995). First Nations literature in Canada and the voice of survival. *The London Journal of Canadian Studies, 11,* 60–76.

Mitchell, C., & Pithouse-Morgan, K. (2014). Expanding the memory catalogue: Southern African women's contributions to memory-work writing as a feminist research methodology. *Agenda, 28*(1), 92–103.

Mitchell, C., & Weber, S. (1998). The usable past: Teachers (re)playing school. *Changing English, 5*(1), 45–56.

Mitchell, C., & Weber, S. (1999). *Reinventing ourselves as teachers: Beyond nostalgia.* London: Falmer.

Mkhize, N. (2004). Sociocultural approaches to psychology: Dialogism and African connections of the self. In K. Ratele, N. Duncan, D. Hook, N. Mkhize, P. Kiguwa, & A. Collins (Eds.), *Self, community & psychology* (pp. 5–31). Lansdowne: University of Cape Town Press.

Ndaleni, T. (2013). *Teaching English oral communication to isiZulu-speaking learners in a secondary school: A self-study* (Unpublished master's thesis). University of KwaZulu-Natal, South Africa. Retrieved from http://researchspace.ukzn.ac.za/handle/10413/11506.

Pence, A., Rodriquez de France, C., Greenwood, M., & Pacini-Ketchabaw, V. (2007). Indigenous approaches to early childhood care and education: Introduction. *The Canadian Journal of Native Education, 30*(1), 1–4.

Pithouse, K. (2011). "The future of our young children lies in our hands": Re-envisaging teacher authority through narrative self-study. In C. Mitchell, T. Strong-Wilson, K. Pithouse, & S. Allnutt (Eds.), *Memory and pedagogy* (pp. 177–190). New York: Routledge.

Pithouse-Morgan, K. (2016). Finding my self in a new place: Exploring professional learning through found poetry. *Teacher Learning and Professional Development, 1*(1), 1–18. Retrieved from http://journals.sfu.ca/tlpd/index.php/tlpd/article/view/1.

Rahman, M. M. (2010). Teaching oral communications: A task-based approach. *ESP, 9*(1), 1–11.

Samaras, A. P. (2011). *Self-study teacher research: Improving your practice through collaborative inquiry.* Thousand Oaks: SAGE.

Samaras, A. P., Hicks, M. A., & Berger, J. G. (2004). Self-study through personal history. In J. J. Loughran, M. L. Hamilton, V. K. LaBoskey, & T. Russell (Eds.), *International handbook of self-study of teaching and teacher education practices* (Vol. 2, pp. 905–942). Dordrecht: Kluwer.

Storrs, D. (2012). 'Keeping it real' with an emotional curriculum. *Teaching in Higher Education, 17*(1), 1–12.

Strong-Wilson, T. (2008). *Bringing memory forward: Storied remembrance in social justice education with teachers*. New York: Peter Lang.

Van Manen, M. (1990). *Researching lived experience: Human science for an action sensitive pedagogy*. Albany: State University of New York Press.

Ethically Significant Moments in Stirring up Memories

Claudia Mitchell, Sifiso Magubane, Casey Burkholder and Sheeren Saloojee

Abstract "Ethically Significant Moments in Stirring Up Memories" by Claudia Mitchell, Sifiso Magubane, Casey Burkholder, and Sheeren Saloojee, points to the issue of ethics in artful engagement as an area that is under-explored in memory-work and self-study. Sifiso Magubane, a South African teacher-researcher, considers the emotional challenges in getting permission to use the photograph of a close friend of his who has died. Casey Burkholder, studying at a Canadian university, considers some of the tensions in preservice teachers producing cellphilms about their own personal histories and, especially, the politics of exclusion. Finally, Sheeren Saloojee, who is completing a doctoral study at a South African university, addresses an issue seldom discussed in relation to vulnerability in social research—that of the emotional well-being of the researcher, especially in relation to what it means to carry around and represent the stories of the participants. The three mosaic pieces highlight situational ethics and ethics of the personal, both aspects of "doing most good" and "doing least harm" that rarely appear in any guide or any ethics policy.

Keywords Arts-based research · Canada · Cellphilms · Ethics · Interviews Memory-work · Photographs · South Africa · Teacher professional learning

---

C. Mitchell (✉)
Department of Integrated Studies in Education, McGill University, Montreal, Canada
e-mail: claudia.mitchell@mcgill.ca

C. Mitchell · S. Magubane · S. Saloojee
School of Education, University of KwaZulu-Natal, Durban, South Africa
e-mail: daddmagubane@gmail.com

S. Saloojee
e-mail: sheereensaloojee@gmail.com

C. Burkholder
Faculty of Education, University of New Brunswick, Fredericton, Canada
e-mail: casey.burkholder@unb.ca

© Springer Nature Switzerland AG 2019
K. Pithouse-Morgan et al. (eds.), *Memory Mosaics: Researching Teacher Professional Learning Through Artful Memory-work*, Studies in Arts-Based Educational Research 2, https://doi.org/10.1007/978-3-319-97106-3_10

1 Setting the Scene

This chapter highlights the ways in which memory-work through narrative and the visual carries with it particular ethical challenges. It is a chapter this is, we think, long overdue in that it pertains to tensions and quandaries that often left out of the procedural ethics of Institutional Review Boards (IRBs). As Posel and Ross (2012) observed:

> Much attention has been paid to professional codes of ethics and disciplinary ethical guidelines, as well as to theoretical and philosophical reflections on the manner of appropriately ethical research practice. A far smaller proportion of the books and articles on the subject deal with ethical conflicts and conundrums that arise in the thick of fieldwork, when researchers have to respond as human beings as much as exponents of disciplinary ethical codes, and when the unanticipated complexities of social relationships in the field throw up the latent tensions or ambiguities in the codes themselves (p. 1).

While—for good reason—there has been extensive attention given to informed consent in working with vulnerable populations such as children and young people, the mosaics in this chapter draw attention to the various forms of vulnerability in doing memory-work. We describe these ethical concerns—in relation to ourselves and to others (colleagues, students, and family members) as revealed through our stories. What does it mean to do "least harm" and "most good" in our work with teachers and memory-work? As Strong-Wilson et al. (2014) and Strong-Wilson et al. (2016) highlighted in their consideration of multidirectional memory-work through the digital, self-study research involving innovative arts-based approaches such as photography and digital media can raise new questions in relation to ethical issues. At the same time, the issue of stirring up memories in self-study and memory-work research goes beyond the visual. What can we learn, then, by looking across a range of case studies and arts-based methods?

The order of the exemplars highlights working with different arts-based frameworks, starting with the visual and running to the narrative. The first two exemplars deal with the visual. Sifiso Magubane's self-study research at a South African university looks at the significance of intrinsic motivation for learning, focusing on particularly sensitive issues in working with photographs. A second set of ethical dilemmas is described by Casey Burkholder, who at a Canadian university used cellphilms (cell phones + video) with preservice teachers in order to explore issues of personal history in the teaching of primary and secondary school social studies curriculum. As a third exemplar, Sheeren Saloojee considers the role of ethics in her "stirring up memories" arts-based, feminist work with women in a postgraduate program at a South African university. In her work, she highlights some of the ways in which feminist research might in and of itself contribute to particular ethical challenges.

Ethically Significant Moments in Stirring up Memories

2 Three Sets of Ethical Moments

2.1 The Emotional Ethics of Data Generation: Behind Every Lesson There Is Another Lesson

by Sifiso Magubane

Setting the Scene

I am a schoolteacher working in a historically black township in the province of KwaZulu-Natal in South Africa. I am an isiZulu speaker who grew up in a rural area of KwaZulu-Natal. In this mosaic piece, I reflect on ethical issues I encountered during the master's of education research I conducted as a Grade 9 technology teacher (Magubane 2014).

In my self-study research in which I draw on the work of Samaras (2011) and others, I looked at my own practices as a teacher in the context of cultivating intrinsic motivation for learning technology in a township high school. Intrinsic motivation can be viewed as engagement in a task being driven by the feeling of pleasure, delight, and excitement (Lee et al. 2005). I explored how I as a teacher could try to ensure that my learners would remain intrinsically motivated so as to make learning technology more enjoyable and interesting for them.

Memory-Work Self-Study

My first critical question for my self-study research was: "What can I learn about cultivating intrinsic motivation for learning by remembering my most motivational or 'demotivational' experiences as a learner?" The method I used to respond to this question was memory-work self-study, which as Samaras (2011) wrote, "is used to represent autobiographical inquiry with critical and reflective revisiting" (p. 103). Memory-work self-study allowed me to deeply engage with my educational past and learn from it. In order to trigger and represent relevant memories, I used the research practices of oral storytelling and artefact retrieval.

Oral Storytelling

To enhance my personal memory-work, I invited two former school friends to help me relive, through oral storytelling, the experiences we shared as learners and friends. This pair of participants consisted of two black African men who are between 30 and 40 years old and are professionals in other fields of work. Their names are Sipho and Mandla (pseudonyms). For data generation with these school friends, I organised a 1-day informal meeting, which was more like reunion. I first explained to them that I was conducting a study and that I might use whatever would transpire in our meeting as data for the study. They gave consent for me to draw on our discussion for my research. As Masinga (2012) explained, through telling stories of the past, important events are evoked, and the manner in which they are later recalled is valuable to the formation and reformation of self. I found sharing school stories with my friends to be very evocative of our long forgotten experiences. As we were narrating our lived stories together, when the teller missed a certain event in a story others would stop him and remind him. This helped me to capture many significant events of our lives.

As the three of us come from a Zulu cultural heritage that is traditionally characterised by oral storytelling, this activity became very easy and enjoyable for us. The Zulu people are known as a nation that has a rich history of passing their cultural beliefs from one generation to the next through oral storytelling rather than through writing them down. Our oral storytelling sometimes brought back some painful experiences that I may have wanted to quickly forget about and move on. But, having my friends to share these stories made me feel more comfortable in exploring past experiences, whether positive or negative. I think the issue of trust played a major role here. It was through mutual trust that we managed to laugh together about what were some really painful stories.

The exercise of reminiscing about our past seemed to be very touching to all three of us because the stories that we discussed were about all of us. I remember how Mandla seemed to be touched by the remembrances of how he managed to start his tertiary education after his family had made it clear that they could not afford to pay for his education. I also remember the admiration we all had for our community members and our parents after Sipho reminded us about their contribution to our education.

Artefact Retrieval
An artefact, as a symbol, can stand for, signify, and help us to articulate our research interests in a non-linguistic manner (Samaras 2011). Mitchell et al. (2009, p. 127) affirmed that "photographs act as powerful memory prompts." For example, through reviewing my high school photographs, I was able to realise the roles played by my teachers, friends, parents, and the community in my educational life. My high school photographs had been in my photo album for more than 20 years, but when I looked at them as artefacts, they give different meaning to my educational life. When I began to look at my high school photographs through a researcher's lens, various emotions were triggered. For example, I felt sad when reminiscing about my high school classmates and teachers who had passed on. I felt the tears in my eyes as I recalled how one of our classmates was brutally killed in 1994 during political violence and also when I recalled the day I was injured when I was playing soccer at school. Through reliving these emotions, I gained a deeper insight into how those past encounters have shaped my life.

In the case of photographs where people's faces were visible, I chose to meet with these people to explain everything verbally and I received their consent to use the photographs in my research. Figure 1 is an example of such a photograph.

In the background of the photograph, there are two blocks of the school where I completed my high school education. Viewing these buildings in this photograph brings back many memories of my high school years, both positive and negative. I remember those elderly women who came to school during break time, to sell to us *amakota* (a tasty quarter of bread cut into two equal slices buttered with margarine, with a roasted egg or slice of polony). Although I did not always have money to buy

Fig. 1 Sifiso: The student by day, warrior by night. This is a photograph of myself (on the left) with my two friends who were pretending to be fighting

ikota, everytime when I had money, I would buy one for myself. That was indeed a mouthwatering meal and when we ate it, we enjoyed it.

The photograph also reminds me of the harsh conditions of the rural school with no electricity, no running water, and no computer even in the principal's office. Our classes had broken windows that forced us to sit very close to each other in winter in order to keep each other warm during lessons. The school was built of bricks and the roof was made of corrugated iron without a ceiling board, which made the classrooms very cold in winter and unbearably hot in summer. I remember that when there was heavy rain during teaching hours, the teacher could not continue with the lesson because of the noise caused by the rain as it hit the roof of the classroom. We learners used to love that because it meant that we would be left unattended and to find time to make noise and chase each other around in the classroom. When I think about this now, I believe it is not that we did not want to learn, but, like most children, we loved playing more than learning.

One of the friends who appear in this photograph passed on in the early 2000s. Therefore, I went to his family to ask for permission to use the photo in my research. I did this for the purpose of addressing ethical issues because among the three of us in the photo he is the only one who had died and therefore I could not get the permission directly from him. I had to be cautious about this because of the emotions involved. I got the authority to use that photograph from his family members and his younger brother asked me if I could give him a copy of my thesis as a memento. He further told me how he missed his brother. I too felt emotional. Also, the other friend who appears in the photograph asked me to give him a copy of the photograph because it reminded him of "those days." To me, these responses indicated the significance for others of remembering one's personal history.

Conclusion

While in a process of addressing ethical issues, we may uncover very important things and that includes even changing lives of some people. Amazingly this will happen when we least expect it because when we plan to meet those people, very often we cannot foresee the possible aftereffects of that interaction. Hence, we do not cater for or even think about what can transpire from those meetings. When I reflected on my encounter with my high school friends, I learned that the spontaneity and the originality of the feelings that both the researcher and the participants go through during that interaction are very important. As part of writing this mosaic piece, I decided to go back to Mandla and Sipho to find out about the aftereffects of the meeting that we had about four years ago. I simply asked each one to write a brief e-mail and send it to me. I also asked their permission to draw on their e-mails for this chapter. Below is an extract Mandla's e-mail in which he shared with me an effect of our encounter:

> My experience was that interview was more of a conversation than a formal interview i.e. question/answer session. That conversation led me to an introspection. The introspection was on whether or not I had reached all my educational goals or maximum potential. The answer was no, and I asked myself what to do next. I thought, "further education."

From this extract, I draw attention to the word *introspection*; this is what I referred to as the aftereffect because it happened after our meeting. I now realise that it was all left to Mandla to deal with the aftereffect; I was not even aware that after our meeting my friends had to deal with such questions from within.

In the e-mail Mandla further mentioned that he was "silently afraid to do a master's degree prior to the meeting/interview, but after realising that a person [such as me] who comes from [his] background is doing it [he] believed that [he] could also do it." On Monday after the weekend of our meeting, Mandla went to the university to start the registration process for a Master of Laws (LLM) degree. On the 7th of April 2017, he graduated and he asked me to accompany him to the graduation ceremony. In his e-mail, he wrote: "If it was not for that meeting we had, I would not have even thought about doing LLM."

My other high school friend, Sipho, is also now doing his fourth year in a Bachelor of Arts programme, specialising in community development. He told me that after our meeting he decided to change his place of work. At the time of our meeting, he was working for the same employer but in a branch that is in the deep rural area where it was going to be very difficult to further his studies while working there. Therefore he decided to move to a city branch where studying would be easier because the university is nearby. I also had an opportunity to talk to him about his academic development after we had that meeting. He shared similar views to Mandla about how he felt after our meeting. Sipho said he felt our school days' spirit of "never say die" being revived within and that he was motivated to further his studies. He told

Ethically Significant Moments in Stirring up Memories

me that he has decided that when he finishes the degree that he is currently doing, he is going for a master's degree. He kept on saying, "We laid a good foundation for ourselves."

From my self-study research, I learned how significant emotional aspects are to the process of addressing ethical issues. Therefore, I learned that we as researchers need to be careful at all times when we interact with other people in the course of our studies, thus ensuring that we do least harm and most good. For example, I quote what Mandla wrote about his involvement in my study:

> It just reminded me where do I come from—the life battles that I conquered, the motivational figures in my life and the people who see us as exemplary in our community. It brought back victor feeling that I had not felt in a long time.

If Mandla went through these serious emotions as a consequence of that meeting, then I feel that we have many souls that we touch daily either positively or negatively as we undertake our studies. Sadly, we do not often make time to go back to find out how have we impacted on the lives of people who became part of our studies. A key lesson that I have learned is about the importance of being sensitive when you generate data with your participants. This became evident when I observed how certain activities that you do with your participants can sometimes stir emotions. I learned that the line that separates sad and happy memories is very thin; therefore, if the method of data generation is memory-work self-study, we need to be very careful. Failing to take necessary precautions, we may find ourselves causing more harm and less good.

2.2 Personal History in Teaching History: A Case for Visual Ethics in Teaching Social Studies

by Casey Burkholder

Introduction

Memory-work has infused my practice in my work as a social studies teacher educator in Prince Edward Island, Canada. As Conrad et al. (2013, p. 10) argued:

> Reflecting on the past is a learned skill, and many Canadians are adept at it. Others have only an unconscious sense of the role that history plays in defining their identity and agency. Canadians weave fabrics of meaning from a warp of personal, deeply felt, highly connected memories, and a woof of critical, distant, disconnected histories…. As a vehicle for legitimizing or destabilizing power relations, maintaining or undermining community identities, and challenging the way we see ourselves collectively and individually, history can take us in many directions.

In this context, I like to begin my social studies methods course with two activities. For the first activity, I ask students to describe the object that they have with them that is the most valuable. Some students have talked about their credit cards, laptops, or their smartphones, while others described heirloom jewellery, notebooks, or digital artefacts (such as a saved voicemail from a loved one) and the memories connected with these items. I do this exercise to get the students thinking about what it means to give value to certain items over others, hoping to make connections between our ideas of value and the people, events, and spaces that are valued within social studies curricula. These decisions are subjective and personal, and even the definition of *valuable* creates a great deal of discussion within the classroom.

The second activity teaches a simple poetry lesson, while asking learners to remember their hometowns. This "I am From" poetry activity was introduced by a colleague during my teacher education at Acadia University in 2006. The instructor prompts the learners to "picture their hometowns." Then, the learners are guided to fill in a series of statements with three descriptive adjectives. "Title: I am from _____. I see _____. I hear _____. I smell _____. I taste _____. It is _____. _____ [Name of hometown]." The students fill in the blanks, and then they are advised to delete the prompts, "I am from, I see, I hear, I smell, and so forth." What remains is a poem that evokes their hometown. I always begin by sharing my own "I am From" poem before eliciting student responses.

> Fort Smith.
>
> Skinny pines, candy-coloured government housing, graffiti on the pavement after high school grad.
>
> The roar of the Slave River, stories from elders, someone calling out, "Bear! Get the kids inside!"
>
> Fall's wild cranberries, Winter campfires, Spring's first crocuses.
>
> Smoked fish from the Salt River, bannock over a fire, trapper butter (lard + maple syrup).
>
> Garden capital of the North, a place to learn about place and privilege, both a small and big town.
>
> Fort Smith.

These two activities lead into work with the visual, specifically working with cellphilm production. Students are prompted to identify values and the ways in which personal histories are intimately connected to specific images. This connection between memory, history, and the visual is then brought forth in the course material, in particular through cellphilms (cell phone + video making) as explored by Dockney and Tomaselli (2009), MacEntee et al. (2016), and Mitchell and de Lange (2013).

What About the Visual?

Exploring personal histories is necessary in critical social studies methods education, as preservice teachers explore curricular spaces where they feel included and excluded. However, this becomes more complex when memory-work includes the visual. Personal and community histories infuse teachers' understanding of and response to state-sponsored curricula. Intersections of privilege and confirmations of dominant identities and histories are rife in state-sponsored curricula. What does this mean for critical social studies teacher education, and what does memory-work have to do with it? By exploring personal and family histories, preservice social studies teachers may begin to wonder: whose histories and experiences are included in social studies curricula? Whose histories and experiences are excluded? How might we go about teaching an inclusive social studies method that both problematizes dominant national discourses and deepens an understanding of why certain histories and experiences are excluded? At the same time, looking back on personal histories become more ethically complex when preservice teachers are asked to create visual representation of their histories through short cellphilms. What ethical concerns arise from asking preservice teachers to mine their personal histories and family artefacts to create visual representations of their own histories through cellphilms? And, what procedures may be put in place in order to address these ethical concerns and complexities as teachers employ visual artefacts such as archival photographs of family and friends? What happens to these cellphilms over time, and how might they be shared?

What Is Included in a Cellphilm Assignment?
With these questions in mind, I describe a cellphilm-making assignment that I conducted with a group of nine preservice secondary social studies teachers in 2014, as well as the procedures that I have implemented to address visual ethics in the projects. I asked the preservice teachers to create a 60–90 s cellphilm that explored the prompt, "Histories, Geographies, and Notions of Citizenship." I began by prompting with the following suggestions to guide the preservice teacher cellphilms, though students were not bound to these suggestions:

- Present an aspect of history, geography, or citizenship (an actor, a place, an issue, an event, or time period).
- Illuminate questions, issues, or even gaps that arise in making sense of Canadian history, geography, and/or citizenship education (as we understand it today).
- Interrogate your role as a social studies educator who will teach students about citizenship and Canadian history (historically and moving forward).

  Keep in mind:

- Your cellphilm must be shot on a cell phone. You can shoot the whole thing in one shot (or using a pause button), or you can use an in-phone editing application, shoot multiple takes, or use stop motion animation, and so forth.
- You should try to keep the audience in mind. Who do you imagine your audience to be? What might they want to know? Is it me (Casey) the instructor? Is it your colleagues? Is it your future students? Your family? Your audience will shape the way in which you tell the story (particularly what you choose to disclose, and what you choose to edit out of the story).
- Your cellphilm must be at least 60 s long, and should be no longer than 90 s in length.

After presenting these general directives within one 3-h class period, I took the students through a modified cellphilm workshop. Briefly, the cellphilm workshop included a brainstorming session, where students decided if they wanted to work in groups or individually, and they thought about a narrative that might speak to (or speak back to) the prompt. Students then created a 6-panel storyboard where they planned dialogue, narration, music, and the specific images that would accompany before moving onto the filming. Because of their existing media-making practices (avid users of social media video sharing on sites like Instagram and YouTube), I encouraged the students to download and experiment with a free in-phone editing application while they filmed. The students returned to the classroom with their video, spent some time editing it, and then we sat down to screen the student cellphilms. Following the screening, we decided to create a playlist of the cellphilms that we might choose to show in our future teaching practices, but we decided not to share the playlist on social media. Since then, some cellphilms have been removed from the playlist, while a few remain. After the workshop was completed and I had provided feedback for the assignment,[1] some ethical considerations remained.

Ethical Considerations

I asked the students to ensure that they did not film people in any identifiable way without their consent, and suggested that they might instead film crowds from a distance, or close-ups of hands or feet to ensure that people not be identified. Of course, not all the students listened to these directives. In fact, some of the most persuasive cellphilms—including one where a student filmed an antiabortion protest on campus and spoke to the protestors—used identifiable images through a documentary style, though the students insisted that they had received prior informed consent from any participants. The issue of identifiable images is a critical ethical concern in this work because the students created a narrative that linked antichoice protest with specific identifiable actors. What becomes increasingly complex is what happens to the cellphilms over time. While the cellphilm participants might absolutely consent to being filmed for a few moments at the time, what happens when the cellphilm remains "out there" in a digital archival space, like YouTube? What happens if those people who protested were identified by others, such as employers? Here, the space between cellphilm as research artifact, cellphilm as assignment, and cellphilm as art piece becomes blurry. In a piece of film, or art, people might be filmed without their consent as fair use. But, what about these pedagogical projects where preservice teachers might share the cellphilms or even screen them at a later date with their students? What about preservice teachers who take cellphilming on with their own students? Will they remember to discuss ethical issues, such as anonymity and using unidentifiable imagery with their students? And what happens if they don't? Ethical risks abound, particularly when creating identifiable images in cellphilm work with youth.

Another issue that arose during the student cellphilms was the use of archival photographs, including images of children and people who are now deceased. Does informed consent pass on when a person has gone? Who decides if and how these images might be included or excluded in the student cellphilms? Each of the students who used these archival images chose photographs that showed themselves as chil-

---

[1] The students were provided with a pass/fail grade, with formative feedback (comments and a rubric). A failing grade would result in a redo but in this iteration, no student was asked to redo the assignment.

Ethically Significant Moments in Stirring up Memories

dren, or family members who had an impact on them (such as grandparents). While anonymity is an important factor in the research in terms of receiving informed consent from all participants pictured in the cellphilm, as I mention above, this becomes complex when the students believe that they have consent from family members who cannot give consent (e.g., they are no longer living).

Other ethical challenges emerged in the cellphilm assignment related to issues of ownership, audiences, and archiving the cellphilms. While participants sent their cellphilms to my e-mail through their own YouTube accounts, and I created an unlisted[2] playlist of the cellphilms on YouTube, this practice is not entirely confidential. Any person who viewed the cellphilms on the playlist might highlight the individual videos and learn about other videos that the filmmaker had previously uploaded. This practice can be problematic for preservice teachers (or any research participant) who might not want one video to lead to their other videos. In later iterations of this assignment, and in later research projects, I have taken this into consideration by creating a YouTube account where all participants share the password. Going forward, however, participants may choose to delete their cellphilms from the instructor-created YouTube playlist (see Burkholder 2016).

Beyond these considerations, it is important to consider, specifically as it confronts issues of the personal and confronts curricular exclusions, how to create upfront, ongoing, and culturally safe consent (Flicker et al. 2015; Schwab-Cartas 2012) in ethnically and culturally heterogeneous classrooms and research spaces. In this classroom, the instructor was a white, middle-class woman, and the students were all white, middle class, and most had grown up in Prince Edward Island. The histories presented in the social studies curricula largely included the stories of some ancestors (white, European) to the exclusion of others. In Prince Edward Island, in particular, complex representations of Mi'kmaq peoples, their histories, and ties to the land have been largely excluded from much of the curriculum.

A key question that remains for me is how an ethic of culturally safe consent can be brought to the cellphilm assignment when it is used in different contexts, such as classroom spaces with heterogeneous groups, including Indigenous peoples, African-Canadians, and other people of colour. In Indigenous spaces, how might elders and knowledge holders be brought into the cellphilm process to provide guidance about what should be included in curricular spaces? How can the cellphilm assignment be tailored to ensure that students are given space to speak back to curricular exclusions, but at the same time do not feel pressured to put their own cultures and histories on display if they do not want to share?

---

[2]When a user uploads a video to YouTube, they have the option to choose three privacy settings: private (where only the video maker can see the video), unlisted (where the video may be viewed by anyone who has the link), and public (where any YouTube user may see the video).

2.3 Stirring Up Memories

by Sheeren Saloojee

Introduction

In this mosaic piece, I reflect on ethical moments in my doctoral study (Saloojee 2017). The focus of my narrative inquiry was on exploring educational experiences of African postgraduate women students at my university in the province of KwaZulu-Natal, South Africa. In the study, I worked with two coresearchers, Zanele and Thabile,[3] and their experiences of learning at the university as postgraduate women students from African countries outside of South Africa. Being an African postgraduate woman student myself, my interest was in finding out about their lived lives and daily experiences.

At the beginning of the study, I was conscious of the advice of DeVault (1996) who believes feminist researchers are united through various efforts to include women's lives and concerns in accounts of society, to minimize the harms of research, and to support changes that will improve women's status. Knowing that women's experiences have been historically subject to interpretation by men or there has been an assumed incorporation of women's experiences as the same as men (Smeal 1984), I wanted to position myself as a feminist researcher by seeking to benefit or empower my female coresearchers. In preparing to interview Zanele and Thabile, I was fully aware that they would reflect on their past and recall memories. I felt that I needed to be a person who the women would want to talk to and I needed to create an atmosphere where they could speak openly, knowing that they would be heard. In this way, I prepared myself to elicit rich, cocreated stories from Zanele and Thabile.

From the start of this study, my coresearchers, Zanele and Thabile, were keen to be engaged, especially because their voices have been silenced in the past. They said they felt "powered" by my interest in their lives as African women postgraduate students. In order to try to balance the power relations in eliciting Zanele and Thabile's lived experiences and diversity I tried to present a clear picture of myself to them—as a South African Muslim woman, a mother of three, middle class, and a schoolteacher. This meant that I was similar in many ways to them, but also different in many ways.

This Constant Feeling of Guilt

Thabile, one of my coresearchers, became extremely emotional during her interview when relating an experience of her young days trying to make it in the big world. She talked of some form of abuse where sex was involved and how ashamed she was. She then became fearful at the thought that her secret was now in the open. In the past, I have had family and friends who poured their hearts out to me and I could contain them, but I felt that I could not contain Thabile. As a novice researcher, I must admit that I was not prepared to handle the situation with Thabile who had experienced this kind of trauma. I immediately questioned myself on how was I to manage this sensitive issue because there was always a concern that this research

---

[3] Both names are pseudonyms.

Ethically Significant Moments in Stirring up Memories

must be ethical, in that it must not cause any harm to those being researched, and that it must give voice to the voiceless. I remember reading about the notion of, the *dialectic of trauma* put forward by Herman (1992, pp. 47–50), where she suggests that individuals who have suffered trauma are motivated simultaneously to forget (repression) and to remember (through intrusions) the trauma. The former is in order to avoid the painful effects of trauma. A feeling of failure overcame me as I could not believe that, as the researcher, I could then be responsible for evoking these traumatic memories of Thabile as part of the data producing process.

I realized that the reemergence of this traumatic episode in Thabile's life was debilitating when it resurfaced in her memory, as she spoke. I immediately stopped the audio recording and gave her hug and assured her that everything was fine. After about 20 min, her crying became more of a panic attack. She was anxious that her supervisor and boyfriend, whom I know very well, might find out what she said in the interview. I reassured that I was ethically and professionally bound to observe confidentiality and could not relate anything she had said to them but she kept on questioning me and her hand movements made me extremely scared. The fact that she exhibited such extreme emotions made me feel sad because I felt that as a woman I was evoking pain on another woman, something feminist scholars warn against (DeVault 1996). It was therefore a very emotional interview for me. When Thabile became so emotionally disturbed by the data production process it became an ethical dilemma for this study and it brought up serious ethical concerns about whether or not I, as a novice researcher, was in the position to research women's lives directly.

Nevertheless, I had to deal with this challenge. In keeping with confidentiality, I erased the audio recording in front of Thabile. Even though the interview of her experiences would have been rich data for my study, I took a decision that no data was more important than her well-being. A few hours later on that same day I called her to see how she was doing, but the phone just rang and rang. The same thing happened the next day. It was only when I put my caller identity off did she take the call. We chatted and even laughed at a point. But she never allowed me to interview her again and opted out of the study. Although I took steps to mitigate the challenges and dilemmas I faced with her, in the end I was left feeling as though I had let her down. There was a constant feeling of guilt. I was indeed disturbed by this.

As I work with the study at present, I constantly feel that I have not resolved this ethical dilemma. But in my heart, I still feel that this study could have being an opportunity for her to "set the record straight." I constantly think of her and question whether I failed to give her voice.

From the experience I encountered with Thabile, I have come to believe this is just what the research is all about. As researchers, we seem to prepare our coresearchers for events that could not go as planned but seldom do we prepare ourselves on how to cope with such deviation. This also bears testimony to how life history interviews are time consuming and never go as planned (Boyce and Neale 2006; Patton 2002). The literature more often describes interviews where the researcher is the guest of the participant (Finch 1984; Limerick et al. 1996; Oakley 1981), suggesting a power imbalance in favour of the participant. The balance of power in my study seems to be a complex and shifting dynamic.

"That's Not what I Said!"

Dealing with Thabile's issue, I thought, was the ultimate dilemma I as the researcher could face in my study. Little did I realize that an issue with the other coresearcher, Zanele, could force me to want to put an end to my study. Zanele had just completed her master's degree and was deciding to register for her doctoral studies. When I initially e-mailed Zanele a copy of her reconstructed story, she responded simply by indicating that I had misspelt the name of her village and that she had enjoyed reading it.

Soon after this, a personal tragedy hit my family. My eldest sister took ill one day and passed on the next day, leaving behind four children, who became my responsibility. So, for a year I had to put my study on hold as it became too difficult for me to prioritize my postgraduate student identity. When I recommitted myself to my study after a year and got immersed with analysing the data, I found that when answering my last research question, most of the data generated with Zanele was initially concurring with what the literature was saying around her experiences of postgraduate studies. This is definitely not a bad thing but as doctoral students we are always told that our study should produce new knowledge—otherwise, why do the study? This forced me to revisit the raw data and try to identify a surprise element that I could have overlooked. I was most stunned when after reading and rereading the data, I identified that surprise element which I then added to Zanele's reconstructed story.

Zanele was then invited to read and reflect on the changes made to her story. I must admit I was most apprehensive and worried because it was more than a year since I made contact with her and I had given in my intention to submit my thesis by the end of year, just three months away. But I knew that this process was important because it demonstrated the value of collaboration between me, as the researcher and her as the coresearcher. However, when Zanele replied via a text message a few days later, I was astonished that she said that I had included details about her life that could allow anyone who had met and talked to her to identify her. The details pertaining to Zanele's biographical history were always there from the initial stage of writing her reconstructed story. A year previously, she had never once shared that this was a problem. On the same day, she also responded with an e-mail indicating that the inserts highlighted in yellow, were a misrepresentation of what she had said and indicated that she rewrote some parts to make the story read better. I could not believe this was happening to me. At first I was shocked and then a little angered because I felt I was being accused of not portraying her as she told, and of distorting her story.

From the start of the study, I had always thought that I was privileging Zanele as my coresearcher because this is what a feminist researcher would do. However, my emotion got the better of me and the professional frustration crept in when she asked me to remove details from her story. It became too overwhelming for me because time was against me and my analysis for the other two research questions was already complete and included pertinent data from the sections she wanted me to remove. However, the final straw for me was when she wrote the words, "you are supposed to represent me as a women but it seems like this is not happening in my story." These

Ethically Significant Moments in Stirring up Memories 189

words broke me and I completely lost it. My anxiety levels went up and a subtle form of depression began to set in. No scholarly work could have prepared me to deal with this. I was not coping as a researcher, as a mum, and as a teacher. These words played on my mind even when I was teaching in my class or having my lunch in the staffroom.

Two days after the incident, I took early leave from school because I was not dealing well with having been accused of misrepresentation of what she said and, even more, her saying that I included words that she did not say. Amidst the anger, anxiety, and depression, I went home and pulled out all the raw data that I generated with Zanele via different sources like the interview, collage making, and artefact retrieval. I put a sign on my study door saying, "hell will break loose if you dare come in" and immersed myself with the raw data, listening to all the recordings and going through all my notes. I found that what she said was misrepresentation was indeed there in her own words, and words she said I had added were audible too. Armed with the evidence to back me, I headed to my research supervisor, Daisy Pillay, to tell her of what transpired with Zanele. She listened to my outburst and then calmly said,

> Zanele has given you her time and her story about her life. Not everyone will be brave to do this. Don't you think she has the right to feel how she felt when she read her story at a different time and space from the previous reading? Expressing her concerns, is allowing her to speak out with what she's uncomfortable with in the story. Don't you think she deserves this? Why are you feeling so upset? This is what research is about… more importantly, how you will go forward with this? (Audio recording, Daisy Pillay, September 2017)[4]

Feelings of guilt overcame me and deep down I knew that my supervisor was right. How did I get to this point as a feminist researcher where I failed to embrace the concerns, emotions, and position of Zanele and only prioritized my feelings? Why did I fail to acknowledge that she did not want some of her account of her life being put in the public domain?

Like other feminist researchers, I had to embrace the interpersonal and mutual relationships I formed with Zanele. I called her and apologized if I had caused her any discomfort. I believe that I put her at ease when I explained that she was at liberty to remove any part of the story. The next day she e-mailed me her changes to the story. After reading her story I was compelled to revisit my analysis chapter for research questions one and two and to delete sections. This meant that I also had to restructure the organization of the chapter, which was indeed painful for me. But in the end, I can sleep peacefully knowing that I have honored feminist ethical obligations in that, although I wrote the story, Zanele is still the owner of her story.

My Learning
At the onset of my study, I was aware of more commonly discussed ethical considerations such as informed consent, the right to exit at any stage, confidentiality, and the right to information about the processes and purposes of the study. However, I found that there were many grey areas in the issue of ethics, considering that it is

---

[4]Published with permission.

sometimes not possible to follow ethics in their absolute sense and that we are not fully prepared to handle the ethical dilemmas that arise when research data is based on interviews with participants who have to recount their experiences (McCormick 2012). Little did I know that this research would be a life changing experience for me. Studying other women's lives became a trigger for my mental distress and deep-rooted psychological issues that came to the fore and forced me to seek medical help. It pushed me into spaces that were uncomfortable for me.

Although feminist research holds many ethical challenges in terms of doing research and, also, holding researchers to very high expectations, one of the biggest ethical challenges faced by researchers concerns potential harm to coresearchers, which feminist researchers seek to avoid. After my experience with Thabile and Zanele, I hope as feminist researchers we can find ways to help avoid potential harms in relationships with the women we wish to study. My learning from Zanele's experience is that in research there will always be the risk of inducing or exacerbating emotional distress, and that individuals who participate in research may experience anxiety, depression, embarrassment, or acute stress reactions as they recall, reexamine, and reveal their experiences (Jorm et al. 2007). Therefore, as a novice researcher researching women's lives directly, I must learn to adhere to professional organizations, regulatory bodies, and institutional review boards that require that researchers identify and minimize potential risks and ensure that the benefits of the research outweigh these risks (Barnbaum and Byron 2001). When Zanele displayed emotional and traumatic distress that became a risk to the study, I should have developed strategies other than the promise of anonymity to minimize harm done to her. Various researchers address the need for such strategies (Griffin et al. 2003; Hawton et al. 2003). These strategies might include employing interviewers who are trained to handle psychological distress, consistent monitoring of emotional reactions, and providing information on available psychological or social services as written on our ethical clearance application.

3   Discussion: Looking Across the Mosaic Pieces

The three exemplars presented here draw attention to situational ethics and ethics of the personal, both aspects of "doing most good" and "doing least harm" that seldom appear in any guide or any ethics policy. We may be asked on an ethics form if we anticipate any harm, but as the three mosaic pieces highlight, it is often the unanticipated in our fieldwork that takes us aback and leaves us in states of heightened emotion, guilt, anxiety about misrepresentation and with many questions. What should Sifiso have done with the photograph of his friend who died and what if he had stayed away from the boy's family for fear of causing further grief? In Casey's example, how do we think of history as bringing along a shifting and future-oriented set of ethical responsibilities? Could Sheeren have handled the charge of misrepresentation any other way, and what role can supervisors play? These are questions that strike us as ones that go far beyond any one thesis or research project and, as

Ethically Significant Moments in Stirring up Memories

such, take us further and deeper into the possibilities for arts-based approaches to self-study through memory-work and personal history. At the same time, each of the three exemplars serve to locate personal memory and self-study within broader frameworks of social and political history. Casey is writing in the Canadian context while both Sifiso and Sheeren are writing of South Africa. It is clear in these mosaic pieces that issues of social inclusion and social exclusion run deep, and the challenges of taking into consideration histories and especially the question of "whose histories?" remain as central to what Sifiso has referred to as "emotional ethics." This work is messy and complex but surely that is what professional learning is all about.

Acknowledgements We are grateful to our reviewer, Lungile Masinga of the University of KwaZulu-Natal, South Africa.

References

Barnbaum, D. R., & Byron, M. (2001). *Research ethics: Text and readings*. Upper Saddle River: Prentice Hall.

Boyce, C., & Neale, P. (2006). *Conducting in-depth interviews for evaluation input*. Watertown: Pathfinder International.

Burkholder, C. (2016). We are HK too: Disseminating cellphilms in a participatory archive. In K. MacEntee, C. Burkholder, & J. Schwab-Cartas (Eds.), *What's a cellphilm? Integrating mobile technology into participatory visual research and activism* (pp. 153–168). Rotterdam: Sense Publishers.

Conrad, M., Ercikan, K., Friesen, G., Létourneau, J., Muise, D., Northrup, D., et al. (2013). *Canadians and their pasts*. Toronto: University of Toronto Press.

DeVault, M. L. (1996). *Liberating method*. Philadelphia: Temple University Press.

Dockney, J., & Tomaselli, K. G. (2009). Fit for the small(er) screen: Films, mobile TV and the new individual television experience. *Journal of African Cinema, 1*(1), 126–132.

Finch, J. (1984). *It's great to have someone to talk to: The ethics and politics of interviewing women*. London: RKP.

Flicker, S., O'Campo, P., Monchalin, R., Thistle, J., Worthington, C., Masching, R., et al. (2015). Research done in "A good way": The importance of Indigenous elder involvement in HIV community-based research. *American Journal of Public Health, 105*(6), 1149–1154.

Griffin, M. G., Resick, P. A., Waldrop, A. E., & Mechanic, M. B. (2003). Participation in trauma research: Is there evidence of harm? *Journal of Traumatic Stress, 16*(3), 221–227.

Hawton, K., Houston, K., Malmberg, A., & Simkin, S. (2003). Psychological autopsy interviews in suicide research: The reactions of informants. *Archives of Suicide Research, 7,* 73–82.

Herman, J. L. (1992). *Trauma and recovery*. New York: Basic Books.

Jorm, A. F., Kelly, C. M., & Morgan, A. J. (2007). Participant distress in psychiatric research: A systematic review. *Psychological Medicine, 37,* 917–926.

Lee, M. K. O., Cheung, C. M. K., & Chen, Z. (2005). Acceptance of Internet-based learning medium: The role of extrinsic and intrinsic motivation. *Information & Management, 42*(2005), 1095–1104.

Limerick, B., Burgess-Limerick, T., & Grace, M. (1996). The politics of interviewing: Power relations and accepting the gift. *Qualitative Studies in Education, 9*(4), 449–460.

MacEntee, K., Burkholder, C., & Schwab-Cartas, J. (2016). *What's a cellphilm? Integrating mobile technology into participatory visual research and activism*. Rotterdam: Sense Publishers.

Magubane, S. E. (2014). *Cultivating intrinsic motivation for learning technology: A teacher's self-study* (Unpublished master's thesis). University of KwaZulu-Natal, South Africa. Retrieved from http://researchspace.ukzn.ac.za/handle/10413/12883.

Masinga, L. (2012). Journeys to self-knowledge: Methodological reflections on using memory-work in a participatory study of teachers as sexuality educators. *Journal of Education, 54,* 121–137.

McCormick, M. (2012). Feminist research ethics, informed consent, and potential harms. *The Hilltop Review, 6*(1), Article 5. Retrieved from http://scholarworks.wmich.edu/hilltopreview/vol6/iss1/5.

Mitchell, C., & de Lange, N. (2013). What can a teacher do with a cellphone? Using participatory visual research to speak back in addressing HIV&AIDS. *South African Journal of Education, 33*(4), 1–13.

Mitchell, C., Weber, S., & Pithouse, K. (2009). Facing the public: Using photography for self-study and social action. In D. Tidwell, M. Heston, & L. Fitzgerald (Eds.), *Research methods for the self-study of practice* (pp. 119–134). New York: Springer.

Oakley, Ann. (1981). Interviewing women: A contradiction in terms. In H. Roberts (Ed.), *Doing feminist research*. London: Routledge & Kegan Paul.

Patton, M. Q. (2002). *Qualitative evaluation and research methods* (3rd ed.). London: Sage.

Posel, D., & Ross, F. C. (2012). Opening up the quandaries of research ethics: Beyond the formalities of institutional ethical review. In D. Posel & F. C. Ross (Eds.), *Ethical quandaries in social research* (pp. 1–26). Cape Town: HSRC Press.

Saloojee, S. (2017). *Exploring educational experiences of African postgraduate women students at UKZN: A narrative inquiry* (Unpublished doctoral dissertation). University of KwaZulu-Natal, South Africa.

Samaras, A. P. (2011). *Self-study teacher research: Improving your practice through collaborative inquiry*. Thousand Oaks: Sage.

Schwab-Cartas, J. (2012). Learning from communities: Personal reflections from inside. In E-J. Milne, C. Mitchell, & N. de Lange (Eds.), *Handbook of participatory video* (pp. 383–396). Plymouth: AltaMira.

Smeal, E. (1984). *Why and how women will elect the next president*. New York: Harper & Row.

Strong-Wilson, T., Mitchell, C., Morrison, C., Radford, L., & Pithouse-Morgan, K. (2014). Looking forward through looking back: Using digital-memory-work in teaching for transformation. In L. Thomas (Ed.), *Becoming a teacher: Sites for teacher development in Canadian teacher education* (pp. 442–468). Ottawa: CATE.

Strong-Wilson, T., Mitchell, C., & Ingersoll, M. (2016). Exploring multidirectional memory-work and the digital as a phase space for teacher professional development. In M. Knoebel & J. Kalman (Eds.), *New literacies and teachers' professional development* (pp. 151–172). New York: Peter Lang.

Index

A
Aesthetic/aesthetics, 9, 27, 57, 92, 96, 114–116, 129
Affect/affective lens, 109
Agency, 3, 6, 12, 108, 119, 181
AmaZulu people, 166
Analysis, 98, 99, 101, 102, 106, 134, 157, 188, 189
Apartheid, 7, 17, 23–25, 58–63, 68, 137, 141, 149, 157, 164
Artefact/artefactual, 4, 16, 18, 25, 30, 37, 52, 83–85, 115, 116, 122, 124–127, 130, 138, 157, 164, 165, 167, 177, 178, 183, 189
Artefactual retrieval
  digital artefact, 182
Artist, 3, 37, 79, 85, 90, 140, 160
Arts
  literary, 2, 11, 98, 115, 135, 148–150
  visual, 56
Arts-based, 6–9, 11, 12, 30, 36, 37, 78, 79, 85, 115, 124, 127, 138, 142, 157, 176, 191
Arts-informed, 135
Assemblage, 8, 28, 78, 79, 91
Audiencing/Audience, 49, 50–52, 56, 63, 109, 130, 150, 163, 183, 185
Autobiographical remembering, 17, 115
Autobiography/autobiographical, 106, 142, 177
Autoethnography/autoethnographic
  critical autoethnography, 10, 97, 105–107

C
Cellphilms
  workshop, 11, 176, 182–185
Class
  stereotypes, 2, 20, 23, 28, 30, 51, 96, 97, 99, 104, 105, 109, 127
  structures, 10, 107
Co-researcher, 186–188, 190
Collaboration/collaborator/collaborative, 2, 6, 7, 17, 40, 42, 52, 56, 57, 102, 115, 130, 135, 168, 169, 188
Collage/collaging, 3, 4, 8, 9, 12, 30, 36–41, 78, 79, 81–83, 85, 86, 88–92, 124, 189
Collage portrait, 10, 85, 86, 89
Colonial/colonisation/colonization, 2, 7, 97, 157
Creative
  analytical practice, 99, 115
  methods, 30
  narrative, 10, 114, 121, 122, 129
  nonfiction, 10, 115, 116, 130
Creativity, 62, 115, 137, 140, 144, 148
Critical friends, 99
Critical moments, 10, 81, 88, 91, 124
Cultural
  awareness, 159
  capital, 24, 27
  heritage, 178
  identity, 159, 162
  practices, 170
  knowledge, 37, 157, 169

© Springer Nature Switzerland AG 2019

K. Pithouse-Morgan et al. (eds.), *Memory Mosaics: Researching Teacher Professional Learning Through Artful Memory-work*, Studies in Arts-Based Educational Research2, https://doi.org/10.1007/978-3-319-97106-3

Index

Cultural (*cont.*)
  stories/storytelling, 79, 162, 163, 168
  studies, 109
  values, 159
Culturally relevant, 104, 159
Culture, 7, 17, 27, 28, 62, 103, 104, 124, 159, 168, 185
Curating, 9, 36, 37, 49–51, 178

D
Data, 11, 38, 51, 88, 118, 124, 134, 137, 148, 150, 157, 160, 163, 177, 181, 187–190
Decolonise/decolonize/decolonisation/
  decolonization, 7, 12, 36, 50
Democratic, 7, 79
Dialogue/dialogic, 2, 5, 11, 52, 56, 83, 116, 135, 158, 168, 170, 171, 183
Digital storytelling, 96, 97
Disability, 2, 9, 18, 21, 22, 29, 30
Diversity, 24, 125, 186
Doctoral
  dissertation, 106, 116, 142
  research, 9, 10, 16, 42, 78, 97, 98, 169
  student, 10, 43, 78, 115, 119, 158, 188
  studies, 42, 80, 81, 116–118, 122, 163, 188
  supervisor, 78, 80
Drawing/drawings, 2, 4, 6, 8, 9, 12, 18, 23, 39, 56–61, 63, 65–69, 71–73, 85, 89, 103, 115, 119, 123, 138, 156, 160

E
Educational research, 7, 12, 78, 79, 114, 115, 129
Embodied, 3, 16, 17, 22, 26, 27, 29, 31, 88, 91, 118, 120
Emotion/emotions/emotional/emotive, 3, 9, 11, 12, 16, 18, 25, 28, 29, 52, 59, 67, 68, 71, 72, 82, 85, 86, 91, 109, 115, 116, 124, 129, 138, 145, 146, 148, 167, 168, 178, 179, 181, 186–188, 190
Empathy, 66, 72, 109, 110, 135
Ethics/ethical
  confidentiality, 187
  consent, 40
  emotional ethics, 177
  IRBs, 176
  ownership, 185
  personal, 11
  procedural, 3, 176
  visual ethics, 181, 183

Everyday practice, 79, 90, 92
Exhibition, 49

F
Feminist research, 176, 190
Film
  and professional development, 96, 109
  See also Teacher films
Found photographs, 2, 9, 16, 17, 28, 29, 31, 32
Future-oriented remembering, 9, 12, 56, 72

G
Guilt, 187, 189, 190

H
Haudenosaunee people, 158, 159
HIV and AIDS, 36, 38

I
Identity/identities
  personal, 37
  professional, 36, 135
  selfhood, 114
  teacher, 27, 29, 108–110, 115
  teacher-researcher, 9, 78, 91
Image/imaging, 36, 39, 43, 45, 48, 52, 79, 83, 85, 118, 120, 125, 130
Images, 4, 10, 16, 18, 30, 36–40, 42, 43, 46, 48, 50–52, 56, 59, 85, 89, 96, 97, 103, 105, 106, 115, 117, 118, 120–122, 129, 182–184
Imagination/imagined, 29, 31, 43, 83, 86, 90, 91, 98, 114, 115, 117, 123, 129, 140, 145, 149
Indigenous
  education, 159, 163, 169
  knowledge, 4, 169
  language, 4, 163, 168
  methodology, 160
  people, 7, 52, 97, 185
  storytelling, 156, 159, 163
  storywork, 157
Interpret/interpretive/interpretative, 56, 89, 91, 115, 134, 138, 140, 150, 160, 186
Interpretive poetry, 138, 140
Interviews, 36, 38, 39, 42, 118, 124, 157, 187, 190
IsiZulu language, 4, 23, 59, 60, 137, 163, 164, 168, 177

Index 195

J
Juxtaposition/juxtaposed, 8, 73, 78, 80, 85, 98,
102, 171

K
Kanien'kehá:ka people, 158
Kanien'kehá language, 158–160, 162

L
Leadership, 9, 17, 18, 21–23, 30
Learning/co-learning
personal, 62
professional, 2, 4, 5, 6, 10–12, 16, 17, 28,
31, 32, 36, 53, 56, 57, 96, 110, 135,
148–150, 156–158, 168, 169, 170, 191
Life story, 29, 80, 115, 141
Lived experience, 3, 5, 9, 16, 17, 29, 31, 58,
81, 82, 84, 122, 130, 134, 136, 137, 150,
156, 157, 164, 170, 186

M
Master's
research, 58, 63, 68, 122, 157, 163
student, 10, 115, 124
study, 10, 81, 122, 136
thesis, 122, 159
Memory drawing, 9, 56–59, 61–64, 67, 69,
71–73
Memory/memories, 3–5, 6, 8–11, 16, 18, 26,
28–32, 36, 39, 40, 42, 51, 52, 56–63,
65–71, 73, 78, 80, 81, 83, 85, 88, 89, 91,
96, 103, 106, 108, 109, 114–117,
120–124, 126, 127, 135, 136, 138, 142,
144, 150, 156, 157, 163, 168, 169, 170,
176–178, 181, 182, 186, 187, 191
Memory-work
and self-study, 11, 36, 191
looking back and looking forward, 39
Metaphor/metaphorical/metaphorical images,
10, 36, 45, 83, 91, 104, 129
Methodology/methodologies/methodological/
methods
arts-based, 6, 8, 9, 30, 37, 78, 85, 127, 138,
157
creative, 30
Indigenous, 160
participatory, 37, 38, 97, 104
visual, 6, 8, 16, 37, 97
Mi'kmaq peoples, 185
Mosaic, 2, 7–12, 17, 18, 31, 38, 51, 53, 57–59,
63, 67, 69, 72, 73, 78, 97, 100, 102, 109,
110, 115, 116, 122, 124, 130, 136, 140,
142, 148–150, 158, 163, 164, 168, 170,
171, 176, 186, 190, 191

N
Narrative
accounts, 16, 17
cinematic, 97, 99, 109
dialogue, 2
inquiry, 36, 78, 80, 81, 116, 118, 122, 186

O
Oral communication, 24, 157, 158, 164, 165,
167–169
Oral storytelling/oral stories, 4, 11, 156, 157,
159, 164, 168, 177, 178

P
Participatory action research, 118
Pedagogical spaces, 29
Pedagogy of reinvention, 5, 56, 57, 73
Peer educator, 37
Personal history, 3, 21, 23, 63, 67–69, 72,
83–85, 98–102, 157, 164, 167, 168,
176, 180, 191
Personal narrative, 22, 25, 98, 157
Personal-professional, 79, 83
Photo album, 9, 35, 37, 50, 178 *See also*
Curating
Photo elicitation, 9
Photograph/photography/photographic
archival photographs, 183, 184
family photographs, 9, 36, 51
personal photographs, 16
school photographs, 36, 178
Photo-voice, 36, 37, 118
Play, 4, 11, 12, 21, 29, 68, 79, 81, 85, 90, 107,
134, 138, 140, 147, 150, 181, 190
Poem/poetry/poetry in a pocket, 8, 10, 72, 89,
134, 135, 138–142, 145–150, 170, 182
Poetic
inquiry, 10, 134–136, 148–150
language, 134, 135, 148–150
professional learning, 10, 135, 149
writing, 134
Polyvocal, 11, 115
Productive remembering, 5, 6
Prompts/probes
Bad Teacher, 97, 103, 104
Histories, Geographies, and Notions of
Citizenship, 183

R
Reflection, 2, 9, 17, 18, 21, 28, 30, 31, 38, 39,
42, 50, 56, 57, 73, 80, 83, 91, 96, 97, 99,
102, 118, 138, 143, 145, 158, 168, 169,
176
Reflective, 102, 127, 177

Reflexive/Reflexivity, 26, 28–30, 37, 142
Re-membering, 11, 156–158, 168, 171
Representation, 9, 11, 12, 25, 28, 36, 37, 52,
    103, 114, 116, 141, 142, 148, 150, 183,
    185

S
Scholarship/scholarly, 5, 9, 10, 16, 32, 57, 92,
    115, 129, 130, 135, 149, 158
Self-awareness, 2, 9, 21, 30, 32
Self-insight, 135
Self-recognition, 51
Self-study, 9, 18, 22, 36, 37, 49, 52, 57–59, 62,
    63, 68, 72, 78, 84, 96, 97, 100, 110,
    136–138, 140–142, 149, 157, 164, 176,
    177, 181
Self-transformation, 5
Sexuality education, 9, 96
Social
    change, 4, 32, 37, 49–51, 78, 135
    justice, 2, 7, 9, 18, 51
    narrative, 114
    research, 11, 56, 72
    science, 5, 10, 134, 135, 149, 157
Sociocultural, 10, 24, 101, 136, 150, 169
Story/Stories/storied, 3, 2, 11, 31, 42, 43, 49,
    50, 52, 58, 62, 67, 72, 73, 79–81, 86, 97,
    98, 106, 114–116, 118, 124, 129, 138,
    156, 159, 163, 171, 178, 188, 189
Storytelling, 4, 11, 97, 116, 156–160, 165,
    167–170, 178
Storywork, 157, 170

T
Teacher
    as producer, 36, 41
    English, 4, 96–98, 100, 103
    development, 78, 115, 124, 138
    education/educator, 3, 4, 10, 16, 57, 58, 78,
        83–85, 87, 88, 91, 96, 98, 115, 145,
        158, 163, 181, 182
    films, 10, 95, 96, 97, 98, 109
    history, 96
    learning, 16, 30, 163, 171

preservice, 9–11, 36–38, 42, 97, 182–185
social studies, 181, 182
Teacher-researcher, 2, 10, 11, 16, 29–31, 56,
    78, 80, 83, 89–92, 115, 129, 141, 149,
    150, 158, 171
Television series, 2, 10, 97, 103, 106, 107, 109
Textual, 114, 128, 130
Transformation/transformative, 4, 6, 12, 91,
    134, 170
Trauma, 186
Truth and Reconciliation Commission, 7

U
Ubuntu, 167

V
Values, 17, 24, 25, 27, 31, 84, 107, 116, 125,
    127, 157, 159, 163, 167, 182
Video, 6, 37, 50, 96, 104, 115, 184, 185
Viewing, 2, 10, 41, 52, 96, 98, 105, 106, 109,
    110, 178
Visual
    encounter, 2, 29
    ethics, 183
    knowing, 16
    meaning, 9, 16, 32
    methodologies, 37, 38, 97
    methods, 16
    studies, 36
Vulnerable/vulnerability, 11, 27, 31, 51, 176

W
Women, 5, 9, 35, 36, 41–49, 108, 113,
    115–122, 127, 128, 176, 178, 186, 188,
    190 *See also* feminist research
    African postgraduate female students, 186
    as late entry doctoral students, 9

Y
Youth activists, 38
Youth As Knowledge Producers (YAKP), 36,
    37, 41, 52